ENCYCLOPEDIA *of* DISCOVERY

Reptiles
and Insects

ENCYCLOPEDIA *of* DISCOVERY

Reptiles
and Insects

CONSULTANT EDITORS

Reptiles & Amphibians   Dr Glenn Shea

Insects & Spiders   Dan Bickel

FOG CITY PRESS

Published by Fog City Press
814 Montgomery Street
San Francisco, CA 94133 USA

Copyright © 2003 Weldon Owen Pty Ltd

Chief Executive Officer: John Owen
President: Terry Newell
Publisher: Lynn Humphries
Managing Editor: Janine Flew
Design Manager: Helen Perks
Editorial Coordinator: Kiren Thandi
Production Manager: Caroline Webber
Production Coordinator: James Blackman
Sales Manager: Emily Jahn
Vice President International Sales: Stuart Laurence

Editorial Coordination: Jessica Cox, Jennifer Losco
Project Editors: Helen Cooney, Kathy Gerrard
Project Designers: Avril Makula, Cliff Watt
Consultant Editors: Dan Bickel, Dr Glenn Shea
Indexing: Puddingburn Publishing Services

ISBN 1-877019-90-9

Color reproduction by SC (Sang Choy) International Pte Ltd
Printed by SNP Leefung Printers Limited
Printed in China

A Weldon Owen Production

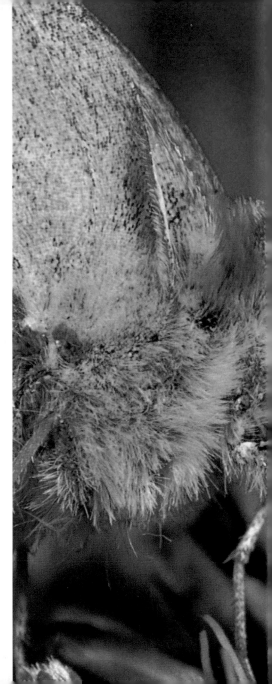

CONTENTS

Reptiles & Amphibians

Insects & Spiders

ENCYCLOPEDIA *of* DISCOVERY

Reptiles &
Amphibians

CONSULTANT EDITOR
Dr Glenn Shea

FOG CITY PRESS

Contents

USING THE GUIDES

The two guide sections of this book (commencing on pages 58 and 156) give a detailed introduction to a wide range of reptiles and amphibians. Each animal is described and information given on its unique characteristics, reproduction behavior, size, diet, and where to find it. Strong visuals increase our understanding and assist our identification of these fascinating creatures in their natural habitats.

The taxonomic data at the top of each entry indicates the order each reptile or amphibian belongs to. When a suborder further defines the division of the groups, this is listed below the order.

The common name for each family or animal is followed by the scientific family name and the number of genera and species within that family.

SQUAMATA
SAURIA

Skinks
Scincidae
About 85 genera/about 1300 species

■ PINK-TONGUED SKINKS
There are more than 1,300 species of skink, making this the largest of the lizard families. Although it can climb small shrubs and trees, the Australian pink-tongued skink usually forages for its prey among ground litter and low vegetation. When threatened, it usually tries to bolt for cover. It shelters under loose tree bark or rock shelves, or in cracks and crevices.
Characteristics This skink's prehensile tail—which accounts for half its length—along with

SNAPS

LENGTH 17 inches
DIET Mainly slug some insects
HABITAT & DISTRI in rainforests an forest areas alo eastern Austral South Wales to of Queensland

its strong claw climbing. Lik has smooth, The newborr rather than **Reproducti** the pink-to birth to liv is usually young, bu are very s

248 KINDS OF REPTILES

Captions and labels draw attention to interesting features or information on each reptile or amphibian.

Photographs and illustrations
support the text with a visual
identification for each reptile
and amphibian.

COLOR OF THE FOREST
The skink's mottled green
color ensures that it is well
camouflaged in its tropical
forest habitat

■ EMERALD TREE SKINK
This Asian–Pacific skink
Lamprolepis smaragdina has a
long tail, depressed head, and
slender snout. Its well-developed
limbs assist as it climbs and
scuttles along tree trunks.
Characteristics The skink's
underside ranges from yellow to
greenish white. It is active during
the day and is a tree dweller,
although it occasionally descends
to the ground in search of food.
It is swift in movement and very
agile as it darts along tree trunks
and branches.
Reproduction This is an egg-
laying species, laying its two eggs
in humus or rotting timber on or
above the ground

SNAPSHOT

LENGTH 4 inches (10 cm) in body
length; tail is equally long
DIET Mainly insects, but it will
also eat fruit and flowers if insects
are not available
HABITAT & DISTRIBUTION Prefer
larger forest trees but have
adapted to human settlement
They are found in Asia and the
Pacific, from Taiwan and the
Philippines through several Pacific
islands to Indonesia, New Guinea,
and the Solomon Islands

LIZARDS 249

and

w
xip

or
s, it
cales.
bluo

skinks,
ives
litter
to 25
lizards

L CRUSHERS
pink tongued
ks have broad,
ened teeth at the
k of the jaws for
shing snail shells.

Snapshot panels give vital
at-a-glance information about
the animal's size, diet, habitat,
and distribution.

INTRODUCING REPTILES AND AMPHIBIANS

Reptiles and amphibians have evolved an astonishing array of behaviors and survival strategies. They have lived successfully for millions of years.

What Are Reptiles and Amphibians?

CLASSIFICATION AND ORDERS

The ancestors of today's amphibians were the first vertebrates to leave the water and spend some of their time on land. Early reptiles evolved from these first amphibians. The differences between reptiles and amphibians are more obvious than their similarities, but the joint study of reptiles and amphibians under the name "herpetology"—from the Greek *herpo*, to creep or crawl—is a scientific tradition dating back nearly two centuries.

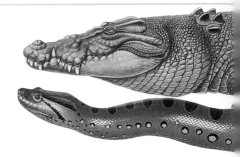

DIVERSITY OF SIZE Reptiles and amphibians vary enormously in size, from tiny frogs only ½ inch (1 cm) long to some crocodiles and snakes that can reach lengths of nearly 30 feet (10 m).

CLASSIFYING ANIMALS

Scientists divide the animal kingdom into several major groups—based on their body characteristics and evolutionary descent—for classification purposes. It provides a logical way to organize information and to show how animals are related to each other. Animal classes, such as reptiles and amphibians, are divided into orders, families, genera, and species (going from the most general to the specific). There are three orders of living amphibians and four of reptiles.

AMPHIBIAN ORDERS

The three amphibian orders are salamanders and newts (order Caudata); frogs and toads (order Anura); and caecilians (order Gymnophiona).

REPTILE ORDERS

The four reptile orders are turtles and tortoises (order Testudinata); crocodiles and alligators (order Crocodilia); tuataras (order Rhynchocephalia); and lizards, amphisbaenians, and

snakes (order Squamata). The squamates are divided into three suborders: Sauria (lizards), Amphisbaenia (amphisbaenians), and Serpentes (snakes).

SPECIES DIVERSITY

There are 7,400 species of living reptiles. The reptiles have evolved adaptations to suit almost every habitat in the temperate and tropical regions of the world. They therefore vary enormously in size and structure. Because of their greater dependence on moisture, the amphibians tend to be less diverse in shape and size. There are 5,000 species of living amphibians. In both groups, there are species that are unremarkable in color, but others with bold, bright patterns and gaudy hues.

TEMPERATURE CONTROL

Every activity of an animal's life—hatching, feeding, reproducing, escaping from predators, even just moving about—depends on its having a body temperature that allows it to function normally. Reptiles and amphibians are unable to control their temperature by internal, physiological means and must rely on external sources of heat to create energy. This is why they are often called "cold-blooded."

PRIME POSITION Many lizards adopt different positions during the day to regulate their body temperature.

BEHAVIORAL CHANGES

Reptiles and amphibians control or regulate their temperature by their behavior.

Warming up Many lizards warm up by moving into the sun or onto a warm surface. To cool down, they expose as little of their body as possible to the heat, or they move into the shade or to a cooler place. However, tropical lizards and snakes are active at night because the nighttime temperatures are mild. Most amphibians are nocturnal and are only active when their surroundings are

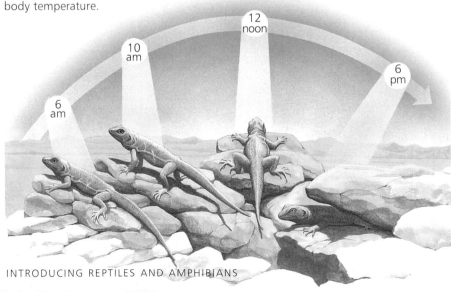

6 am

10 am

12 noon

6 pm

FLAT OUT This basking alligator stretches out to absorb heat from the sun so it has energy to hunt later in the day.

moist enough to stop them becoming dehydrated. Some frogs in cooler climates bask to raise their body temperature, but only if they live near water to prevent moisture loss. Many tiger salamanders and tadpoles increase their temperature by moving into shallow water on sunny days.

SHUTTING DOWN

While being "cold-blooded" can have disadvantages, such as being sluggish at low temperatures and therefore more vulnerable to predators, it also has advantages. Amphibians and reptiles can "shut down" when conditions are unsuitable. In colder climates, lizards and frogs hibernate underground during the winter,

and alligators can survive freezing temperatures in shallow pools. Shutting down enables the animals to avoid wasting energy to produce heat when they are not required to be active.

COLOR CONTROL In the early morning and late afternoon, the skin of the rhinoceros iguanas is dark so it absorbs heat. During the hottest parts of the day, their skin becomes lighter to reflect as much heat as possible.

AN EGG START

A reptile or amphibian's life starts with an egg. Reptiles produce eggs within which the embryo develops and then hatches (or is born, in the case of live-bearing species) into what is generally a miniature replica of the adult. Amphibians, however, have a two-stage lifecycle. The eggs hatch into aquatic larvae, such as tadpoles, which often differ markedly from the adult. The larvae have gills, take in oxygen from the water, and eventually metamorphose into adults which breathe air and live mostly on land. Occasionally the entire tadpole stage takes place within the egg or within the mother's body.

AMPHIBIAN EGGS

Amphibians lay eggs varying in number from a single egg to many thousands laid in clutches. The eggs do not have a waterproof covering and are always laid in water or damp places so they do not dry out.

Fertilization Amphibians fertilize their eggs both externally and

JELLY CAPSULE Each fertilized amphibian egg is surrounded by a dense jelly and contains yolk to nourish the developing young. Waste products permeate out through the jelly.

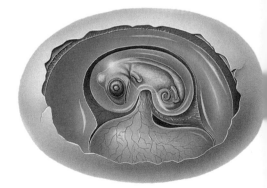

HARD SHELL A hard, waterproof shell enables a reptilian embryo to develop on dry land. Nourished by a yolk sac, the embryo is cushioned by the amnion, a fluid-filled sac.

internally. Most frogs fertilize externally. The male clasps the female with his forelimbs and, as she lays the eggs, expels his sperm over them. Most salamanders fertilize their eggs internally.

REPTILIAN EGGS

The reptile egg is more complex than the amphibian egg and better adapted to survival on land. It is a self-contained system with oxygen entering the egg through a sac called the chorion, a yolk sac, a waste sac, and a cushioning fluid-filled sac, which also prevents the embryo from drying out. In those reptiles where the young develop inside the mother's body, the eggs do not have a shell but the various sacs function in the same way.

Fertilization Reptiles fertilize their eggs internally. All male reptiles (except the tuatara) have well-developed organs for inseminating the females.

GROWING UP Just before metamorphosis into a frog, the tadpole loses its gills. The lungs that have been developing during the tadpole stage take over.

FULLY FORMED All the embryo's needs are met within the closed system of a reptilian egg. This allows it to grow into a miniature adult.

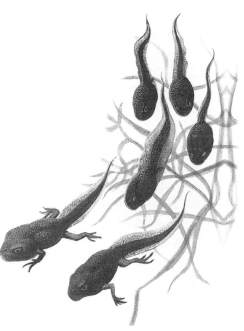

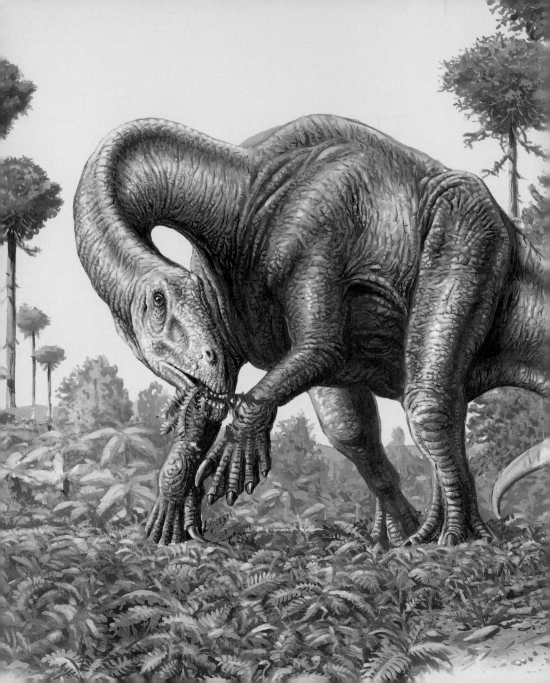

The Origins of Amphibians and Reptiles

THE FIRST AMPHIBIANS

In the process of evolution, life takes every opportunity it gets to increase its chances of survival. In the late Devonian and the early Carboniferous periods, one of the greatest of all opportunities for life presented itself: expansion onto land. The first vertebrates to make the transition from water to land were the amphibians. About 360 million years ago they became the first tetrapods; that is, the first backboned animals with four jointed limbs. It was from these animals that reptiles, birds, and mammals evolved. The earliest known amphibians were *Ichthyostega* and *Acanthostega*.

Millions of years ago	Era	Period		
245	Paleozoic	Permian		More sophisticated reptiles evolved, both plant- and meat-eaters.
290		Carboniferous		The age of amphibians, with some developing into primitive reptiles.
362		Devonian		The age of the fish and the first vertebrate land animals to evolve.
408		Silurian		Land plants and giant sea scorpions appeared.
439		Ordovician		Jawless fish were followed by sharks and bony fish.
510		Cambrian		Sponges, segmented worms, and the first hard-shelled animals appeared.
570	Precambrian	Proterozoic		The first multi-celled animals evolved, resembling worms and jellyfish.
2,500		Archaean		The earliest forms of life were algae and single-celled bacteria.

Origin of Earth

LIFE IN THE SEA

Before amphibians, life started in the sea with algae and single-celled bacteria. The first hard-shelled animals appeared 2,000 million years later. Within 100 million years, a wide variety of marine animals had appeared. It is thought that the amphibians evolved from lobe-finned fish that had lungs and enlarged fins supported by bones and muscles.

Development Amphibians developed into many diverse forms and became the dominant animals of the day. Many were aquatic and possessed gills, but many more made the transition to land.

MODERN AMPHIBIANS

The direct ancestors of today's amphibians are unknown as there are no fossil records linking them to the ancient Paleozoic forms. The first frog fossil is 245 million years old; the first salamander fossil is 150 million years old; and the first caecilian fossil, 65 million years old.

CLOSE RELATIVE The lobe-finned fish *Eusthenopteron* was close to, but not directly on, the evolutionary line that led to amphibians.

FIRST ON LAND *Acanthostega* had a skull similar to its fish ancestors and other fishlike characteristics, such as a tail fin and scales. However, unlike fish, it had a short neck and, to support it on land, four limbs, a greatly thickened backbone, and a well-developed rib cage.

REPTILES RULE

About 50 million years after the first amphibians appeared, the first reptiles evolved from an amphibian ancestor. The development of a dry, scaly skin and an egg with a waterproof shell improved a reptile's chance of surviving on land. Another 100 million years on they had replaced the amphibians as the dominant land-dwelling animals. This was the beginning of the age of the dinosaurs, by which time most of the ancient amphibians were extinct. The earliest known reptile was *Hylonomus*, which looked like a small lizard. Later reptiles included pterosaurs, plesiosaurs, dinosaurs, lizards, snakes, crocodiles, turtles, and tuataras. While dinosaurs ruled the land, marine reptiles dominated the sea. Dinosaurs died out 140 million years later, but the ancestors of today's reptiles survived to evolve into thousands of different species. The only living representatives of those original ruling reptiles, the archosaurs, are the crocodiles.

Carboniferous
362–290 mya

Coelurosauravus, 16 inches (40 cm) long, glided from tree to tree like a flying lizard today.

Although *Dimetrodon* was a reptile, it was also related to the ancestors of mammals.

Hylonomus is known only from fossils found trapped in fossilized tree trunks.

Proganochelys had much in common with living tortoises.

Planocephalosaurus, 8 inches (20 cm) long, resembled the New Zealand tuatara.

THE AGE OF REPTILES From 245 to 65 million years ago, reptiles were the dominant land animals. Their habitats also included the air and sea, with birdlike pterosaurs and fishlike ichthyosaurs.

nian	Triassic	Jurassic	Cretaceous
45 mya	245–208 mya	208–145 mya	145–65 mya

Stegosaurus, a 30-foot (9-m) long dinosaur, had sharp spikes on its tail, probably for defense.

Pteranodon, a pterosaur, had a 23-foot (7-m) wingspan. It fed on fish like a pelican.

Deinosuchus, at 49 feet (15 m) long, may have been the largest crocodile ever to have lived.

Archelon, 12 feet (3.7 m) long, had weak jaws and a toothless beak, so probably ate jellyfish.

Ichthyosaurus, 7 feet (2 m) long, was streamlined and ate fish like a living dolphin.

Elasmosaurus, a 46-foot (14-m) long plesiosaur, had the longest neck of any marine reptile.

Mighty Dinosaurs

■ Dinosaurs were found on every continent during the Mesozoic Era (Triassic, Jurassic, and Cretaceous periods). They were divided into two groups depending on how their hip bones were arranged: the Saurischia had a reptile-like pelvis and the Ornithischia had a birdlike pelvis. Some dinosaurs walked on two legs, though most used four. The Ornithischia were all plant-eaters. Some of the Saurischia evolved into the biggest meat-eaters the world has ever known, fierce hunters like *Allosaurus* and *Tyrannosaurus*.

Others became plant-eating giants. *Diplodocus* reached a length of 100 feet (30 m) and *Brachiosaurus* was 65 feet (20 m) long and stood 40 feet (12 m) high. Dinosaurs walked with their legs tucked under their bodies rather than sprawled out like other reptiles. No other reptiles have been able to do this. It allowed the dinosaurs to breathe more easily while running quickly, and to grow bigger and walk farther than any other reptiles. This was the key to their enormous success.

LIVING TOGETHER A plant-eating *Plateosaurus*, in a scene from the late Triassic world, has little to fear from two meat-eating *Coelophysis*. They are more interested in smaller reptiles.

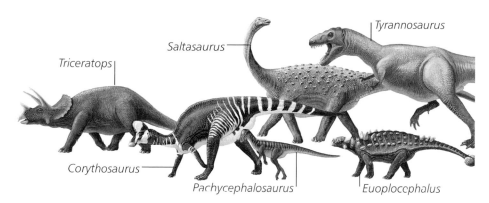

Triceratops
Saltasaurus
Tyrannosaurus
Corythosaurus
Pachycephalosaurus
Euoplocephalus

END OF AN ERA

The reign of the dinosaurs came to an abrupt end when, around 65 million years ago, a catastrophic event wiped them out, along with most of the other large reptiles, except the crocodiles and turtles.

DINOSAUR PARADE More species of dinosaurs evolved during the Cretaceous period than during the Triassic and Jurassic combined. This group shows how diverse these animals had become by the Cretaceous.

TERRIBLE LIZARDS

The word dinosaur means "a fearfully great, or terrible lizard." Sir Richard Owen, a famous British scientist, created the term in 1842 from two ancient Greek words, *deinos* and *sauros*.

An *Ankylosaurus* successfully defends itself, using its massive club-like tail, against a fearsome *Tyrannosaurus*.

THE WORLD OF AMPHIBIANS

Amphibians display a stunning variety of voice, shape, color, habitat, ways of getting around, and ways of life.

Where Do Amphibians Live?

AMPHIBIAN HABITATS

The word amphibian comes from the Greek word *amphibios,* which means "a being with a double life." Most amphibians do indeed live two different lives—in water as larvae and on land as adults—but some live their whole lives in water and others never leave the land.

SALAMANDERS AND NEWTS

Most salamanders and newts live in cool, shady places in regions with temperate climates. They live in a variety of habitats, but all are damp or wet. Aquatic species can be found in rivers, lakes, mountain streams, swamps, and underground caves. Some, like sirens, congo eels, and the olm, are almost limbless and swim like snakes. Others, like the giant salamanders, hellbenders, and mudpuppies, have normal limbs and crawl about on the bottoms of lakes and rivers. Terrestrial species usually live under rocks and logs, but some burrow into the soil and others live in trees.

CHANGE OF HABITAT Mole salamanders only leave their sub-terranean habitats to reproduce near ponds and streams.

FROGS AND TOADS

The most numerous and diverse of the amphibians, frogs and toads

WATERWORLD Frogs that live in water have webbed toes to help propel them.

TREE DWELLER Special finger and toe pads help tree frogs cling to smooth surfaces.

can be found in nearly all habitats, from deserts, savannas, and mountains to tropical rainforests. Most live in water for at least part of their lives, usually the tadpole stage. Nearly all frogs can swim, though some are better at it than others.

On land, frogs can be found under logs, among the leaf litter on forest floors, or in damp rock crevices. Some burrow into soft dirt or mud either for daytime retreats or for long periods of estivation during very dry seasons. Other frogs live in shrubs and trees. Some tree-dwellers lay their eggs in tree holes or in the base of epiphytic plants so the tadpoles can live in the pools that collect there.

CAECILIANS

These legless, wormlike creatures usually live underground in tropical forests. They move along tunnels they build by pushing their head through loose mud or damp soil. All caecilians burrow. Aquatic caecilians burrow into the soft mud and gravel on the floor of their watery habitats.

TIME OUT A Great Plains toad burrows into the sand.

DISTRIBUTION

Amphibians occur throughout much of the world. The only places where native amphibians do not occur are Antarctica, the northernmost parts of Europe, Asia, and North America, and most oceanic islands.

SALAMANDERS AND NEWTS

Almost all salamanders and newts (caudates) are found in the Northern Hemisphere; in Europe, central, northern, and Southeast Asia, northwestern Africa, North America, and Mexico. A few species occur in South America as far south as central Bolivia and southern Brazil. Caudates are found from sea level to about 14,700 feet (4,500 m). Most occur in temperate regions, though the lungless salamanders occur in tropical parts of Central and South America.

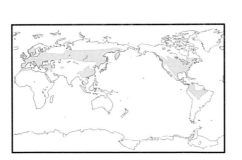

NORTHERN EXPOSURE Most salamanders are found in the Northern Hemisphere (as shown on the map). The fire salamander *Salamandra salamandra* (above) occurs in Europe and northwest Africa.

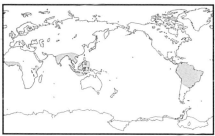

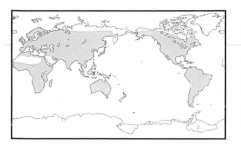

FROGS AND TOADS

There are frogs and toads on most oceanic islands and on every continent except Antarctica. Three species, the common frog and moor frog of Europe and the wood frog of North America, have ranges that extend north of the Arctic Circle. While many frogs and toads have successfully colonized the temperate regions, more than 80 percent of species are found in the tropics and subtropics.

CAECILIANS

Caecilians are confined to tropical and subtropical regions of the world. In Asia they can be found in southern China, southern Philippines, Southeast Asia, Sri Lanka, and India. Elsewhere they occur in equatorial East and West Africa, the Seychelles, and in tropical Central and South America. Aquatic species are restricted to South America. Because of their burrowing habits caecilians remain poorly known.

MANY HOMES The Fowler's toad is found near marshes, ditches, backyards, and temporary rain pools. It is widespread throughout North America.

SOFT MUD BURROWER This eel-like caecilian *Typhlonectes natans* is strictly aquatic. It is found in lakes and rivers in South America.

AMPHIBIANS ON THE DECLINE

Today, there are fewer species of amphibians than of any other class of vertebrate. The most obvious cause of this decline was habitat loss through construction of roads, towns, and the spread of farming. However, there has been recent recognition that many amphibian populations worldwide are also declining through the effects of disease, pollution, and climate change. Many frogs, even in apparently unaltered habitats, are rapidly declining, or have even become extinct.

SENTINEL SPECIES

Amphibians are regarded as "sentinel species." Because of their intimate contact with air, water, and earth they are the first to be hit if something is wrong. Deformities in frogs in Canada and northern USA have been caused by certain parasites, but pesticides are increasingly suspected. During the 1980s, golden toads, *Bufo periglenes* (below), found only in Costa Rica's cloud forests, suffered a mysterious extinction. Biologists now blame global warming for creating intolerable dry weather by pushing moisture-giving clouds beyond the forest's range. Ultraviolet (UV) light can alter DNA in cells and suppress immune responses. Massive die-offs of frogs' eggs in Oregon, USA, are thought to be caused by the increased UV radiation escaping through the thinning ozone layer.

SHARING THE PLANET

Declining amphibian populations are the barometer to unseeable changes in the environment we share with them. When frogs are affected, there is a chance these changes will be affecting us too.

CROSSING THE BARRIER The eggs and skin of amphibians are highly permeable and easily absorb toxic substances that are taking their toll on amphibian populations.

Amphibian
Anatomy

■ A Close View *42*

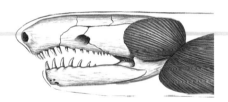

A CLOSE VIEW

Amphibians share a basic tetrapod vertebrate skeletal structure. However, some have become highly modified, such as the frog, whose efficient jumping has been achieved by replacing several vertebrae with a long, supporting bone, and the powerful caecilian skull that is used to ram through the earth. An amphibian's skin has special functions and, as for most vertebrates, sight, hearing, and smell are critical survival tools.

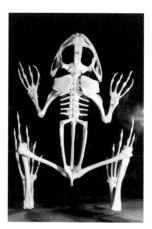

SPRINGBOARD This frog skeleton shows the long, supporting bone, called a urostyle, and the long legs needed for efficient jumping.

SPECIAL SKIN

The skin of most amphibians is thin and needs to be kept moist to function effectively. One of its important functions is water balance: the skin is highly permeable, allowing water to be absorbed or lost. Most amphibians have lungs, but respiration also occurs through the skin. There are many glands in an amphibian's skin. Secretions from the mucous

WASTE DISPOSAL Digested food is absorbed by the small intestine. The remaining waste moves down the large intestine to the cloaca—a chamber that opens to the outside of the body. Waste products, as well as eggs and sperm, pass out of the body through the cloaca.

SLIMY CHARACTER This California newt shines from the secretions produced by its skin glands.

glands keep the skin moist. Other glands secrete the poisons with which many species defend themselves. Amphibians continue to grow after sexual maturity and shed the outer layer of their skin several times a year.

SENSE ORGANS

For most amphibians three senses are critical for survival: sight, hearing, and smell. Frogs and toads can hear a wider range of sounds than salamanders and caecilians. Most amphibians have good eyesight, which helps them to catch their prey. However, caecilians have little use for sight in their underground burrows and their eyes are either very small or absent. Most amphibians smell by passing on scent particles to the sensory cells of the Jacobson's organ in the roof of their mouth.

Built for Burrowing

■ The caecilian skull is powerfully constructed with a pointed snout and an underslung lower jaw—features that allow the head to be used as a ram to push through soil or mud. This is just one of the many adaptations the caecilians have for burrowing.

ROD AND TUBE

The body muscles of caecilians are arranged so the body can act like a rod moving within a tube. The "tube" is the skin and outer layer of body muscles. The "rod" is the head, backbone, and the muscles attached to the backbone. With the tube fixed in position in a tunnel, the rod can be pushed slightly forward through the soil to extend the tunnel. When the tip of the rod—the head—has gone as far forward as it can, the tube is pulled forward and fixed in position so the rod can again be pushed through the soil.

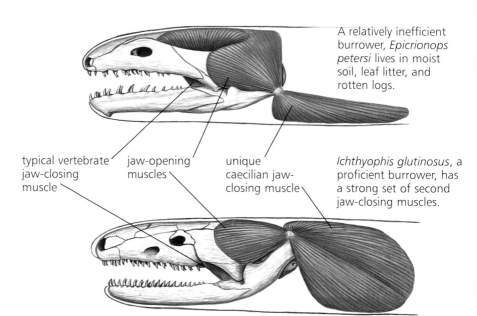

A relatively inefficient burrower, *Epicrionops petersi* lives in moist soil, leaf litter, and rotten logs.

typical vertebrate jaw-closing muscle

jaw-opening muscles

unique caecilian jaw-closing muscle

Ichthyophis glutinosus, a proficient burrower, has a strong set of second jaw-closing muscles.

JAW MUSCLES

Typical vertebrates have a single set of jaw-closing muscles that pull on the lower jaw from a point in front of the jaw hinge. Caecilians have these muscles, too, but they are the only vertebrates with a second set of jaw-closing muscles. These help close the jaw by pulling back and down on a special extension behind the lower jaw hinge in much the same way as pushing down one end of a seesaw causes the other end to swing up. These muscles improve burrowing efficiency.

Better burrowers Some caecilian species are better burrowers than others. The more efficient burrowers make more use of the second set of muscles, reflected by the increased muscle size shown in the illustrations. They also have more rigid skulls and their mouth is more recessed.

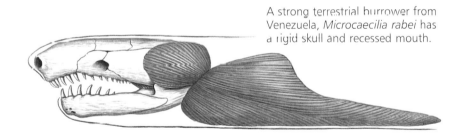

A strong terrestrial burrower from Venezuela, *Microcaecilia rabei* has a rigid skull and recessed mouth.

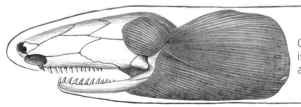

Crotaphatrema lamottei is a good burrower with a strongly recessed mouth.

Life
and Death

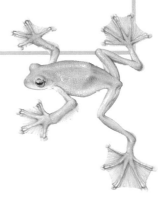

PREY

Adult amphibians are all carnivorous. Most amphibian larvae are vegetarian, except for salamanders and newts, which are carnivorous at all stages in their lifecycles. Most amphibians snatch prey with a flick of their tongue or a snap of their mouth.

SALAMANDERS AND NEWTS

Small invertebrates such as insects, spiders, crustaceans, mollusks, and worms are usually the prey for salamanders and newts. However, the larger species also prey on small vertebrates, such as small fish, and cannibalism can occur in both larvae and adults.

FROGS

Frogs will eat whatever small animals share their habitat and fit into their huge mouths. Some of the larger frogs, such as the North American bullfrog, can take birds and mice, small turtles and fish,

READY FOR ACTION This spotted salamander investigates a worm.

THE RIGHT SIZE Few frogs are large enough to eat other vertebrates. This leopard frog of North America eats what it can manage—a worm.

young snakes, and even smaller frogs of their own and other species. Tadpoles are mostly vegetarian. They filter organisms from the water or scrape algae from rocks. But some scavenge on carrion, or prey on invertebrates or other tadpoles.

Catching prey Most frogs simply sit and wait for prey to come within reach. Some species ambush their prey from hiding places. A few heavy-bodied frogs lure agile prey by waving the long toes on their hind feet. Other frogs, especially the small poison frogs of tropical America, forage for small insects among the leaf litter by day.

CAECILIANS

Land-dwelling caecilians feed on worms, beetles, and other insects. Aquatic species eat worms, insects, and other invertebrates.

A VICIOUS CYCLE A carpenter frog chases a cricket. However, when food is scarce, a carpenter frog becomes the meal for a larger, more fearsome predator, the North American bullfrog.

PREDATORS AND ESCAPE

A dult amphibians have many predators, including snakes, birds, and mammals. Frogs, in particular, have many enemies, from spiders and birds to humans. The amphibian larval stage, too, is a perilous time. Almost any meat-eater will find them a succulent morsel. To protect themselves, amphibians use many methods—from simply staying out of sight to toxic secretions.

HEAD FIRST This red-backed salamander, a lungless salamander, could have escaped from the jaws of this ring-neck snake if it had been caught by its tail.

PROTECTION AND ESCAPE

Salamanders defend themselves by secreting foul-tasting or toxic substances. Some have poison glands on the back of their neck. Other salamanders and newts display their brightly colored underside to warn that their skin is toxic. Some mole salamanders even head-butt their enemies. If seized, lungless salamanders can shed their tail, growing a new one later.

Many frogs can avoid danger by camouflage or jumping. Sometimes, though, an enemy has to be

faced and other defenses are necessary. These include toxic skin secretions, feigning death, or puffing up the body to make it look bigger. Some frogs from South America have brightly colored eyespots on their rump which they display to deter an attacker.

Caecilians have poison glands in their skin. Most species are dull-colored, but some are brightly colored and patterned, perhaps to warn enemies of their toxic skin secretions. Still, caecilians are often eaten by snakes and introduced predators.

A FIRM HOLD Some invertebrates eat frogs. This leopard frog has been captured by a giant water bug.

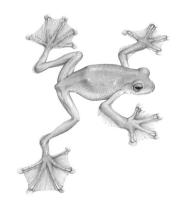

GLIDE AWAY The Wallace's tree frog glides to escape from predators. It uses its toe "wings" to glide between branches, steer in midair, and slow its fall.

DON'T TOUCH The bright skin colors of the funereal poison frog warn potential predators of the dangers of its toxic skin.

New Life

CALLING FOR A MATE

Frogs croaking at dusk is a common sound in many parts of the world. In some tropical areas thousands of frogs may call at once, creating a chorus that can be heard more than a mile away. A male frog calls to attract a female ready to mate and to repel other males from its territory. In some species, one sort of call serves both purposes; other species may add extra notes for the territorial call or change the "tune" entirely. Each frog species has a unique call to which only members of that species will react.

HOW IT IS DONE

Frogs were the first animals to develop a true voice. The frog forces air from its lungs through

the larynx, causing the vocal cords to vibrate and produce sound. The sound is amplified and given its characteristic timbre by the vocal sac or sacs. These are pouches of skin beneath the floor of the mouth or at the corner of the mouth with openings into the mouth cavity. When calling, a frog keeps its nostrils and mouth closed and uses muscles of the body wall and throat to shunt air back and forth between the vocal sac and the lungs across the vocal cords.

MORE THAN A CROAK

Calls range from simple, brief clicks to long, drawn-out trills of several minutes, depending on the pattern of the air flow. Different calls have been described as plonks, honks and unks, whistles, warbles and chuckles, as well as bleats, barks, and duck-like quacks, to list but a few in the huge repertoire of the frog chorus. The frequency level of the call is largely determined by the frog's size, with small frogs having high-pitched calls and large frogs having low-pitched calls, but this pattern can be varied somewhat according to species.

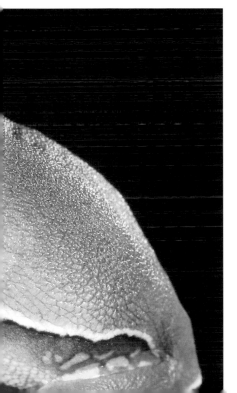

WARMING UP The call of the male Pine Barrens tree frog is a nasal *quonk-quonk-quonk*. It is repeated about 25 times in 20 seconds on warm nights and more slowly on cooler ones.

LIFECYCLES

Almost all amphibians produce eggs, varying in number from a single egg to many thousands, which are deposited in water or in humid spots on land. Frogs and toads fertilize the eggs outside the female's body, whereas most salamanders and caecilians fertilize inside the female's body. The lifecycle for salamanders, and for frogs and toads, continue on their different paths.

SALAMANDERS

There is no one lifecycle that applies to all the diverse members of this order. However, there are three general types that cover many species: entirely terrestrial, entirely aquatic and, by far the most common, the amphibious lifecycle where the female or both sexes return to the water to breed. In this lifecycle, much of the development occurs outside the

THE AMPHIBIOUS LIFECYCLE
1 Eggs laid in water, usually in large clutches.
2 Larva with gill buds.
3 Larva with developing gills, forelimbs, and hindlimb buds.
4 Larva with fully developed limbs and gills.
5 Terrestrial adult.

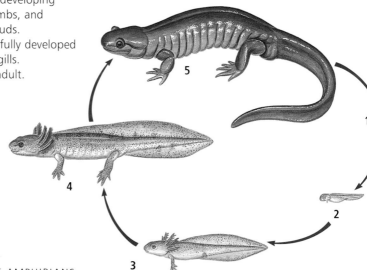

egg. The larva metamorphoses, losing its external gills and the fins on its back and tail, and changing in other external and internal parts of its body. Depending on the species, this may take from a few days to several years.

FROGS AND TOADS

About three-quarters of the world's frogs and toads lay eggs in water that hatch into tadpoles that grow and metamorphose into adult frogs (as shown above with the European common frog). Within each of these stages many variations occur. Many species do not have free-living tadpoles but lay eggs that hatch into froglets. Development takes place entirely inside the egg, which hatches into a fully metamorphosed froglet. In a few species the eggs stay in the female's oviduct where they develop before the froglets are born.

THE FROG LIFECYCLE

1 The male clasps the female under the arms, hangs on until she lays the eggs, then inseminates them. On contact with the water, the jelly around the eggs swells and they float to the surface.

2 The eggs hatch after about two weeks. The tadpole feeds on weeds and algae and breathes through external gills.

3 The lungs become functional and the gills disappear after about three weeks. After four weeks the tail begins to shrink as the limbs gradually appear.

4 At about six weeks metamorphosis is complete. The frog leaves the water, switching from a vegetarian diet to one of mainly insects.

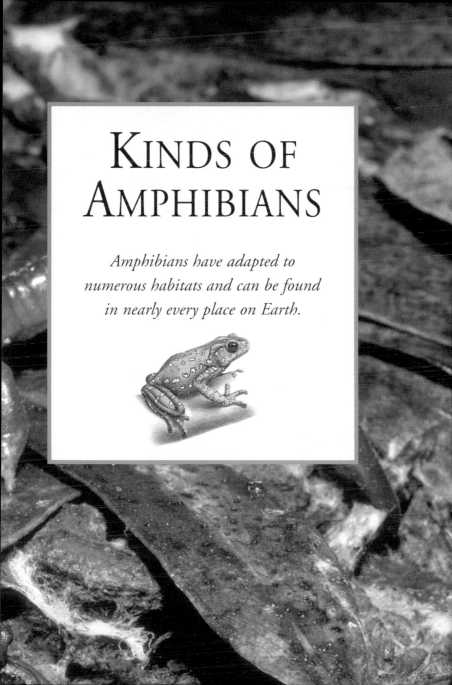

KINDS OF AMPHIBIANS

Amphibians have adapted to numerous habitats and can be found in nearly every place on Earth.

Salamanders and Newts

Hellbenders and Giant Salamanders

Cryptobranchidae

2 genera/3 species

S N A P S H O T

LENGTH Up to 6 feet (180 cm)
DIET Any small animal that shares their habitat: worms, insects, crayfish, fish, snails, and smaller salamanders
HABITAT & DISTRIBUTION Always live in flowing rivers and streams. Hellbenders are found in the USA, and giant salamanders are found in Japan and China

■ GENERAL
These bulky animals, the largest of all the salamanders, never leave the water. They feed mostly at night and spend the day under rocks. With poor vision, they lie in wait for their prey, relying on smell and touch to locate it.

■ CHARACTERISTICS
Hellbenders and giant salamanders breathe through their lungs but they also have skin folds along their flanks that increase the surface area for oxygen taken in via their skin from the water.

■ REPRODUCTION
One of the few families to have external fertilization. The female lays up to 450 eggs, in paired rosary-like strings. The male releases sperm on the eggs and guards them until they hatch 10 to 12 weeks later.

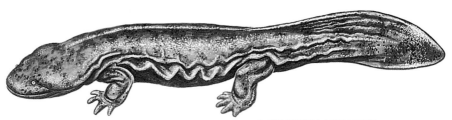

A GIANT SALAMANDER
The Japanese giant salamander grows to about 5 feet (150 cm) in length.

Sirens

Sirenidae

2 genera/3 species

■ GENERAL

With their long, slender bodies, small forelimbs, and no hind-limbs, sirens look rather eel-like. They are often nocturnal, and spend the day burrowed in mud and weeds. Like eels, they can cover short distances on land at night during rainy periods. If their habitat dries out, they can survive for months embedded in the mud, enveloped by a kind of mucous cocoon with only the snout poking out.

SNAPSHOT

LENGTH 4–35 inches (10–90 cm)
DIET Variety of invertebrate animals and plants. Greater siren also eats small fish
HABITAT & DISTRIBUTION The shallow water of ponds, swamps, and ditches with muddy bottoms and rich aquatic vegetation. Found in southern USA and Mexico

■ CHARACTERISTICS

Sirens do not metamorphose so they retain larval structures, such as external gills, throughout their life.

■ REPRODUCTION

Eggs have been found attached to submerged plants, either singly or in small clumps. The female guards the eggs until they hatch. It is not known how fertilization occurs.

SMALL AND SLENDER
The dwarf siren
Pseudobranchus striatus
of North America is a
fully aquatic salamander.

Waterdogs and the Mudpuppy

Proteidae

2 genera/6 species

S NAPSHOT

LENGTH 9–30 inches (22–75 cm)
DIET Feed on a variety of animals, including insects, crayfish, and fish
HABITAT & DISTRIBUTION Streams, rivers, and lakes, sometimes in running water, sometimes in stagnant, muddy water

■ GENERAL

The waterdogs and mudpuppy of North America are totally aquatic. They forage for prey at night and hide themselves under rocks and debris during the day. Their red or purple external gills look like miniature ostrich feathers. These vary in size depending on the oxygen content of the water where they live.

■ CHARACTERISTICS

All members of the Proteidae family retain their gills. They have large, flat heads, stout bodies, and small limbs. They usually have a mottled appearance.

■ REPRODUCTION

A female lays 20 to 180 eggs, attaching them to the undersides of rocks and logs. They are guarded by the male until they hatch.

FEATHERY GILLS

The gills of the mudpuppy *Necturus maculosus* are largest in the warm swamps in the southern part of its range.

Congo Eels

Amphiumidae

1 genus/3 species

SNAPSHOT

LENGTH Can be over 3 feet (1 m)
DIET Feed on crayfish, frogs, fish, and small snakes
HABITAT & DISTRIBUTION
Swamps, streams, and drainage ditches in southeastern USA, spending much of their time in burrows in the mud

■ GENERAL

If it were not for the presence of four tiny limbs, these large salamanders could easily be mistaken for eels, hence their common name. They live in water and, like eels, burrow into the mud and can move across wet ground. Despite their permanently aquatic way of living, congo eels breathe air through lungs by periodically poking their nostrils above the surface of the water. They are active at night, when they search for prey.

■ CHARACTERISTICS

The adults retain some larval characteristics. Even though they lose their external gills, they retain internal gills and can use these, in addition to lungs, for breathing.

■ REPRODUCTION

The eggs are laid in shallow, muddy water under shelters such as a log, in long strings, each containing up to 150 eggs or more. The female coils her body around them until they hatch. If the water has dried up when they hatch, the young have to find their way to water, usually when it rains.

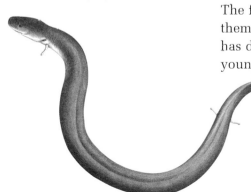

EEL-LIKE AMPHIBIAN
The three species of Congo eel have different numbers of toes on their tiny limbs. *Amphiuma means* is the two-toed species.

Mole Salamanders

Ambystomatidae

2 genera/31 species

■ GENERAL

The mole salamanders of North America spend their adult life almost entirely underground, emerging from their subterranean world only to return to the ponds or streams where they reproduce. In some areas there are members of various species where the adults retain their larval form even when they reach sexual maturity. The most famous of these is the Mexican axolotl.

■ CHARACTERISTICS

Mole salamanders have broad heads, strong limbs, and heavily built, squat bodies. Some of them have brightly colored markings on their smooth, shiny skin.

■ REPRODUCTION

Fertilization, often preceded by a nuptial dance, is immediately followed by the laying of up to 200 eggs. Most species lay their eggs in water attached to submerged objects such as logs or roots. Others bury their eggs on land where water will fill the nest when it rains. Only the marbled

LARVAL FORM
Under certain environmental conditions the axolotl
Ambystoma mexicanum
is permanently aquatic
and larval in form.

salamander, which lays its eggs in dry pond beds, has been observed guarding the eggs. She coils herself around them until the rains come.

■ DISTRIBUTION

Mole salamanders are found from southern Alaska and Canada, throughout the USA to most of Mexico,

STRIPED SALAMANDER
The tiger salamander *Ambystoma tigrinum mavortium* is one of the largest terrestrial salamanders.

SNAPSHOT

LENGTH Usually less than 14 inches (35 cm)

DIET Depending on their size, they will eat earthworms, many kinds of insects, spiders, frogs, tadpoles, and even small snakes and mice

HABITAT In burrows or under litter on the forest floor, returning to still ponds and lakes to breed

Lungless Salamanders

Plethodontidae

27 genera/220 species

■ GENERAL

This is the largest family of salamanders. As their common name suggests, they have no lungs. Lungless salamanders breathe through their skin and the lining of their mouth. Because their skin must remain moist to absorb oxygen, these animals spend much of their time hidden away in damp places. They shelter in caves, crevices in rocks, spaces between roots and stones, or under logs, and will only venture out when it is humid enough and the temperature is mild, usually on rainy nights.

BRIGHT AND BOLD
The red salamander
Pseudotriton ruber is found near brooks and springs in Central to North America.

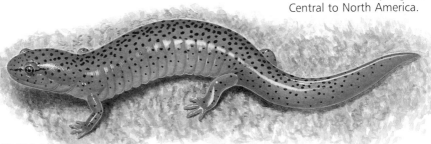

AWAY FROM HOME
This Dunn's salamander in
a forest beside a stream
in Oregon, USA, is more
often found under stones
in moist areas.

young hatch as miniature adults. Aquatic species lay their eggs in water and the eggs hatch into larvae. In both cases the female guards the eggs.

■ DISTRIBUTION

Most species occur in the Americas—from Nova Scotia and British Columbia south to Bolivia and Brazil. A few species are found in France, Sardinia, and Italy.

■ CHARACTERISTICS

Lungless salamanders have long, slender bodies and tails. Their color varies, but many are spotted, mottled, or striped. Unlike other salamanders, they have a groove, lined with glands, which runs between the lip and nostril and which transfers chemicals from the salamander's moist environment to sensory receptors inside the nostril.

■ REPRODUCTION

After fertilization, terrestrial species lay their eggs on the ground or on vegetation, and the

---

S N A P S H O T

LENGTH Just over 1 inch and up to 12½ inches (3–32 cm)
DIET Variety of invertebrates, including slugs, snails, worms, beetles, ants, mites, and flies
HABITAT Most species are totally terrestrial, covering a range of damp habitats from burrows and caves to rocks and trees. Others have an aquatic larval stage, and a few are completely aquatic, living in fast-flowing streams

Newts and "True Salamanders"

Salamandridae

14 genera/53 species

■ GENERAL
The term "newt" refers to the members of ten genera in the Salamandridae family that are partly or entirely aquatic in their adult form. Most newts spend at least half the year in water. Here they court, lay eggs, and build up the fat reserves needed to survive the winter on land. Adults of the rest of the salamanders in the family, the true salamanders, are predominantly or entirely terrestrial. They are secretive animals, usually active only on mild, damp nights.

■ CHARACTERISTICS
Salamandrids have slender bodies, well-developed limbs, and a long tail that is finlike in aquatic forms. Male newts have bright colors, which develop in the breeding season, to attract females. Newts, unlike other salamanders, have rough skin.

■ REPRODUCTION
Fertilization typically occurs after a long and elaborate courtship. Nearly all the salamandrids lay eggs in water. Two mountain-dwelling

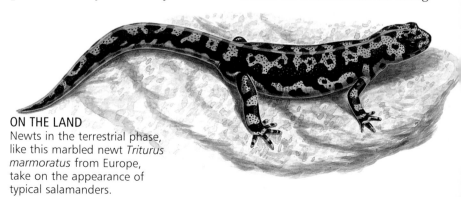

ON THE LAND
Newts in the terrestrial phase, like this marbled newt *Triturus marmoratus* from Europe, take on the appearance of typical salamanders.

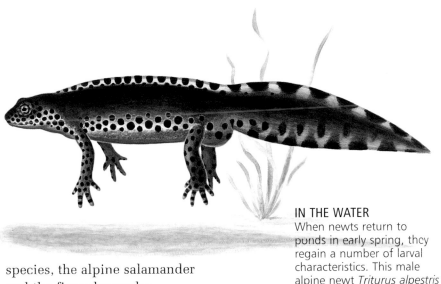

species, the alpine salamander and the fire salamander, give birth to completely metamorphosed young.

■ DISTRIBUTION

Terrestrial species occur only in Europe with the exception of the fire salamander, which reaches the Middle East and northwest Africa. Newts are more widespread, occurring in Europe, the Middle East, Asia, and North America. In their aquatic phase they live in ponds and streams. When on land they live under logs, rocks, and dense ground litter.

SNAPSHOT

LENGTH 3–12 inches (7–30 cm)
DIET Whether they live on land or water, newts and true salamanders feed on small invertebrates, including worms, slugs, insects, and crustaceans. Some aquatic forms prey on tadpoles
HABITAT In burrows and under logs and stones in moist woodlands and subalpine meadows

Frogs and Toads

Tailed Frog

Ascaphidae

1 genus/1 species

SNAPSHOT

LENGTH 1–3 inches (3–7 cm)
DIET Frogs eat insects and other invertebrates. Tadpoles eat algae
HABITAT & DISTRIBUTION Semi-aquatic, lives in and around cold, fast-flowing mountain streams in northwestern USA and southwestern Canada

■ GENERAL

The tailed frog *Ascaphus truei* does not have a true tail but rather a small appendage, present only in the male, which is adapted to insert sperm directly into the female. It is one of the few frogs to have internal fertilization. It is most active at night around the streams where it lives.

■ CHARACTERISTICS

The tailed frog has a slender body and slightly webbed toes.

■ REPRODUCTION

The eggs are attached to the undersides of rocks in water. Tadpoles take three years to develop. They have large suckers on their mouths, which they use to cling onto rocks while feeding.

TAIL OF A FROG
The small appendage of the tailed frog ensures that during fertilization the sperm is not washed away in the rapidly flowing water where the frogs mate.

Painted Frogs

Discoglossidae

5 genera/14 species

■ GENERAL

Painted frogs are usually found at the edges and in the shallows of streams, lakes, and ponds. Often they can be seen sitting in shallow pools with their heads just above the surface of the water. On land they shelter under logs or in rocky crevices. They are usually active at night but some are also active during the day.

SNAPSHOT

LENGTH 2–3 inches (5–7 cm)
DIET A wide variety of insects, spiders, and other invertebrates
HABITAT & DISTRIBUTION Near ponds, streams, or lakes or in woodlands and rocky areas. They are found in western Europe, the Middle East, and northwest Africa

■ CHARACTERISTICS

Some species have quite plump bodies, but others are slender. Their color patterns are often highly variable.

■ REPRODUCTION

The eggs are laid in water and the tadpoles are aquatic.

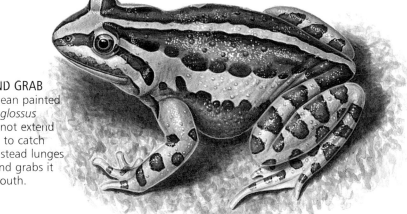

LUNGE AND GRAB
The European painted frog *Discoglossus pictus* cannot extend its tongue to catch prey, so instead lunges forward and grabs it with its mouth.

New Zealand Frogs

Leiopelmatidae

1 genus/3 species

■ GENERAL
There are only three frog species native to New Zealand. They are small, secretive, nocturnal animals that shelter by day under stones and logs or in damp crevices.

■ CHARACTERISTICS
These frogs are mainly shades of brown and sometimes green with flattened heads and pointed snouts. Hochstetter's frog has some webbing on its toes, the others have very little. The frogs are almost silent, making no sound other than faint chirps.

SNAPSHOT
LENGTH 1–2 inches (3–5 cm)
DIET Insects and spiders are the main part of the frogs' diet, but they will eat any prey that they can catch
HABITAT & DISTRIBUTION Damp, forested areas. Hochstetter's frogs live on edges of shady creeks on the North Island. Archey's frogs are restricted to a small area of the North Island and Hamilton's frogs to two small islands

■ REPRODUCTION
They lay their one to nineteen large, yolky eggs in moist soil under rocks and logs. Archey's frog and Hamilton's frog lay their eggs on land. When the tadpoles hatch, they climb onto the male's back where they stay until they metamorphose. The tadpoles of the semi-aquatic Hochstetter's frog develop in water.

NATIVE FROG
Three frogs are endemic to New Zealand. All are small, nocturnal, egg-laying species.

Mexican Burrowing Toad

Rhinophrynidae

1 genus/1 species

SNAPSHOT

LENGTH About 3 inches (7 cm)
DIET Feeds mostly on ants and termites. Tadpoles are filter feeders; they eat small particles suspended in water
HABITAT & DISTRIBUTION Drier lowland areas from southern Texas to Costa Rica

■ GENERAL

The Mexican burrowing toad *Rhinophrynus dorsalis* spends most of its life underground, emerging only to breed after heavy rain. When frightened or calling, it becomes so inflated with air that it looks like a balloon.

■ CHARACTERISTICS

The toad has a rotund, oval-shaped body with a pointed snout and short legs. Its tongue projects straight out of its mouth instead of flipping over itself as in most frogs. Its bright colors are unusual for a burrowing frog.

■ REPRODUCTION

Many eggs are laid in ponds caused by heavy rains. The tadpoles hatch after a few days and take one to three months to metamorphose into adults.

BURROWING TOAD
On the inner edge of each hind foot is a "spade", which the frog uses to dig as it shuffles backward into the earth.

Tongueless Frogs

Pipidae

4 genera/26 species

■ AFRICAN CLAWED FROGS
These frogs rarely, if ever, venture out of water. Along with the other members of the Pipidae family, they have no tongue but rely heavily on their hands to capture food.

SNAPSHOT

LENGTH 1½–4½ inches (4–11 cm)
DIET Mainly arthropods, also fish and other amphibians. Tadpoles filter the protozoan-rich mud
HABITAT & DISTRIBUTION Ponds, rivers, and stagnant pools in Africa, south of Sahara Desert

Characteristics The frogs have flattened bodies, powerful legs, and large, fully webbed feet with clawlike structures on three toes.
Reproduction Unlike most frogs, courtship is a quiet affair, its call being a faint chirping made under water. The eggs are laid singly and may be attached to aquatic plants, rocks, or debris.

WAIT AND SEE
African clawed frogs hang just below the surface of the water, arms outstretched, waiting for prey to swim by.

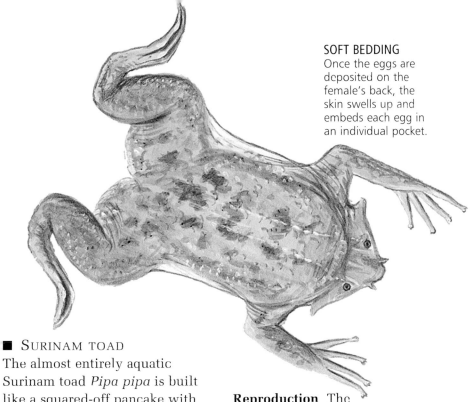

SOFT BEDDING
Once the eggs are
deposited on the
female's back, the
skin swells up and
embeds each egg in
an individual pocket.

■ SURINAM TOAD

The almost entirely aquatic
Surinam toad *Pipa pipa* is built
like a squared-off pancake with
a limb at each corner. During
breeding, the male distributes the
eggs over the female's back where
they sink into spongy tissue. Here
they develop into tiny, fully
formed froglets.

Characteristics The Surinam toad
has large, fully webbed feet and
powerful hindlimbs. Its flat head
has a pointed beak and tiny,
lidless, black eyes. It has no
tongue but uses its sensitive
fingers to capture prey.

Reproduction The
female lays about 100 eggs in
a single clutch and carries them
on her back for three months.

SNAPSHOT

LENGTH 1½–7 inches (4–18 cm)
DIET Worms, insect larvae,
and other bottom-dwelling
invertebrates
HABITAT & DISTRIBUTION Swamps,
streams, lakes, and other water
bodies in South America

Asian Horned Toad

Megophryidae

7 genera/74 species

■ GENERAL

The bizarre shape of the Asian horned toad *Megophrys nasuta* and its coloration provide excellent camouflage for its life among the leaf litter on the rainforest floor. The males become more noticeable during rainy periods when they sit in shallow streams making strangely metallic clanking noises.

BLENDING IN
With its ribbed, mottled brown skin, the Asian horned toad looks like a dead leaf.

S N A P S H O T
LENGTH **Up to 4½ inches (11 cm)**
DIET **Large prey such as rodents and smaller frogs. Tadpoles feed from the water's surface with funnel-shaped mouths**
HABITAT & DISTRIBUTION **Among the leaf litter on the floors of rainforests near rivers and streams in Southeast Asia**

■ CHARACTERISTICS

This large toad has flexible projections of skin on its upper eyelids and snout, which resemble horns.

■ REPRODUCTION

The eggs are laid in water, but little else is known of its reproductive habits.

Spadefoot Toads

Pelobatidae

2 genera/10 species

■ GENERAL
They spend the day and long, dry periods—most of the year if rain is scarce—in their deep, almost vertical burrows. On warm, moist nights they may come out to eat, and when it rains they emerge to breed in temporary pools.

■ CHARACTERISTICS
Spadefoots are plump toads with short limbs and large eyes.

SNAPSHOT
LENGTH Up to 4 inches (10 cm)
DIET Almost any terrestrial arthropod. The rain brings insects and a few nights' feeding allows them to survive months underground. The tadpoles eat algae and other plant material, while some cannibalize their pond mates
HABITAT & DISTRIBUTION Most live in dry areas with sandy soils. Found in North America, Europe, northwest Africa, and western Asia

■ REPRODUCTION
The tadpoles have to develop quickly before the breeding pools dry up. Egg laying to metamorphosis can take less than two weeks.

DIGGING TOOL
Spadefoots have a digging tubercle on each hind foot that they use to dig rapidly backward, circling as they descend.

New World Southern Frogs

Leptodactylidae

51 genera/about 750 species

S N A P S H O T

LENGTH **About 8 inches (20 cm)**
DIET **Anything it can swallow: insects, frogs, lizards, even small mammals, small birds, and snakes**
HABITAT & DISTRIBUTION **Tropical rainforests in Argentina. It can also survive in more arid regions**

■ ORNATE HORNED TOAD
The ornate horned toad *Ceratophrys ornata* has been called a "mouth with legs" because of its enormous, wide mouth. The toad is a robust, aggressive predator with a big appetite and it will attack an animal many times its own size. It cannot move quickly, so lies partially buried among leaf litter on the forest floor and ambushes its prey.

Characteristics Almost as wide as it is long, its common name comes from the folds of skin over its eye, which resemble small horns.

Reproduction Small clusters of eggs are laid hidden under rocks and logs.

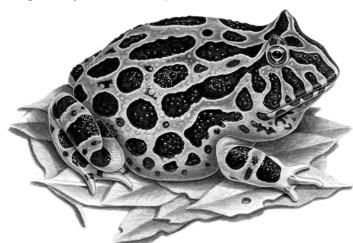

A TOUGH CHARACTER
The ornate horned toad usually lives in tropical rainforests but its range extends to more arid areas where it will estivate in mud or clay during the dry season.

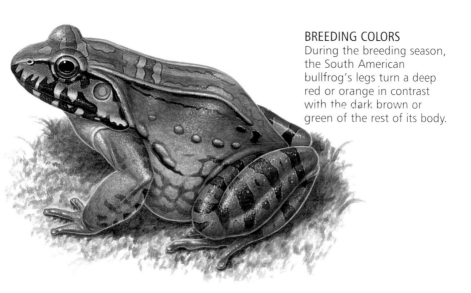

BREEDING COLORS
During the breeding season, the South American bullfrog's legs turn a deep red or orange in contrast with the dark brown or green of the rest of its body.

■ SOUTH AMERICAN BULLFROG

Like some other members of the genus, the South American bullfrog *Leptodactylus penta dactylus* is a very large frog that is often eaten by humans. In the West Indies the meat of the hind legs is served up as "mountain chicken." Because of its value as a food source to humans and others, really large examples are not plentiful.

Characteristics The South American bullfrog is a large and chunky frog. The male has a prominent black spur on its thumb and others on its breast to assist in holding the female during mating.

Reproduction This species lays its eggs in foam "nests" which are constructed while the frogs mate. The male uses his feet to whip the mixture of eggs and seminal fluid into a froth. The nest protects the fertilized eggs, and then the tadpoles, from enemies.

S N A P S H O T

LENGTH Up to 8 inches (20 cm)
DIET A variety of small invertebrates
HABITAT & DISTRIBUTION Most of Central and South America

Australian Southern Frogs

Myobatrachidae

21 genera/about 120 species

SNAPSHOT

LENGTH About 2 inches (5 cm)
DIET Wide range of small invertebrates, including insects, spiders, worms, and springtails
HABITAT & DISTRIBUTION Near streams, ponds, marshes, and other temporary water in woodlands, shrublands, and grasslands. It is widespread in eastern Australia

■ SPOTTED GRASS FROG
The semi-aquatic spotted grass frog *Limnodynastes tasmaniensis* is usually found in marshy, wet areas or near streams and ponds with grassy edges. During the day it sits under stones, fallen timber, and debris close to the water's edge. In hot, dry periods it shelters in cracks in the ground, usually under large rocks, where temperatures are lower.

Characteristics This medium-sized frog has a pointed head and strong limbs, and its toes are slightly webbed.

Reproduction The eggs are laid in a white, foamy mass on the surface of still water. They are usually attached to vegetation and exposed to sunlight.

DISTANT COUSIN
The spotted grass frog is similar in appearance to many ranid frogs of the Northern Hemisphere, but is not closely related to them.

The corroboree frog's yellow stripes match the color and pattern of the sphagnum moss and sedges in the swamps it inhabits

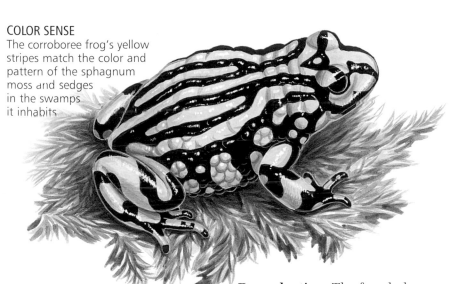

■ CORROBOREE FROG

The vivid coloration of the tiny corroboree frog *Pseudophryne corroboree* is similar to the striped ocher and charcoal decorations which the Aboriginal people of Australia paint on their bodies for ceremonial dances, or corroborees. Although its skin is toxic, it is thought that the bright colors are also useful in deterring predators.

Characteristics This small, squat frog has a rather toad-like gait, walking slowly on its short limbs and making occasional short leaps.

Reproduction The female lays about 26 eggs in a burrow in sphagnum moss. The tadpoles hatch when rain floods the nest in winter or when the snow melts in spring. If conditions are not wet enough, hatching is delayed.

S N A P S H O T

LENGTH Just over 1 inch (3 cm)

DIET Mainly ants and sometimes other small invertebrates

HABITAT & DISTRIBUTION Burrows in damp places such as bogs, seepages, and marshes. It is found at altitudes above 5,000 feet (1,500 m) in the Australian alps in New South Wales. Its numbers have declined dramatically in recent years

LENGTH About 2 inches (5 cm)
DIET Ants and termites
HABITAT & DISTRIBUTION Semi-arid slopes and plains west of the Great Dividing Range in southern Queensland and New South Wales, Australia, especially the black soils of inland river floodplains

■ CRUCIFIX TOAD
The crucifix toad *Notaden bennetti* is well adapted to life in dry areas where rainfall is sparse and seasonal. It spends much of its time buried underground and is seldom seen or heard except when it emerges to mate, feed, and breed after heavy rain.

Characteristics This medium-sized, squat, short-legged toad has warty skin and a blunt snout. It has a spade on each hind foot that it uses to dig backward into loose soil.

Reproduction The toad spawns in temporary pools caused by heavy rain. The tadpoles have to develop quickly before the water evaporates, usually within two or three weeks.

ALL BLUFF
When threatened, the toad rises on all fours, puffs out its body, and secretes a sticky, yellow liquid to deter potential predators.

True Toads

Bufonidae

24 genera/about 350 species

SNAPSHOT

LENGTH Up to 5½ inches (14 cm)
DIET Usually small invertebrates
HABITAT & DISTRIBUTION Prefers deep waterholes, dams, and other watery habitats. It is a native of southern Africa

■ LEOPARD TOAD

With its dry, warty skin, short limbs, and large parotid (toxin-producing) glands behind the eyes, the strikingly marked leopard toad *Bufo pardalis* is a typical true toad. Like all members of the *Bufo* genus, the leopard toad is a ground dweller that hides during the day, usually in holes, and emerges at night to hop about looking for prey, which it snaps up with its long, sticky tongue.

Characteristics This is sometimes called the snoring toad because of its deep, pulsating, snoring sound. It makes one call every three or four seconds. Its distinctive, warty back is symmetrically patched; the underside is whitish.

Reproduction Huge numbers of eggs are laid in paired strings in permanent water such as dams or waterholes. The jelly surrounding the eggs is quite bad tasting, thus discouraging fish and other animals from eating them.

TOOTHLESS TOAD
On close inspection, the leopard toad, like all toads, is toothless.

SNAPSHOT

LENGTH Males up to 3 inches (7 cm); females can be an inch longer

DIET Small invertebrates

HABITAT & DISTRIBUTION In Asian rainforests, usually well hidden in bushes and small trees in the dense parts of the forest

■ ASIATIC CLIMBING TOAD
The tree-dwelling Asiatic climbing toad *Pedostibes hosii* is well adapted to its arboreal life, with long limbs and broad, adhesive pads on the digits. Males are brown or blackish above with distinct bars or crossbars on the limbs. Females are purplish in color, with bright yellow spots, or olive green with chrome yellow spots on the sides and beneath.

Characteristics The body of the Asiatic climbing toad is quite stout, and the skin on the upperside is covered with small, scattered warts. The underside is light and finely granular.

Reproduction Little is known of its reproductive biology, although it lays large numbers of eggs.

ADAPTATIONS
The adhesive pads on this female toad's digits enable it to grip slippery leaves and branches.

■ VARIABLE HARLEQUIN FROG
Looking more like the unrelated
poison frogs than its relatives the
toads, the variable harlequin frog
Atelopus varius of South and
Central America is brilliantly
colored, a clear warning that its
skin secretes potent toxins. As
the variable harlequin frog is
slow moving and active during
the day, this warning is probably
a powerful deterrent to help fend
off potential predators.

Characteristics The strong colors
of this frog are its most distinctive
feature, and its common name is
apt, for it resembles the bright
hues of a circus harlequin. The
front digits are elongated to
enable better purchase.

Reproduction Eggs that are large
and unpigmented are laid in fast-
flowing streams. The tadpoles
have sucker-like mouths as well
as an adhesive disk on their
abdomen so they can stay put
while feeding.

S N A P S H O T
LENGTH 1–2½ inches (3–6 cm)
DIET Small invertebrates
HABITAT & DISTRIBUTION Costa Rica to Bolivia, the Guianan region, and coastal eastern Brazil

True Tree Frogs

Hylidae

40 genera/about 770 species

■ GREEN AND GOLDEN
  BELL FROG

The semi-aquatic green and golden bell frog *Litoria aurea* is usually found among bullrushes and reeds either in or near the edge of permanent water. Active at night and during the day, it enjoys basking in the sun, slipping into the water to cool off when necessary. It is a voracious feeder and catches its prey by lunging forward and seizing it with both hands.

Characteristics This frog has strong limbs, unwebbed fingers, and almost fully webbed toes. It is bright green and a rich metallic golden bronze in color, with the pattern varying between individuals.

Reproduction A loose mass of eggs is deposited among vegetation floating in water. The eggs hatch within a few days and the tadpoles metamorphose about four to six weeks later.

ENDANGERED
The green and golden bell frog, previously abundant, is now dangerously threatened by urban development and disease.

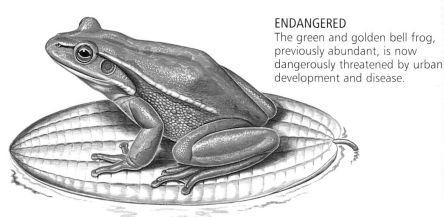

LENGTH About 4 inches (10 cm)
DIET Small invertebrates and sometimes small mammals
HABITAT & DISTRIBUTION Tropical forests, coastal areas, and arid inland regions in northern and eastern Australia

■ WHITE'S TREE FROG

Also known as the green tree frog, White's tree frog *Litoria caerulea* is one of Australia's best-known frogs due to its habit of visiting houses and buildings. While its natural environment is on the branches or in the hollow limbs of trees it can often be found in bathrooms, downpipes, watertanks, letterboxes, or any other damp and shaded place where it can shelter.

Characteristics A large, rather rotund frog, White's tree frog is usually bright green in color, but frogs that spend more time on the ground tend to be brown. It has large climbing pads on each toe and some webbing on its hind feet.

Reproduction Large clumps of 2,000 to 3,000 eggs are laid in still water in the wet season. They sink to the bottom of the pool where they hatch into tadpoles that take up to six weeks to metamorphose.

FROGS' CHORUS
The distinctive call of the White's tree frog is loud and deep, and when thousands of frogs gather to breed the noise can be deafening.

SNAPSHOT

LENGTH About 2 inches (5 cm)
DIET Insects that share its tree habitat such as caterpillars, flies, beetles, ants, and tree crickets
HABITAT & DISTRIBUTION Trees such as birch, oak, or apple trees. It is common in eastern North America and can be found on mossy or lichen-covered ledges or posts

■ GRAY TREE FROG
With skin that resembles lichen, the gray tree frog *Hyla versicolor* is beautifully camouflaged when it rests on a tree. This and its ability to stay perfectly still for hours at a time provide excellent protection. If an enemy gets too close and the frog decides to flee, it has orange "flash" markings on its groin that become visible only when it leaps away, thus startling and confusing a predator.

Characteristics The gray tree frog has a short, broad head and a stout body with large, adhesive pads on its fingers and toes.

Reproduction The frogs mate after their winter hibernation. The eggs are attached in small groups or singly to grass or plant stems near the surface of the water in ponds or rivers. About seven weeks after the eggs are laid the tadpoles complete metamorphosis and leave the water.

FEELING SAFE
The gray tree frog is perfectly camouflaged as it waits in a tree for potential prey to pass by.

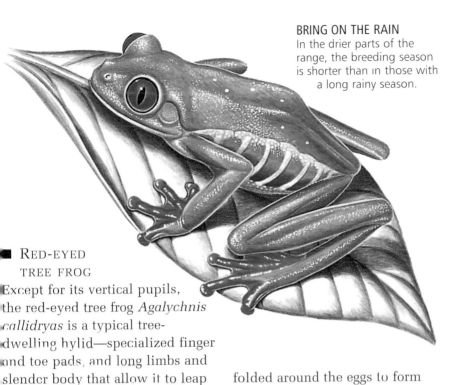

RED-EYED TREE FROG

Except for its vertical pupils, the red-eyed tree frog *Agalychnis callidryas* is a typical tree-dwelling hylid—specialized finger and toe pads, and long limbs and slender body that allow it to leap from one leaf or branch to another and to hold onto its perch.

Characteristics The red-eyed tree frog has vivid red eyes with vertical pupils, and barred flanks and bluish tinges on the limbs.

Reproduction When the red-eyed tree frogs mate, the males come down from the canopy of the rainforest to the low-growing foliage and, in a chorus of raucous croaking, call the females out of the treetops. The eggs are laid on the underside of a leaf that is then folded around the eggs to form a tube. The tube is plugged at each end with jelly. The tadpoles hatch about six days later, wriggle through the jelly and drop into the water below.

SNAPSHOT

LENGTH 1½–3 inches (4–7 cm)
DIET Adults feed on insects and other small invertebrates. Tadpoles eat decaying plant matter
HABITAT & DISTRIBUTION In the dense and damp rainforests of Central America

---

SNAPSHOT

LENGTH 1–5 inches (3–12 cm)
DIET Depending on the species, a range of invertebrate prey is eaten
HABITAT & DISTRIBUTION Tropical and temperate parts of Africa and Asia, including Madagascar and Japan

Oriental Tree Frogs

Rhacophoridae

12 genera/about 300 species

■ GENERAL

The rhacophorids, most of which are tree frogs, are relatives of the largely aquatic and terrestrial ranids or "true" frogs.

■ CHARACTERISTICS

The terminal segment of each finger and toe of many tree frogs is expanded into a specialized toepad that enables the frogs to adhere to vertical surfaces.

■ REPRODUCTION

Most rhacophorid frogs lay their eggs in foam "nests." As the eggs are produced, the mating frogs use their feet to beat the eggs and seminal fluid into a froth which hardens to protect the developing eggs. The larvae remain in the nest for some time before dropping into the water to complete their development.

NOT CLOSE
Despite the similarities in habits and appearance, the rhacophorid frogs, such as this dark-eared tree frog, are not closely related to the true hylid tree frogs.

WALLACE'S FLYING FROG
Wallace's flying frog *Rhacophorus nigropalmatus* has huge, fully webbed hands and feet, with fringes of skin along its limbs that enable it to glide from tree to tree. This is usually done to escape from predators as the frog rarely launches itself unless it feels threatened.

Characteristics This tree frog has a rather flattened body, with well-developed toe disks and loose skin on its belly to help it adhere more securely to the leaves and branches of its rainforest habitat. Its upper skin is smooth or finely

SNAPSHOT

LENGTH Up to 4 inches (10 cm)
DIET Like other tree frogs, the Wallace's flying frog feeds on small invertebrates
HABITAT & DISTRIBUTION Wallace's flying frog has quite a restricted distribution. It can be found on trees and bushes in the canopies of tropical rainforests of Malaysia and Borneo

granulated; the underside is coarser. Wallace's flying frog is green above, with minute white markings and one or two white patches on the thigh. Its underside is yellowish white.

Reproduction Like many other rhacophorids, this frog lays its eggs in a foam "nest" in a tree.

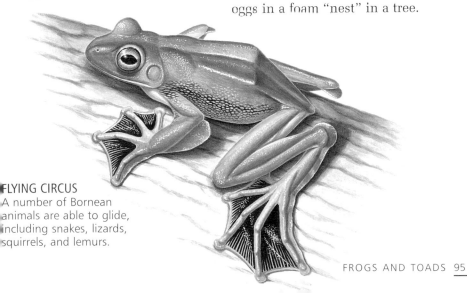

FLYING CIRCUS
A number of Bornean animals are able to glide, including snakes, lizards, squirrels, and lemurs.

Poison Frogs

Dendrobatidae

8 genera/about 170 species

■ GENERAL

These are some of the most colorful and interesting frogs. Their bright, gaudy hues are a warning that their skin glands secrete poisons that act on the nervous system. The toxin of one species, *Phyllobates terribilis*, is so potent that it is used by Colombian Indians to poison their blow-gun darts. Poison frogs are lively little foragers. They hop about among the leaf litter on the forest floor, rarely still for longer than a second or two.

■ CHARACTERISTICS

Most of the poison frogs are small and, unlike most frogs, they are active during the day. Some species have adhesive pads on their fingers and toes, and climb shrubs and trees.

SNAPSHOT

LENGTH 1–2 inches (3–5 cm)
DIET Most species seem to prefer ants and similarly sized arthropods, which they snap up with their tongue. Unlike most frogs, they actively hunt for their prey, moving about in short hops as they search
HABITAT Most live on the forest floor, though some are tree dwellers, and they are often found in areas near small streams

TADPOLE CARRIER
Although it is usually the male that carries the tadpole to water, in the strawberry poison frog *Dendrobates pumilio* it is the female.

The orange and black poison frog *Dendrobates leucomelas* was named from preserved museum specimens in which the bright yellow colors had faded. "Leucomelas" means black and white.

■ REPRODUCTION

Mating takes place after an elaborate courtship. Small numbers of eggs are laid in moist places and a parent, usually the male, guards the eggs. When the tadpoles hatch, they wriggle onto the parent's back and are carried to water to complete their development. In some species the female releases the tadpoles into a water-holding bromeliad plant, returning occasionally to deposit an unfertilized egg into the plant as food for the tadpoles.

■ DISTRIBUTION

Poison frogs inhabit moist, tropical forests in Central and South America, from Nicaragua to southeastern Brazil and Bolivia.

TOXIC ARTHROPODS

The skin toxins of poison frogs, such as this funereal poison frog, are probably obtained from the arthropods they eat.

True Frogs

Ranidae

Over 40 genera/over 500 species

■ WOOD FROG

The wood frog *Rana sylvatica* is the most terrestrial of the North American frogs. Its brown and gray coloring blends in with the forest floor, and when it is still it is almost invisible. The frog has very long legs and is a powerful jumper.

Characteristics The wood frog's long legs are twice the length of its head and body. It has partially webbed feet and a flat, slender body with a broad, pointed head. Its coloring can be various shades of brown, from a pinkish color

SNAPSHOT

LENGTH 2–3 inches (5–7 cm)
DIET Insects, earthworms, and other small invertebrates
HABITAT & DISTRIBUTION Found in damp woods in northern North America and its range extends north of the Arctic Circle. It can survive temperatures as low as 21°F (-6°C)

through to dark brown, and it has a distinct dark mask over the side of its face.

Reproduction The wood frog emerges from hibernation to breed in the early spring. A globular mass of 1,000 to 3,000 eggs is attached to submerged vegetation in a shallow pool. If the water later freezes, the eggs do not die, but continue developing as soon as higher temperatures return.

CATCH ME IF YOU CAN
The wood frog never jumps twice in the same direction. This confuses predators and makes the frog harder to catch.

LENGTH 2½–4 inches (6–10 cm)
DIET Little is known about the Solomon Islands tree frog's feeding habits
HABITAT & DISTRIBUTION This frog prefers the humid tropical forests of its Solomon Islands habitat

■ SOLOMON ISLANDS
   TREE FROG

The Solomon Islands tree frog *Platymantis guppyi* is one of several species in the genus, all of which have limited distributions within Asia and the South Pacific. All the frogs of this genus live on islands, ranging from the southern Philippines to New Guinea and eastward through the Solomon Islands and Fiji.

Characteristics This tree frog is well adapted to its arboreal life. It has well-developed suction pads that enable it to attach itself to tree ferns and other rainforest plants. The fingers and toes are only partly webbed.

Reproduction This frog lays a few, large eggs with a big yolk sac. Larval development occurs inside the egg, and the young hatch as froglets without an intermediary aquatic larval stage.

ANCIENT TRAVELER

Oceanic islands typically do not have native frogs. It is assumed that the frog's ancestors either rafted between islands on floating vegetation or used ancient land connections.

SNAPSHOT

LENGTH 2–3 inches (5–7 cm);
male is smaller than the female
DIET Insects such as flies, beetles,
butterflies, caddis flies, gnats, and
caterpillars as well as snails and
small crustaceans
HABITAT & DISTRIBUTION Live on
the margins of brooks, marshes,
streams, and cold springs in
eastern North America, as far
north as Hudson Bay in Canada

■ PICKEREL FROG

The pickerel frog *Rana palustris*
lives in and around brooks and
streams, spending more time out
of the water than in it. It retreats
to the water to breed, to avoid
predators such as snakes and
birds, and to cool off.

Characteristics This brown-
spotted, smooth-skinned frog is an
agile, powerful jumper, with long
legs and webbing on its feet. It
has an orange-yellow belly that
"flashes" when it jumps.

Reproduction An irregular mass
about 2 inches (5 cm) in diameter
and containing 2,000 to 3,000 eggs
is laid in shallow water in spring.
The eggs hatch within a few days.
The tadpoles metamorphose at
different rates, some taking two,
three, or four months, others
waiting till the following spring
to turn into frogs.

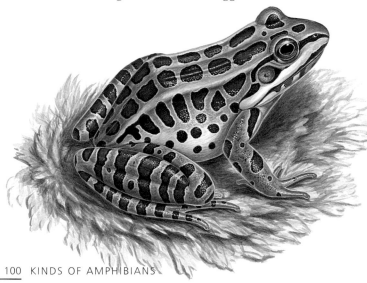

FOUL SMELL
The frog produces
an irritating
secretion on its skin,
which has a very
unpleasant odor.

■ ORNATE BURROWING FROG
The ornate burrowing frog *Hildebrandtia ornata* is an African species. Ranid frogs are most diverse in Africa, where there are 16 endemic genera. The ornate burrowing frog usually emerges from its burrow only after rain. It has a squat body, short limbs, and a large digging spur on the heel.

Characteristics This mottled brown frog can sometimes be distinguished by the green stripe along its body. Its throat is dark with a pair of distinctive, white Y-shaped markings. Its pupils are horizontal. Although the fingers lack webbing, the toes are webbed.

Reproduction The small eggs are laid individually in shallow water. The tadpoles have heavy jaws and fat bodies. They grow to quite a large size before metamorphosing into adult frogs.

SNAPSHOT

LENGTH Just over 2 inches (5.5 cm)
DIET Little is known about the specific food preferences of this elusive species
HABITAT & DISTRIBUTION Inhabits open bushland and savanna in tropical and subtropical southern Africa

Gold Frog

Brachycephalidae

2 genera/2 species

SNAPSHOT

LENGTH Less than ½ inch (1.2 cm)
DIET Little is known about the food preferences of this species
HABITAT & DISTRIBUTION The humid coastal region of south-eastern Brazil

■ GENERAL

This tiny frog, named for its bright golden-yellow color, builds burrows among the leaf litter on the forest floor of its restricted Brazilian habitat. On its back the gold frog *Brachycephalus ephippium* has a peculiar, cross-shaped bony shield that is fused to its backbone. This shield is probably used to plug the entrance to its burrow.

■ CHARACTERISTICS

These are small frogs, with greatly reduced phalanges. They have only three functional toes on each foot and two on the hand. The horizontal pupil is remarkably large for such a diminutive frog.

■ REPRODUCTION

A small number of large eggs are laid on land. Direct development takes place in the eggs, which hatch into tiny froglets, omitting the tadpole stage.

SMALLEST AMPHIBIAN
The gold frog is one of the world's smallest amphibians.

Eastern Narrow-mouthed Frog

Microhylidae

Over 60 genera/over 300 species

SNAPSHOT

LENGTH 1–1½ inches (3–4 cm)
DIET A variety of insects, however it prefers ants
HABITAT & DISTRIBUTION Near still water and under moist decaying plant litter. It is found mainly in southeastern USA with a few populations in northern USA

■ GENERAL

The eastern narrow-mouthed frog *Gastrophryne carolinensis* is completely nocturnal. It is rarely seen except in the breeding season when it can be found floating in pools with only the tip of its pointed head visible. At the first sign of danger it disappears beneath the surface of the water.

■ CHARACTERISTICS

A stout, short-legged frog that has a small, pointed head with tiny, beady eyes and a narrow, slit-like mouth. It is a smooth-skinned, brown-patterned frog with a loose fold of skin extending across the head behind the eyes. It has a croak which sounds like the weak bleat of a sheep.

■ REPRODUCTION

The frogs usually mate after rain. Small eggs are laid in stagnant water where they float on the surface in a thin sheet.

OUT OF SIGHT
An excellent burrower, this frog can disappear into leaf litter or loose soil very quickly.

African Tree Frogs

Hyperoliidae

19 genera/about 300 species

SNAPSHOT

LENGTH About 1 inch (2 cm)
DIET Flying insects such as damsel flies, mosquitoes, and mites
HABITAT & DISTRIBUTION On the edges of lakes, ponds, and swamps in Africa and Madagascar

■ REED AND LILY FROGS
During the day these small frogs rest on reeds and sedges at the edge of water, often still for hours at a time. At dusk they set up a shrill chorus and begin to look for food. They are often boldly colored and patterned, and there can be considerable variation in the markings within the same species. Some species, such as the arum frog, are almost the same color as the lilies they inhabit. When it hides in the calyx of the arum lily, eating insects attracted by the nectar, this tiny, ivory-colored frog is almost invisible.

Characteristics Most are smooth-skinned, but the two species of spiny reed frogs have minute spines on their head and back, which can be seen only with a magnifying glass.

Reproduction Some deposit their egg masses on floating vegetation, others on plants or rocks under the water. Some lay them on leaves overhanging water. When the tadpoles hatch, they drop into the water below.

TINY CLIMBER
Like all reed frogs, the painted reed frog *Hyperolius marmoratus* has expanded toe-pads and is a good climber.

■ RUNNING FROGS

These ground-dwelling frogs prefer to walk or run rather than hop. They have bold, dark stripes that provide camouflage among the grasses in which they live. The underside is white, and ranges from smooth to slightly granular. The pupils are vertical, and the fingers lack webbing, although the toes are slightly webbed.

Characteristics These are slow-moving, medium-sized frogs. The body is elongated and the limbs slender, with long digits. Their cryptic color provides good camouflage in their savanna environment.

BREEDING CALLS
Male running frogs such as this Senegal running frog, issue a loud, clear "quoip" sound, with long intervals between calls.

Reproduction Small, pigmented eggs are laid attached to submerged vegetation. Each egg is surrounded by a jelly capsule, but eggs may adhere together in small clusters.

SNAPSHOT

LENGTH About 1½ inches (4 cm)
DIET Mainly insects
HABITAT & DISTRIBUTION Open grassland areas from the sea-shore almost to the snowline. Three species are widely distributed in southern Africa

---

Paradox Frog

Pseudidae

2 genera/7 species

SNAPSHOT

LENGTH About 3 inches (7 cm)
DIET Small aquatic invertebrates
HABITAT & DISTRIBUTION Still,
richly vegetated bodies of water
in the tropical lowlands of
northern South America

■ GENERAL

The paradox frog *Pseudis paradoxa* is an excellent swimmer and lives in shallow lakes, ponds, and swamps where there is plenty of plant life. The frog floats among the vegetation, searching for food by stirring up the mud with its fingers and toes. The paradox frog survives very dry periods by burying itself in mud.

■ CHARACTERISTICS

It has extremely powerful hindlimbs, huge, fully webbed feet with long, slender fingers and toes. It has extraordinarily slippery skin and cryptic coloring, which help it to elude predators such as snakes and fish.

■ REPRODUCTION

The eggs are laid in a frothy mass on the surface of the water. The tadpoles reach lengths of up to 10 inches (25 cm) before metamorphosing into the more moderate-sized adults. The tadpoles reach their full size in four months.

FROG FREAK
The paradox frog is famous for its gigantic tadpoles that can grow up to four times the length of the adults.

Ghost Frogs

Heleophrynidae

1 genus/4 species

SNAPSHOT

LENGTH About 2 inches (5 cm)
DIET It is assumed their main diet is insects
HABITAT & DISTRIBUTION They live around fast-flowing mountain streams in the Cape and Transvaal regions of South Africa

■ GENERAL

These frogs have rather flat bodies and well-developed adhesive pads on their fingers and toes. They are therefore well adapted to fit into crevices and to cling to slippery rocks along the cool, shaded mountain streams where they live.

■ CHARACTERISTICS

These are small to medium-sized frogs that have long legs and heavily webbed feet for swimming. Their underside is covered with thin, white skin, so thin that their digestive organs can be seen through it. They have a flat head and very prominent eyes.

■ REPRODUCTION

The eggs are large and are laid beneath wet stones in shallow backwaters. The tadpoles have sucker-like mouths, which enable them to cling to rocks while feeding in swiftly flowing water.

SEE THROUGH
The ghost frogs' common name may have been coined due to the thin, pale skin on the belly that allows you to see the internal organs.

Fire-bellied Toads

Bombinatoridae

2 genera/8 species

■ GENERAL
These largely aquatic toads are small and warty-skinned with colorful red, orange, or yellow undersides. When they are disturbed, they arch their back and throw up their arms and legs, thus revealing their bright belly and warning predators that their skin secretions are distasteful and

SNAPSHOT

LENGTH 1–3 inches (3–7 cm)
DIET Worms, crustaceans, and other invertebrates
HABITAT & DISTRIBUTION Shallow water at the edges of rivers, streams, marshes, drainage ditches, and in temporary puddles. They are found in Europe and Asia

mildly toxic. Sometimes they expose their belly by turning over onto their back.

■ CHARACTERISTICS
Fire-bellied toads have a flattened body and a disk-shaped tongue. They have an unusual call, producing it during the inhaled breath rather than on the exhalation like most frogs.

■ REPRODUCTION
The eggs are large and are laid either singly at the bottom of ponds, or in groups, often attached to aquatic plants.

LYING IN WAIT
Fire-bellied toads, such as this Oriental fire-bellied toad, catch flying insects that land on the water's surface or fly just above it.

Glass Frogs

Centrolenidae

3 genera/about 120 species

SNAPSHOT

LENGTH 1 inch (3 cm)
DIET Spiders and insects such as beetles and caterpillars, as well as flying insects such as moths and midges
HABITAT & DISTRIBUTION Moist forests in Mexico and Central and South America

◼ GENERAL

Most glass frogs live high up in trees that overhang mountain streams in the cloud forests and rainforests of tropical America. Some larger species live and breed in rocky waterfalls. Their name comes from the transparent skin on their abdomens—the result of a scarcity of pigment—which makes their internal organs visible. In some species the heart can be seen beating.

◼ CHARACTERISTICS

Most species are small and delicate, and bright green. They have a wide, blunt head with small eyes set almost on top of the skull.

◼ REPRODUCTION

Clutches of eggs are laid on leaves overhanging streams. The male remains with the eggs until the tadpoles hatch and fall into the water below. Waterfall dwellers attach their eggs to rocks.

GREEN BONES

This species of glass frog, *Hylinobotrachium fleischmanni,* has white bones like most frogs. However, some glass frogs have green bones.

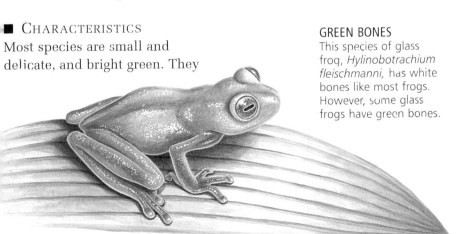

Caecilians

Caecilians

Caeciliidae/Rhinatrematidae/
Ichthyophiidae

34 genera/156 species

■ GENERAL

Caecilians are so little known—
they rarely emerge from their
burrows—that most have no
common name. Caecilians are
capable of moving snakelike
across land, but normally they
live underground. They move
through existing tunnels or create
new ones by pushing their head
through moist soil or loose mud.
Even the most aquatic species are
adept at burrowing into the soft
mud and gravel on the bottoms

S N A P S H O T

LENGTH Vary from 3 inches (7 cm)
to 5 feet (1.5 m)
DIET All caecilians are carnivorous.
Land-dwelling species eat earthworms, insects, and sometimes
small frogs and lizards. Aquatic
species eat insects, earthworms,
and other invertebrates
HABITAT Terrestrial caecilians live
in moist soil, leaf litter, and rotten
logs in tropical forested areas.
Aquatic species live in rivers and
streams and aquatic larvae live in
seepages and streams

and edges of the streams and
rivers where they live.

■ CHARACTERISTICS
Caecilians have numerous skin
folds, or rings, which partially or
completely encircle their body.
Terrestrial caecilians have a

UNDERWATER
Typhlonectes natans is an
aquatic caecilian from
South America, which
gives birth to fully
developed young.

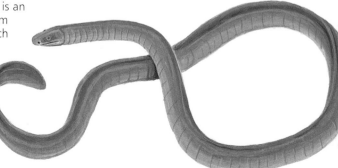

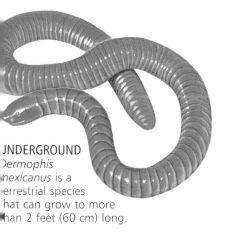

cylindrical body. Aquatic and semi-aquatic species are flattened from side to side and have a fin running the length of their back to facilitate movement through water. Caecilians have smooth skin which, like all amphibians, contains numerous poison glands. Most species are subdued in color, usually shades of bluish gray, but some are boldly colored and marked, perhaps as a warning to predators of their poisonous skin secretions. Caecilians move by undulating their bodies, with the muscle action going from the head to the back. They have a unique pair of sensory organs—probably of taste and/or smell—called tentacles, on each side of the snout between the eye and the nostril.

■ REPRODUCTION

All caecilians have internal fertilization. Some species lay eggs that hatch into water-dwelling larvae that later metamorphose into adults. Some lay eggs that hatch directly into terrestrial juveniles with no larval stage. Other species give birth to live young, again with no larval stage. Females of the egg-laying species remain with their eggs until they hatch.

■ DISTRIBUTION

Caecilians are found in Central and South America, Southeast Asia, India, the Seychelles archipelago in the Indian Ocean, and in equatorial Africa.

STOCKY BUILD
Siphonops annulatus, a fairly stocky and common terrestrial species, is found in Brazil and Argentina.

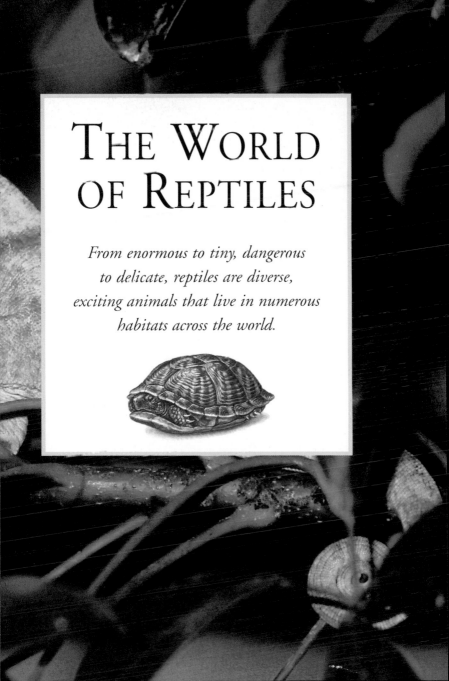

THE WORLD OF REPTILES

From enormous to tiny, dangerous to delicate, reptiles are diverse, exciting animals that live in numerous habitats across the world.

Where Do Reptiles Live?

REPTILE HABITATS

There are reptiles in nearly every habitat on Earth. They live in rainforests, woodlands, savannas, grasslands, mountains, deserts, and scrub. They can be found on the ground, under the ground, in trees, and in water, and some even take to the air from time to time.

TURTLES AND TORTOISES

Sea turtles live in temperate and tropical oceans. Freshwater turtles occur in still water such as ponds and lakes, and in running streams and rivers. The sea turtles and a few species of freshwater turtles leave their aquatic habitats only to lay eggs. The other species are

IN AND OUT OF WATER Amphibious turtles such as these spotted turtles, soak up warmth from the sun before they set off to hunt for food in cool water.

amphibious and regularly move about on land. There are a few land tortoises that live in dry areas where there are no open bodies of water.

BEWARE! Lying submerged in its swampy environment, with only its eyes, ears, and nostrils showing, this alligator is a fierce predator that attacks with a sudden rush.

CROCODILIANS

All crocodilians are semi-aquatic and do not venture far from water. Most species favor the warm, still water of lakes, ponds, swamps, or the lower reaches of rivers, while a few species prefer the cool, clear water of running rivers. Most crocodilians live in freshwater habitats, but a few are at home in the more saline environments of mangrove swamps and estuaries.

TUATARAS

Tuataras live in areas of low forest and scrub, spending the day in burrows on the forest floor.

The thorny devil of central Australia has sharp, spiny scales that are arranged so that they collect rainwater, which is then channeled to the mouth via fine grooves.

LIZARDS

Lizards are found in almost all habitats. Some live in temperate climates, some in extremely hot or cold areas, and some experience both extremes in different seasons. Most lizards are terrestrial or tree-dwelling. They shelter in all sorts of places—in cracks and crevices, under rocks and logs, among leaf litter or clumps of vegetation, in holes in tree trunks or in the foliage—and some burrow into the ground. Lizards are especially numerous in arid areas. Physical adaptations as well as certain ways of behaving allow them to survive where no bird or mammal could. A few lizards are semi-aquatic,

retreating to the water when they are disturbed. The marine iguana is the only lizard that enters the sea.

AMPHISBAENIANS

Worm lizards spend most of their lives underground. They prefer moist habitats in which to build their tunnels, but some burrow through very hard soils.

SNAKES

Snakes occur on almost all parts of the planet except the very

BY THE SEA Marine iguanas from the Galápagos Islands are the only living lizards dependent on the marine environment. They feed almost exclusively on marine algae.

coldest areas, and they live in all kinds of habitats. Most live on the ground, but many live in trees, beneath the ground in burrows, or in fresh or sea water. Some, such as the anaconda, which lies in wait at the water's edge for prey, are semi-aquatic. Others, such as the file snakes, are totally aquatic.

CONCERTINA CLIMBING Some tree-dwelling snakes, like this emerald tree boa, have developed a concertina way of climbing smooth tree trunks.

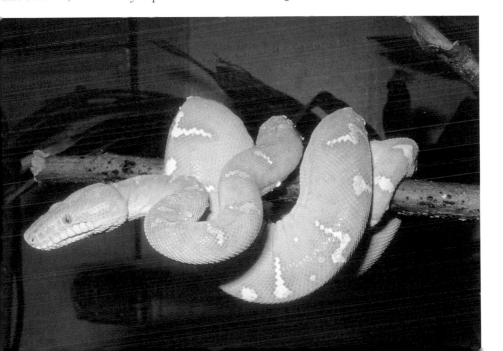

DISTRIBUTION

Reptiles live on all continents except Antarctica and some can be found on tiny, remote islands. Being cold-blooded, the number of species decreases toward higher latitudes and elevations. Nevertheless, the hardy, viviparous lizard and the European viper occur above the Arctic Circle in Scandinavia and, on some mountains, lizards skirt around snow banks in their daily activities.

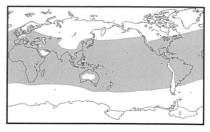

TURTLES AND TORTOISES Turtles and tortoises live in the temperate and tropical regions of the world. Hidden-necked turtles are found on all continents except Antarctica and in all the oceans. Side-necked turtles are found only in Australasia, South America, and central and southern Africa.

CLOSING THE BOX The eastern box turtle *Terrapene carolina carolina* is found in eastern and southern USA and Mexico. It has a hinge that allows the bottom shell to close tightly against the top shell.

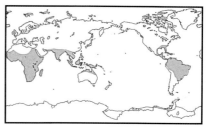

CROCODILIANS Most species occur in tropical areas, but a few, such as the American and Chinese alligators, extend into temperate regions. Alligators and caimans are found in southeastern USA, Central and South America, and eastern China. Crocodiles occur in Africa, Madagascar, Australia, Asia, and Central and South America. The false gharial occurs in Southeast Asia and the gharial in India, Pakistan, Nepal, and Bangladesh.

ISLAND REPTILE The Fijian crested iguana *Brachylophus vitiensis* has a small distribution —Fiji and Tonga. It is now considered an endangered species.

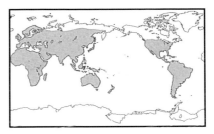

LIZARDS Lizards today occupy almost all landmasses except Antarctica and some Arctic regions of North America, Europe, and Asia. Species occur from sea level up to 16,500 feet (5,000 m). They are particularly numerous in hot, arid parts of the world, but many also occur in temperate climates.

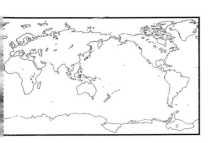

TUATARAS Tuataras once ranged throughout the two main islands of New Zealand, but are now restricted to 30 small islands off the northeast coast of the North Island and in Cook Strait.

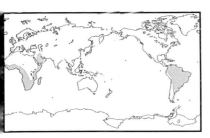

AMPHISBAENIANS Most species live in Central and South America and Africa, but there are a few species in the West Indies and the warmer parts of North America (Florida), the Middle East, and Europe (Spain).

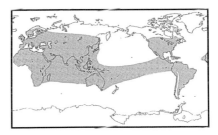

SNAKES Snakes inhabit most parts of the planet outside the polar regions, from alpine meadows to the tropical Pacific and Indian oceans. They occupy all landmasses with the exception of Iceland, Ireland, New Zealand, and some small oceanic islands.

Reptiles at Risk

Reptiles are threatened when their habitats are destroyed for agricultural land, housing divisions, and even sporting activities such as trail riding and scuba diving; when they are hunted for meat and turtle eggs, and skinned for leather; when they are collected as "pets"; and when they are preyed upon by introduced animals such as pigs, foxes, cats, mongooses, and rats.

Species that live on islands or in small areas are especially vulnerable because they often occur in small numbers. The land iguana of the Galápagos Islands is seriously endangered because of predatory dogs and cats. Some sea turtles, which are hunted for their meat and eggs, are now dying after mistaking plastic bags for their main food—jellyfish.

HUMAN INTERVENTION

Humans are the main danger to reptiles, but we also have the power—through awareness and intervention—to ensure the continued success they have enjoyed for 300 million years.

BACK FROM THE DEAD

The re-emergence of the Australian pygmy blue-tongue skink is encouraging. It had not been seen alive for 33 years and was rediscovered in 1992, following the finding of a freshly eaten lizard in a brown snake on the road. It has since been discovered to spend most of its time hiding in abandoned spider burrows in grassland habitats—explaining why it had been so rarely found previously.

A PRECIOUS SPECIES Sea turtles are among the largest species of turtles and they are the most vulnerable. Human contact needs to be one of respect and wonder.

Reptiles Up Close

THE INSIDE STORY

The most obvious feature that all reptiles share is their dry, horny scales. Other special features have also evolved within the different reptile groups that have allowed them to live so successfully for so long.

PROTECTIVE SCALES

Reptile scales are made from keratin—the same material as our fingernails. They not only

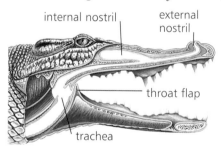

internal nostril · external nostril · throat flap · trachea

UNDERWATER ADAPTATIONS
Crocodilians can struggle with prey underwater without drowning.

protect a reptile from predators—a barrier for the internal organs and aiding concealment—but also prevent it from drying out when water is scarce, and absorb heat to keep the animal warm. Chelonians, crocodilians, and tuataras shed the outer layer of individual scales independently, whereas snakes, lizards, and amphisbaenians shed the outer layer of their scales as a sheet of many scales several times a year.

CHELONIANS

Turtles and tortoises have the unique feature of a shell built into the skeleton that allows them to more or less conceal themselves entirely within the shell. Both the carapace and the plastron are made of interconnected bony

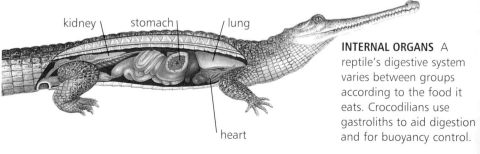

kidney · stomach · lung · heart

INTERNAL ORGANS A reptile's digestive system varies between groups according to the food it eats. Crocodilians use gastroliths to aid digestion and for buoyancy control.

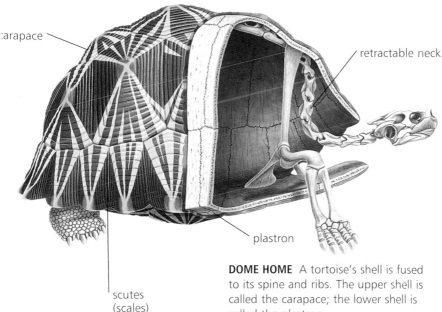

carapace

retractable neck

plastron

scutes
(scales)

DOME HOME A tortoise's shell is fused to its spine and ribs. The upper shell is called the carapace; the lower shell is called the plastron.

plates covered by an outer layer of large, horny plates, or scales.

CROCODILIANS

These fierce predators are able to wait for prey while almost completely submerged because of their external nostrils that stay above the water. Once attacked, prey is dragged underwater and the crocodilians' throat flap is closed to prevent water from entering their trachea. Unlike other reptiles, most crocodilians do not chew their food. They swallow stones and other hard objects, called gastroliths, to break down the food so it can be digested.

SQUAMATES

Lizards, amphisbaenians, and snakes make up the largest group of reptiles. Amphisbaenians have evolved a hard, strong head to burrow through soil. Lizards have evolved many special features to suit their habitats including different body plans, which are highlighted farther on.

Spotlight on Snakes

■ Snakes have evolved many features that allow them to live successfully within their environments. The following adaptations are only a few.

SPECIALIZED FEATURES

The long, slender body of snakes—the internal organs have been reorganized to accommodate this elongation—allows them to enter

REAR, GROOVED FANGS

The venom of rear-fanged snakes travels down grooves along the fangs.

rear, grooved fang

venom gland

HOLLOW, FIXED FANGS

Cobras and their relatives have hollow, fixed fangs in the front of the mouth. Venom travels down the hollow fang and is injected into the prey.

hollow, fixed fang

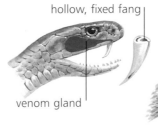

venom gland

SWINGING FANG

Vipers and rattlesnakes have large, hollow fangs that swing forward to the front of the mouth.

hollow, swinging fang

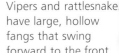

venom gland

INTERNAL REORGANIZATION

A snake's liver and lung are long and thin—their one functional lung runs nearly the length of their body. The reproductive organs and kidneys are arranged one behind the other.

lung

liver

stomach

venom gland

hollow, swinging fang

narrow crevices for food or shelter and also gives snakes a greater degree of control over their body temperature. Snake scales have also been modified to suit the habitats they live in so they can move quickly and effectively.

More than half of all snakes are venomous, some are more dangerous than others. The venom is produced by highly evolved mouth glands and injected through grooved or hollow fangs. The venom immobilizes prey and in some snakes, begins digesting it.

Snakes have many defense tactics, the most famous being the rattlesnake's rattle. It has evolved from the horny scale at the tip of a "normal" snake's tail.

A USEFUL SCALE

Snake scales give us clues about how and where snakes live. Most snakes that live in wetlands and fresh water have keeled scales. These help to balance side-to-side movement and provide a larger surface area for heating and cooling. Snakes that burrow usually have smooth scales, because these make it easier for them to push through the soil. Many water and sea snakes have "granular" scales with a rough, grainy surface like sandpaper, which helps them to grip their slippery prey.

| Keeled scales | Smooth scales | Granular scales |

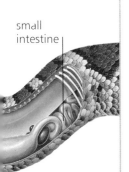

small intestine

RATTLE TAIL
When a rattlesnake's tail is shaken, interlocking shells of hardened skin make a rattling sound. It warns large grazing animals that a rattlesnake is nearby.

interlocking shells

SHAPED FOR SUCCESS

Body shapes and their functions reflect an animal's behavior. Reptiles are ideally shaped to function successfully within their habitat. The thick and powerful tail of a crocodilian is shaped like a paddle and is used to propel it through the water during long-distance swimming. Because they are legless, snakes have a body shape to maximize movement in their different habitats so they can hunt and protect themselves from predators. A chelonian's shell and legs are shaped to suit land or water, or both, as in some species. The array of lizard body shapes reflects their vastly different sizes, habitats, and behaviors.

SHELL HOMES

The shape and structure of a chelonian's shell—from the slow-moving land tortoise to the fast, sleek sea turtle—often points to how it moves and the environment in which it lives.

LAND TORTOISE
Thick, domed shell for protection

SEMI-TERRESTRIAL TURTLE
Semi-domed shell for land and water

POND TURTLE
Small, flattened shell for swimming

SEA TURTLE
Light, streamlined shell for swimming

SUITABLE LIMBS Chelonians' legs have evolved to suit the different environments. Sea turtles have flippers to propel them through the water. Land tortoises have column-shaped legs with claws. Pond turtles need to move on land and in the water, so they have webbing between their claws.

Sea turtle

Land tortoise

Pond turtle

SNAKE SHAPES

Snakes have different body shapes suited to the environments in which they live—trees, water, and land.

A tree snake's body is shaped almost like a loaf of bread so that it can grip small crevices and notches on the branches.

A sea snake has a flattened body. This gives it a larger surface area with which to push against the water.

A ground-dwelling snake has an almost semicircular body. It has strong muscles to grip slippery sand and soil, or rough rocks.

A Lizard's Body Plan

Lizards have developed many features to live successfully in their different habitats. For example, all lizards have ears, but lizards that live beneath the ground do not have external ear openings. Most burrowing lizards also have smooth scales to reduce drag as they plow through the soil. In the same way, the shape of a lizard's body, the type of feet it has, and the style of its tail are adapted to ideally suit its environment.

The flat body of the desert short-horned lizard helps it hide from predators.

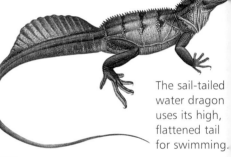

The sail-tailed water dragon uses its high, flattened tail for swimming.

The legless lizard has a streamlined body for moving in narrow places.

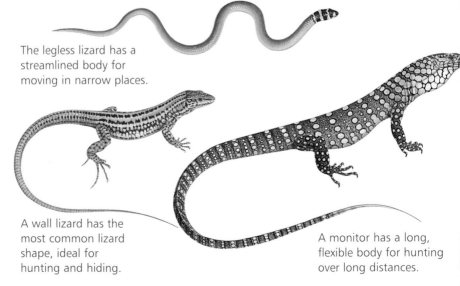

A wall lizard has the most common lizard shape, ideal for hunting and hiding.

A monitor has a long, flexible body for hunting over long distances.

FOOT SPECIALISTS

Many sand-dwelling lizards have webbed feet or fringed toes to help them grip shifting sand. A desert gecko's foot is webbed to help it dig burrows and to move across sand dunes to look for food or to escape from predators. The toes of the fringe-toed lizard have featherlike scales to grip sand when the lizard needs to chase prey or run from predators. The fringes on its toes may also help this lizard to cool its feet so that it does not become too hot.

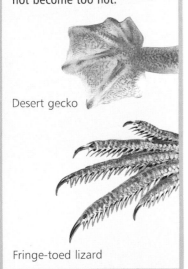

Desert gecko

Fringe-toed lizard

THE TALE OF THE TAIL Lizards' tails can have many functions. Like the rest of its body, they have been adapted to suit its environment.

Tree-living chameleons have prehensile (gripping) tails that help them hang on to twigs when they are moving about.

Australian shinglebacks live in dry places. Their club-like tails store fat—a source of energy and water.

Skinks' tails are long and streamlined. Most skinks can shed their tail if attacked by a predator.

Leaf-tailed geckos live in rock crevices or trees, and have flattened, camouflaged tails.

SURVIVAL SENSES

Reptiles rely on a variety of sense organs to detect their prey, recognize a predator, and find a mate.

SENSE ORGANS

The relative importance of each sense is strongly correlated to a species habitat and behavior.

Sight Most reptiles have good vision, and some can tell the difference between colors. However, amphisbaenians, which live underground, can only distinguish light and dark.

Hearing The hearing of reptiles varies among species. Snakes have limited reception of airborne sounds, as the "hearing" membrane—tympanum—is absent or covered by skin. They compensate for this by sensing vibrations from the ground.

Taste and smell Olfactory senses are moderately to well developed in most reptiles. The most important olfactory organ is the Jacobson's organ that lies in the roof of the mouth. It has a similar function to the taste and smell organs of humans.

Heat sensors Pit vipers, most pythons, and boas have special sensory organs that can detect infrared heat rays from warm-blooded prey.

NIGHT-TIME EYES Nocturnal snakes have small eyes, but many have vertical pupils that open up wide in dim light. They rely on their tongue and, in some species, special heat-sensing organs to sense prey.

DAYTIME EYES Diurnal snakes usually have large, round eyes. Some of the day-active ground-dwelling and tree-dwelling snakes have very acute vision.

HEAT SENSORS

A snake's sensory heat organs are situated in pits on the side of the face of the pit vipers (as shown on this rattlesnake), and on the lips of pythons and boas. With these heat receptors, a snake can detect how far away the animal is and where its heart (its warmest part) is located. This allows the snake to strike accurately, even in total darkness.

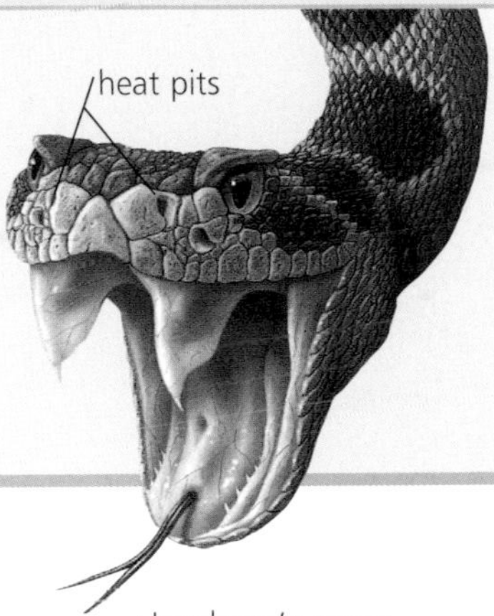

heat pits

Jacobson's organ

sensory cells of Jacobson's organ

nasal passage

nostril

FLICK OF THE TONGUE Reptiles, particularly lizards and snakes, flick their tongue to pick up particles from the air, water, or the ground. The tongue then brings these particles to the Jacobson's organ, which is in the roof of the mouth. There they are analyzed, giving the snake accurate information about the presence of predators or prey.

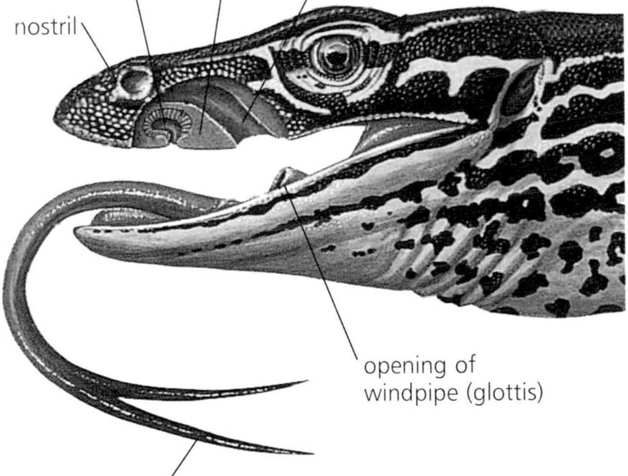

opening of windpipe (glottis)

forked tongue

Staying
Alive

FINDING FOOD

Some carnivorous reptiles actively pursue their prey, while others employ a strategy of "sit and wait" until the prey comes close. When close enough, the reptiles strike.

CROCODILIANS

Crocodilians eat everything from insects, frogs, and snails to fish, birds, turtles, and large mammals. Crocodilians' teeth are designed to grip, not cut. Fish-eating crocodilians have sharp, narrow teeth and long snouts to hold their slippery, struggling prey. Larger crocodiles with broader snouts often ambush land animals when they come to drink. With powerful jaws and strong teeth, a crocodile grasps its prey and pulls it underwater. The crocodile twists and spins its body, which tears large prey to pieces.

TUATARAS

Tuataras come out to hunt at night. Since they are not fast runners, they usually wait for small prey such as insects, snails, and worms to come close before seizing it with their tongue. Larger animals are impaled on the tuatara's sharp front teeth.

LIZARDS

Most lizards are carnivorous, and eat everything from ants and insects to other lizards and animals. Plant-eating lizards, such as large skinks and iguanas, eat mainly plants and fruit with either flattened teeth for crushing or narrow teeth for slicing. The marine iguanas of the Galápagos Islands eat mostly seaweed, which they gather off the rocks at low tide. A few lizards have a long

PRICKLY FOOD A Galápagos Islands land iguana nibbles a cactus plant. It lives in burrows in sandy ground, and feeds on plants and insects.

LONG, STICKY TONGUE A chameleon moves slowly toward its prey. Its incredibly long tongue, which is covered in sticky mucus, shoots out and traps the prey.

tongue that shoots out to capture prey. Other lizards seize prey in their mouths and swallow it when it stops struggling.

AMPHISBAENIANS

If they detect prey such as an insect or earthworm, amphisbaenians can dig very quickly and catch it with their sharp, interlocking teeth and powerful jaws. The larger species can cut and tear pieces from larger prey such as small vertebrates and carrion.

SNAKES

All snakes are carnivores. They eat only animals, their young, and their eggs. Snakes have a number of ways of overcoming their prey. Snakes like boas and pythons kill by constriction. They seize the animal with their sharp teeth, then wrap their coils around it, squeezing it until it suffocates. The venomous snakes inject their prey with venom which paralyzes or kills it. Some snakes swallow small animals live. They suffocate

OPEN WIDE Snakes swallow their prey whole. A snake's upper and lower jaw are attached with elastic connections that allow the bones to part and stretch the snake's mouth wide open

after a few minutes in the snake's stomach. Most snakes eat a single animal, often a large one, and may eat on average once or twice a week. Snakes can survive for long periods without eating.

TURTLES AND TORTOISES

Sea turtles eat shellfish, fish, jellyfish, and seagrasses. Semi-terrestrial turtles hunt on land and water, and eat both plant and animal food. Young land tortoises eat worms and insects as well as plants. Adult tortoises, which move too slowly to catch animals, eat flowers, fruit, and plants.

SHARP JAWS Ancient chelonians had small teeth, but modern chelonians do not have any teeth. They use their sharp-edged jaws to grasp and cut plant and animal food.

DEFENSE AND ESCAPE

Small reptiles have many enemies, particularly birds, mammals, and other reptiles. The main threats for large reptiles are people. Reptiles avoid their enemies with a variety of strategies. Different reptiles have different techniques. If the first technique of defense fails, a reptile will employ another strategy for escape. A few reptiles, such as the horned lizards of North America, are so unpalatable because of spikes that predators will avoid them. However, the first line of defense for reptiles is often camouflage and remaining still so they become "invisible." If noticed, the first instinct for most reptiles is to flee danger. If provoked, slow-moving reptiles can sometimes protect soft body parts by tucking in or curling up. Many small lizards are able to shed their tail if it is grasped by a predator. Other reptiles bluff or play tricks to avoid attack. Large reptiles such as crocodilians, large lizards, and venomous snakes will bite or scratch. The bite from a venomous snake can be fatal.

TUCKED IN The ornate box turtle draws its head and legs into its domed shell to protect itself from predators (and from drying out).

STAYING STILL Tree-dwelling lizards defend themselves by becoming "invisible." Many predators react to small movements, so the lizards keep very still and try to look like part of the tree.

INTIMIDATION A frilled lizard startles a predator by opening its mouth, hissing loudly, and extending the frill behind its neck. A blue-tongued lizard scares a predator away by flashing its blue tongue and hissing.

FALSE COLORS The bright bands of color on the venomous Mayan coral snake (top) warns predators to stay away. The false coral snake copies these color bands to trick predators.

FOOLING THE ENEMY The long, blue tail of the western skink from USA and Mexico distracts a predator from its vulnerable head and body.

MOVING AROUND

Reptiles burrow, crawl, walk, run, climb, glide, and swim depending on their habitat and mode of locomotion. They need to be able to move effectively so they can look for food, escape from predators, and find a mate.

Sea turtles can journey up to 3,000 miles (5,000 km) across oceans to reach their nesting beaches. They can swim at speeds of up to 18 miles (29 km) per hour when escaping from predators, such as sharks. Land tortoises with strong and heavy shells are slow-moving—the most they could move in an hour would be about 300 feet (91 m).

Snakes lever themselves along on the edge of their belly scales, connected by tiny muscles to the

FLYING LEAP The flying gecko of Southeast Asia has flaps of skin along its sides, and glides from tree to tree to escape predators.

ribs, and can move at about 2 miles (3 km) per hour. Sea snakes and other water snakes move just like land snakes—they push against the water (rather than against the land) with the sides of their curved bodies. Sea snakes have flattened tails to give them additional "push." Amphisbaenians move like snakes in confined spaces. They anchor the front part of their body by pressing coils against the side of the tunnel and drawing the rest of the body behind it.

CROCODILE CRAWL Crocodiles crawl or slither on their bellies for short distances, especially when they enter the water from a riverbank and do not want to alert prey by disturbing the water's surface.

CROCODILE WALK On dry land, crocodiles lift their bodies off the ground and walk, dragging their tails.

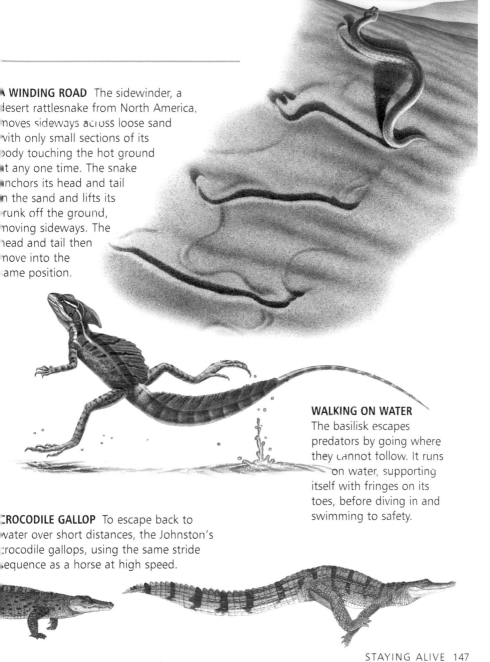

A WINDING ROAD The sidewinder, a desert rattlesnake from North America, moves sideways across loose sand with only small sections of its body touching the hot ground at any one time. The snake anchors its head and tail in the sand and lifts its trunk off the ground, moving sideways. The head and tail then move into the same position.

WALKING ON WATER The basilisk escapes predators by going where they cannot follow. It runs on water, supporting itself with fringes on its toes, before diving in and swimming to safety.

CROCODILE GALLOP To escape back to water over short distances, the Johnston's crocodile gallops, using the same stride sequence as a horse at high speed.

The Next Generation

FINDING A MATE

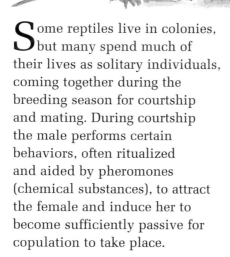

Some reptiles live in colonies, but many spend much of their lives as solitary individuals, coming together during the breeding season for courtship and mating. During courtship the male performs certain behaviors, often ritualized and aided by pheromones (chemical substances), to attract the female and induce her to become sufficiently passive for copulation to take place.

COURTSHIP RITUALS

During the courtship of snakes, the male usually crawls repeatedly over the female and orients his head to hers, at the same time bringing his tail into position next to hers to allow copulation to take place. A male gharial snorts air through the knob on the end of its snout. It makes a buzzing noise that warns rival males to stay away. The male gopher tortoise circles the female on land,

READY TO MATE Marine iguanas are usually a grayish black. When they are ready to mate, the spiny crest and limbs of the males (as shown on this male out of the water) turns green and their body becomes rusty red.

PUSH-UPS A defined territory provides an area for an adult male lizard to hunt for food and find a female. If a rival invades its territory, a collared lizard does "push-ups" to make itself look bigger.

perhaps butting her shell, to induce her to become passive so he can mount her from the rear. Male tuataras inflate their body and elevate the crest and spines to attract females and to advertise their presence to other males. Lizards communicate in a number of ways, such as raising crests, extending or curling dewlaps, waving a front limb or lashing a tail, or changing color. The fork-tongued lizards rely on pheromones to recognize potential mates and rivals.

THE FLUTTERS As male and female turtles usually look the same, they recognize each other through behavior. This male red-eared turtle courts a female by fluttering his claws in front of her face.

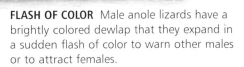

FLASH OF COLOR Male anole lizards have a brightly colored dewlap that they expand in a sudden flash of color to warn other males or to attract females.

STARTING OUT

Most reptiles abandon their eggs after laying, but a few watch over the eggs until they hatch. Crocodilians are the most devoted, and can stay with their young for several years.

TURTLES AND TORTOISES

Most turtles lay their eggs in a funnel-shaped chamber in sand or soil, which the female digs with her hindlimbs. A few lay their eggs in burrows, in the nests of other animals, or under leaf litter or decaying plant matter. Once the eggs are covered, the parents show no interest in the young. In many species, the hatchlings spend the winter in the egg chamber,

RACE TO THE SEA Newborn flatback turtles race to the sea, safety in numbers being the only thing that saves some of them from predatory birds and crabs.

appearing for the first time in the spring. From the day they leave the nest, the young must fend for themselves. It is estimated that less than one turtle in a hundred will live to become an adult.

BRIEF VISIT Female sea turtles leave the sea only to lay eggs, and males never come ashore. They lay several clutches, of 80 to 200 eggs, over two- or three-week intervals.

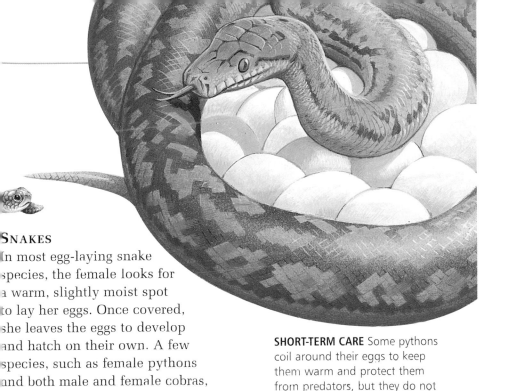

SNAKES

In most egg-laying snake species, the female looks for a warm, slightly moist spot to lay her eggs. Once covered, she leaves the eggs to develop and hatch on their own. A few species, such as female pythons and both male and female cobras, do stay until the eggs hatch.

SHORT-TERM CARE Some pythons coil around their eggs to keep them warm and protect them from predators, but they do not look after the young once the eggs have hatched.

CROCODILIANS

Crocodilians may be ferocious predators, but the females, sometimes with help from the

MATERNAL DEVOTION An American alligator carries her newly hatched babies to a quiet pond, where she will protect them from predators.

male, look after their eggs and young more carefully than most reptiles. Some crocodilians make nests by scraping soil and vegetation into mounds; others bury their eggs in holes dug in sand or soil. The eggs take 60 to 100 days to develop, depending on the species and the temperature of the nest. During this time, the female, and sometimes the male, will remain near the nest to defend it against predators. When the hatchlings first break through the shell, they begin calling from within the nest and the female scrapes a hole in the nest to release them. The mother, and sometimes other adults, guards the babies in groups for periods ranging from a few weeks to years in the case of some American alligators.

Tuataras

As in crocodilians, turtles, and egg-laying lizards and snakes, young tuataras are born with a horny "tooth" on the tip of their snout, which they use to cut their way out of the egg shell. They can move very quickly and are most active during the day—possibly a strategy made necessary by the cannibalistic tendencies of the nocturnal and larger adults.

Lizards

Most lizards lay eggs but some species give birth to live young. Egg-laying lizards may dig holes for nests, make use of ready-made hiding places, or simply bury them in soil or leaves. The eggs usually take from two weeks to three months to hatch depending on the temperature of the nest, though some take much longer. Most lizards bury the eggs and abandon them. A few lizards guard their eggs

LIVE YOUNG The Australian blue-tongued skink gives birth to several live young.

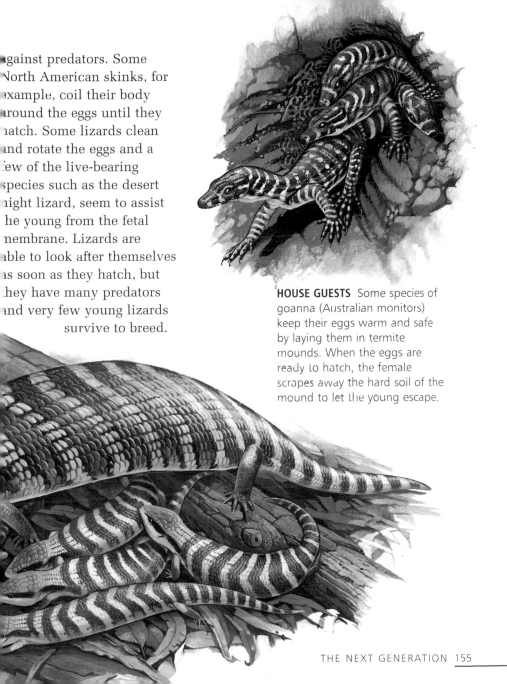

against predators. Some North American skinks, for example, coil their body around the eggs until they hatch. Some lizards clean and rotate the eggs and a few of the live-bearing species such as the desert night lizard, seem to assist the young from the fetal membrane. Lizards are able to look after themselves as soon as they hatch, but they have many predators and very few young lizards survive to breed.

HOUSE GUESTS Some species of goanna (Australian monitors) keep their eggs warm and safe by laying them in termite mounds. When the eggs are ready to hatch, the female scrapes away the hard soil of the mound to let the young escape.

KINDS OF REPTILES

There are 7,400 species of living reptiles. They vary enormously in size and structure, and live in almost every habitat in the temperate and tropical regions of the world.

Turtles and Tortoises

Side-necked Turtles

Chelidae

11 genera/about 45 species

■ GENERAL

The side-necked turtles in the family Chelidae are well adapted to life in fresh water. The long neck of many species allows them to draw breath at the surface of the water without exposing the rest of the body to potential predators, and they can stay underwater for lengthy periods

while searching for food. In seasonally dry areas, some species will burrow deep into the mud at the bottom of lagoons and swamps where they remain dormant until the rain comes again.

CRYPTIC COLORS
The South American twist-necked turtle *Platemys platycephala* is a poor swimmer that walks along the bottom of streams. Its coloration camouflages it on the leaf-strewn forest floor or stream bed.

EXCELLENT SWIMMER
The Sepik turtle *Elseya novaeguineae* is a short-necked turtle that inhabits streams and lakes in New Guinea.

◄ CHARACTERISTICS
The short-necked turtles and snapping turtles have shorter necks and are excellent swimmers. The long-necked species use their long neck to ambush prey by striking at fish moving past.

■ DISTRIBUTION
Side-necked turtles are found in Australia, New Guinea, and South America.

◄ REPRODUCTION
Clutches of 1 to 25 eggs are laid in soil or in sandy riverbanks. The Australian northern snake-necked turtle is the only turtle that lays its eggs underwater.

REPTILE AT RISK
There are only 30 western swamp turtles *Pseudemydura umbrina* from Western Australia remaining.

Helmeted Side-necked Turtles

Pelomedusidae

5 genera/25 species

■ GENERAL

These side-necked, freshwater turtles are aquatic and semi-aquatic. Giant, side-necked river turtles are a common sight on the sandbanks of the Amazon and Orinoco rivers when they are nesting. The African species live in both flowing and still water but prefer to hide in the mud where they find their food and where they bury themselves in the dry season to estivate.

■ CHARACTERISTICS

The African species have strong-smelling musk glands that deter predators.

S N A P S H O T

SHELL LENGTH Range in size from the 5-inch (12-cm) African dwarf mud turtle to the 3-foot (1-m) South American river turtle

DIET Some species eat mollusks, worms, and insects. Others, such as South American river turtles, are predominantly plant-eaters

HABITAT & DISTRIBUTION Some live in and around flowing rivers and streams. Others prefer the still water of ponds and swamps, and even temporary floodwaters. They are found in tropical South America, Africa south of the Sahara, and Madagascar

■ REPRODUCTION

Depending on the size of the turtle, clutches of 4 to 150 eggs are laid in a chamber excavated in soil or in a sandy riverbank.

PLANT-EATER

The yellow-spotted Amazon River turtle *Podocnemis unifilis* is mainly a plant-eater but sometimes filters particles from the water's surface.

Big-headed Turtle

Platysternidae

1 genus/1 species

SNAPSHOT

SHELL LENGTH **Rarely more than 8 inches (20 cm)**
DIET **Emerges at night to hunt snails, crabs, and mollusks**
HABITAT & DISTRIBUTION **Lives in fast-flowing mountain streams in southern China, and northern and central Indochina**

GENERAL

This unique Asian turtle cannot retract its huge head nor its long, heavily armored tail into its shell. It is a poor swimmer, preferring to walk along the bed of the mountain streams where it lives, but it can climb well. It is sometimes seen basking on the lower branches of bushes and trees at the edge of the water.

CHARACTERISTICS

Its flattened shell is too small to enclose the fleshy parts of its body. Both the head and tail are covered with large, horny scales, and it has very strong, beak-like jaws, which it uses to grasp its prey tightly and to bite through their thick shells.

REPRODUCTION

Only one or two eggs are laid in a nest dug by the female in the bank of a stream. In its natural environment, this low birth rate is not a problem as the turtle has few predators.

HEAVILY ARMORED
A big-headed turtle from Vietnam *Platysternon megacephalum shiui* crawls well along the stream bottom by grasping rocks with its strong claws.

Snapping Turtles

Chelydridae

2 genera/2 species

■ GENERAL

The two species of snapping turtles are famous for their swift, savage bite. They lie in wait and ambush their prey, snapping it up with their powerful jaws. The American snapping turtle, the smaller of the two species, spends much of its time in water, though it does like to sunbathe in the mornings on the banks of streams and swamps. The alligator snapping turtle is even more aquatic. Large, older animals rarely leave the water, and then only the females to lay eggs.

SNAPSHOT

SHELL LENGTH American snapping turtle 18½ inches (47 cm); alligator snapping turtle 26 inches (66 cm)
DIET The American snapping turtle is mainly carnivorous, feeding on frogs, salamanders, fish, and small birds and mammals. The alligator snapping turtle eats anything it can capture, including small turtles and mussels
HABITAT & DISTRIBUTION The American snapping turtle lives in freshwater swamps and streams. The alligator snapping turtle lives in rivers, lakes, and large swamps

MEAT-EATER
After a sunbathe, an American snapping turtle *Chelydra serpentina* snaps up a snake.

CHARACTERISTICS

These turtles have a long tail with large scales similar to those of a crocodile. They have a huge, powerful head, which cannot be completely retracted into the shell. The alligator snapping turtle has a line of bony ridges on its carapace, long, soft scales on its neck, and a hooked beak.

REPRODUCTION

Both species dig a nest chamber, usually well away from water, and lay 20 to 40 eggs.

DISTRIBUTION

The American snapping turtle is found from southern Canada to Ecuador. The alligator snapping turtle lives in southeastern USA.

FISHING WITH WORMS

The muddy brown, algae-covered shell and rough, brown skin of the alligator snapping turtle *Macroclemys temmincki* provide it with excellent camouflage on the river bed. It has a pink, wormlike appendage on its tongue that it waves in its open mouth to lure fish and other unwary prey to within reach of its fast jaws.

New World Pond Turtles

Emydidae

10 genera/34 species

■ GENERAL

The best-known pond turtles are the ornamented turtles—the beautiful painted turtles, sliders, and cooters. They have brightly colored shells, heads, and limbs. Many species like to bask in the sun, especially in the early morning when they congregate along the banks of rivers and ponds to raise their body temperature—although they are always prepared to plunge into deeper water if alarmed.

SNAPSHOT

SHELL LENGTH 4½–23½ inches (11–60 cm)
DIET See main text
HABITAT Most pond turtles are semi-aquatic and live in swamps, pools, ditches, rivers, and even coastal lagoons and estuaries. Some, such as the box turtles, are more terrestrial and live in grasslands, prairies, and woodlands far from water

■ CHARACTERISTICS

Pond turtles have a bony shell covered with horny plates, and some species have well-developed hinges on the plastron that can completely close the shell. They also have well-developed limbs with webbed feet. In a number of species, the males are much smaller than the females.

BIG AND BEAUTIFUL
The largest subspecies of painted turtle, *Chrysemys picta belli* grows up to 10 inches (25 cm) long and occurs in western USA.

PROTECTION
The eastern box turtle *Terrapene carolina carolina* can withdraw its head, limbs, and tail into its shell.

DIET

There is considerable variation in diet between species, even between sexes and individuals. For example, the much larger female map turtles, which live in deeper water, have a largely vegetarian diet, while the smaller males favor a more carnivorous diet in the shallows. In some species the adults are more vegetarian while the young feed mainly on insects. Species that live in brackish water eat a broad range of food including crustaceans, mollusks, and aquatic plants.

REPRODUCTION

Most New World pond turtles dig a nest or cavity in which five to ten eggs are laid. Often several clutches are laid in a season.

DISTRIBUTION

New World pond turtles occur in the Caribbean, and North, Central, and South America, with one species, the European pond turtle, in Europe, North Africa, and the Middle East.

SUNBATHING
The painted turtle *Chrysemys picta picta* is fond of basking.

Old World Pond Turtles

Bataguridae

24 genera/56 species

■ GENERAL

There are many similarities between these and the New World pond turtles. Many Old World species are mostly aquatic, leaving the water only to sunbathe or lay eggs. Others are decidedly amphibious. The Mediterranean turtle and Caspian turtle, for example, live in arid and mountainous areas where the streams tend to dry up in the

S N A P S H O T

SHELL LENGTH Range from 11–31 inches (28–80 cm)
DIET River turtles tend to be omnivorous when young, but herbivorous when adult. Most other aquatic species are herbivores, except the Malayan snail-eating turtle, which primarily eats mollusks. Amphibious and terrestrial species tend to be omnivorous, though the land turtles are mostly herbivores
HABITAT Aquatic species live in estuaries, rivers, and lakes; semi-aquatic species in forested ponds, streams, and marshes; and terrestrial species in woodlands and mountain forests

summer. They migrate overland, often long distances, to find new sources of water. If they find none, they bury themselves until it rains.

TERRESTRIAL SPECIES
The spined or cogwheel turtle *Heosemys spinosa* is a forest dweller from Southeast Asia.

AQUATIC SPECIES
The Malayan snail-eating
turtle *Malayemys subtrijuga*
lives in still or slow waters.

■ CHARACTERISTICS

River turtles, the largest of all the
pond turtles, have a distinctive,
solid shell and strong, fully
webbed feet. The amphibious
hinged tortoises of Asia have a
plastral hinge that allows the
turtle to withdraw its head and
limbs into a completely closed
shell. Some terrestrial species
have colors and markings that
provide them with camouflage on
the forest floor. The warm yellow,
orange, and brown patterns of the
Indochinese box turtle make it
almost invisible among the leaf
litter. The shells of the keeled box
turtle and the black-breasted leaf
turtle have serrated edges that,

along with their variegated brown
color, give the turtles a leaf-like
appearance when they are still.

■ REPRODUCTION

Small species lay one or two eggs,
larger species around thirty. The
painted terrapin of Asia often lays
its eggs on beaches. The young
live briefly in the sea then make
their way to estuaries and rivers.

■ DISTRIBUTION

Old World pond turtles are found
in Europe, North Africa, Asia, and
Central and South America.

Land Tortoises

Testudinidae

10 genera/39 species

■ GENERAL

Land tortoises from temperate regions are dependent on seasonal supplies of fresh, herby plants and spend the colder months hibernating underground. In hot, dry regions, land tortoises are active only in the morning and late afternoon. During the heat of the day they rest in the shade of shrubs and trees or in burrows in the earth. Some take refuge in underground burrows during the dry parts of the year.

■ CHARACTERISTICS

Most land tortoises have high-domed, heavy shells that make them slow-moving. The bones

SNAPSHOT

SHELL LENGTH Ranges from 4–51 inches (10–130 cm)
DIET All land tortoises are mainly vegetarian, though they will eat insects, worms, crustaceans, mollusks, and even carrion and the dung of hoofed animals
HABITAT Land tortoises live in various habitats, from deserts to rainforests

FLAT AS A PANCAKE
The African pancake tortoise *Malacochersus tornieri* has a flat, flexible shell that allows it to squeeze into crevices in its rocky habitat.

Land tortoises range in
length from the 4-inch
(10-cm) Madagascan spider
tortoises to the 51-inch
(130-cm) wheel-barrow-sized
giants of the Aldabra Islands.

In the shells of the giant species, such as the Galápagos tortoises, have a honeycomb structure that encloses many small air chambers to make the shell lighter. When threatened, many land tortoises retract their heads and all or most of their limbs into the shell. They have strong, stumpy legs with claws.

REPRODUCTION
The eggs of all land tortoises have a calcified shell that is resistant to damage and drying out. To make digging a nest easier in often hard ground, the females may release urine and water (stored in their anal sac) to soften the soil.

■ DISTRIBUTION
Land tortoises are found in Europe, Africa, Asia, and the Americas as well as on islands such as the Seychelles, Aldabra, and the Galápagos Islands.

TESTUDINATA

SNAPSHOT

SHELL LENGTH Up to 43 inches (110 cm)
DIET Grass and other herbaceous plants and leaves from bushes
HABITAT & DISTRIBUTION The tortoises live on seven islands in the center of the Galápagos archipelago. In the cooler months they live on the grassy lowlands. During the hot, dry season they travel to the volcanic high-lands to wallow in the water, to feed on the plant life there, and to shelter in the shade

■ GALÁPAGOS TORTOISES
Groups of these giant tortoises were isolated from each other many thousands of years ago and as a result, have adapted differently. Tortoises on the large, wetter islands have developed big, dome-like shells, and are known as "domes." Tortoises on the smaller, drier islands where plants grow tall have long legs and a smaller "saddleback" shell.

SADDLEBACKS

A "saddleback" shell is raised in front so the tortoises can stretch their neck to reach up to the plants.

Characteristics Galápagos tortoises weigh 330–440 pounds (150–200 kg) and have elephantine limbs and feet.
Reproduction Mating occurs after the male rams the female with his shell and nips at her legs until she is forced to draw them in; this immobilizes her. The female lays clutches of about ten eggs in a nest in the dry lava soils of the lowlands of the islands. The time of incubation varies from three to eight months, depending on the temperature. Most young tortoises die in the first ten years of life.

Softshell Turtles

Trionychidae

7 genera/23 species

GENERAL

Instead of an outer horny layer on their carapace, the softshell turtles have a leathery skin, which makes their shell light and flexible. They are fast swimmers in open water, and can stay underwater longer than most aquatic turtles. Oxygen can be absorbed from the water through the lining of their throat and also through their skin. They lie hidden from predators on the muddy beds of streams and lakes.

CHARACTERISTICS

Softshell turtles have knife-sharp, horny jaws that they use to defend themselves, and a snorkel-shaped

SNAPSHOT

SHELL LENGTH 12–51 inches (30–130 cm)

DIET Most species are strictly carnivorous, feeding on mollusks, crustaceans, aquatic insects, worms, frogs, and fish. A few will also eat fruit and aquatic plants

HABITAT & DISTRIBUTION These turtles live in freshwater rivers, lakes, and streams, with some inhabiting the brackish estuaries of larger rivers. They are found in North America, Africa, and Asia

snout that allows them to breathe while keeping the rest of their body under the surface. Many species have large flaps of skin on the plastron to cover the hind feet.

REPRODUCTION

Most softshell turtles lay about 10 to 20 eggs. They are about 1 inch (3 cm) in diameter and are laid in a nest excavated on a beach or in a riverbank or a river sandbar.

SPINY SHELL EDGE
The eastern spiny softshell *Apalone spinifera spinifera* is a colorful North American species.

Mud and Musk Turtles

Kinosternidae

3 genera/22 species

■ MUD TURTLES

Most of these are inconspicuous, brown-colored turtles, which spend the greater part of their day walking on the bottom of streams and lakes looking for food. In the mornings they leave the water to bask in the sun. Many species, especially the smaller ones, climb onto shrubs and trees at the water's edge.

Characteristics All species have a solid carapace that is covered by

SNAPSHOT

SHELL LENGTH Range from 6–8 inches (15–20 cm)
DIET All mud turtles are carnivorous. They eat worms, insects, mollusks, crustaceans, fish, and amphibians
HABITAT & DISTRIBUTION The semi-aquatic mud turtles are found in and around the edges of lakes, streams, and ponds in the USA, Central America, and northern South America

strong, occasionally overlapping, horny shields. The plastron is hinged at the front and the back so the turtle can completely close the shell.

Reproduction Several clutches of one to six eggs are laid each year. Some species lay them under leaf litter or in rotting logs, others excavate a shallow nest chamber.

MUD BATH
The yellow mud turtle
Kinosternon flavescens
is found in Mexico
and the USA.

Musk turtles

The four species of musk turtles found in the United States are often called "stinkpot" turtles because of the extraordinarily strong musky smell they release when they are captured or disturbed. Musk turtles from Central America also produce this odor, and they have sharp, horny beaks as well that they use to defend themselves effectively. Musk turtles are closely related to the mud turtles and have similar habitats and behaviors.

Characteristics Most musk turtles have a reduced plastron. In the cross-breasted turtles of Central America it is a strong, bony cross.

SNAPSHOT

SHELL LENGTH Range from 6–8 inches (15–20 cm)

DIET The turtles are omnivorous. They eat insects, spiders, mollusks, fish, amphibians, and aquatic plants

HABITAT & DISTRIBUTION Musk turtles are semi-aquatic and live in lakes, streams, and ponds in central and southern USA and in central America

Reproduction Most species lay several clutches of two to five eggs each season. The eggs are laid under fallen timber or in dense leaf litter, or in a shallow, excavated nest chamber.

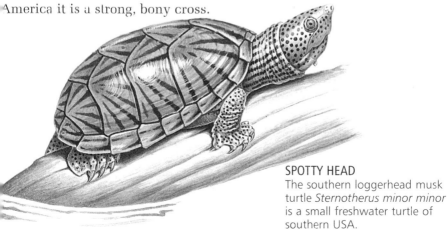

SPOTTY HEAD
The southern loggerhead musk turtle *Sternotherus minor minor* is a small freshwater turtle of southern USA.

Hardback Sea Turtles

Cheloniidae

1 genus/7 species

■ GENERAL

With their flattened, streamlined shells and large front flippers, sea turtles are built for life in the ocean. They can swim at speeds of up to 18 miles (29 km) per hour when escaping from predators, such as sharks. Usually they swim much more slowly, using the ocean currents to help them search for food. The males never leave the water and the females do so only to lay eggs. They often sunbathe at the surface, drifting on floating fields of seaweed, or in shallow water left by the receding tide on coral reefs.

LONG DISTANCE TRAVELERS
Some green turtles migrate from the coast of Brazil to nesting beaches on Ascension Island in the mid-Atlantic Ocean, a distance of 3,000 miles (5,000 km).

ENDANGERED TURTLE
The much sought-after "tortoise shell" of the Pacific hawksbill turtle *Eretmochelys imbricata* ha put this species at great risk.

■ CHARACTERISTICS

The shells of hardback sea turtles have a complete covering of horny plates. Their forelimbs are more strongly developed than their hindlimbs—a feature that distinguishes them from freshwater species—and they are shaped like paddles or flippers. The turtles use their forelimbs to move through the water, the

SNAPSHOT

SHELL LENGTH **Range in size from 28 inches (70 cm) to 7 feet (2 m)**
DIET **Most sea turtles are chiefly carnivorous. They eat fish, jellyfish, sponges, crabs, clams, mussels, and sea urchins. Some species also eat marine plants and the green turtle grazes on sea grasses**
HABITAT & DISTRIBUTION **Sea turtles are found in all the tropical and subtropical oceans of the world**

EYE WASH
Sea turtles produce "tears" from special glands close to the eyes to get rid of salt.

...indlimbs serving chiefly as udders. The shell is lighter than that of freshwater species because there are areas of fibrous skin between the bony plates of the carapace and the plastron. Sea turtles cannot retract their head inside their shell.

■ REPRODUCTION

Sea turtles travel vast distances across the oceans to breed. The two sexes rendezvous and mate at sea near the nesting beaches, often the same beach at which they themselves were hatched. The female comes ashore at night to lay the eggs. She builds a nest in the sand or dunes above the high-tide line. The clutches are large, varying from 80 to 200. Several clutches may be laid at two- or three-week intervals, though she will lay only every two or three years.

RENDEZVOUS AT SEA
Olive ridley sea turtles are found throughout much of the Atlantic and Pacific. They mate offshore from the nesting beach.

Leatherback Turtle

Dermochelyidae

1 genus/1 species

■ GENERAL
The largest turtle alive today
is the leatherback turtle
Dermochelys coriacea, the only
survivor of an otherwise extinct
family. Unlike the other sea turtles,
whose shells are covered by horny
plates, the shell of this species is
covered by a leathery skin.

■ CHARACTERISTICS
The span from the tip of one front
flipper to the tip of the other is
greater than the length of the shell.
The turtles have a large head with
big eyes and a hooked beak.

■ REPRODUCTION
Like all sea turtles, the females
return to the same beaches over
and over again to lay their eggs,
usually the same beach where
they themselves were hatched.
They lay several clutches of 50
to 170 eggs at ten-day intervals,
every two or three years.

SNAPSHOT
SHELL LENGTH Normally less than 5 feet (1.5 m)
DIET Feeds mainly on jellyfish but also eats mollusks, crustaceans such as swimmer crabs, and echinoderms such as sea urchins and sea stars
HABITAT & DISTRIBUTION Found in tropical and temperate seas throughout the world, and sometimes in the colder waters of higher latitudes. They lay their eggs on tropical beaches

FULL STEAM AHEAD

The leatherback turtle is a powerful swimmer and when its huge, paddle-like forelimbs are in motion in the open ocean, the fast-moving turtle is an impressive sight.

Crocodiles
and Alligators

Alligators and Caimans

Alligatoridae

4 genera/7 species

■ AMERICAN ALLIGATOR

When the American alligator *Alligator mississippiensis* spots its prey, it submerges all of its body but the top of its head and swims soundlessly through the water until it is close enough to attack. So smoothly does it glide through the murky swamp water that the vegetation on the surface is

SNAPSHOT

LENGTH Average is about 10 feet (3 m); can reach up to 19 feet (5.8 m)

DIET Young alligators eat insects. As they grow larger, snakes, turtles, snails, fish, small mammals, and birds are added to their diet. Large adults sometimes take small calves and, very occasionally, people

HABITAT & DISTRIBUTION American alligators live in swamps, ponds, rivers, lakes, and estuaries in southeastern USA

scarcely disturbed. This same silent hunter is also the noisiest of all the crocodilians. During the breeding season, a territorial male utters loud, bellowing roars that can be heard 500 feet (150 m) away. Its neighbors respond in choruses that may last half an hour or more.

Characteristics The black American alligator's snout is moderately long and wide, and it

JUMP SHOT
American alligators often hunt near water-bird colonies where they eat the fish that gather to feed on the birds' droppings. Occasionally an alligator will leap from the water to catch a bird such as this egret chick, which has fallen from its nest.

has blunt, broad jaws, which help it catch prey in thick vegetation.

Reproduction The female scratches soil and vegetation into a pile, repeatedly dragging her body over the nest until it is compacted into a mound. She then scoops out a cavity in the center of the mound with her hind feet and lays a clutch of about 35 to 40 large eggs, which take nine weeks to hatch.

WHAT A HIDE!
In the past, American alligators have been hunted for their hides. However, with government protection their numbers have increased again.

WINTER HOME
During winter, American alligators hibernate in dens, which are deep holes that they have dug.

SNAPSHOT

LENGTH Rarely exceeds 7 feet (2 m)
DIET Snails, clams, insects, and rats form the greater part of the alligator's diet
HABITAT & DISTRIBUTION This alligator lives in the muddy waters of the Yangtze River and its tributaries in China. The Chinese alligator is critically endangered because human population pressures and natural disasters such as floods threaten its habitat

■ CHINESE ALLIGATOR
Like its American relative, the Chinese alligator *Alligator sinensis* can tolerate much colder temperatures than other crocodilians. In winter, alligators retreat into burrows under river-banks and in mud holes. Or they move to shallow backwaters where the larger animals can survive freezing conditions by keeping their nose above the water so that breathing holes form when the surface of the water freezes. Here they remain dormant until the temperature rises.

Characteristics The Chinese alligator has a broad, heavy head and its back and neck are heavily armored with overlapping plates.

Reproduction The female builds a mound nest similar to that of the American alligator but slightly smaller. She lays 10 to 40 eggs.

DEEP FREEZE
The Chinese alligator can survive temperatures as low as 41°F (5°C) with full recovery.

CUVIER'S DWARF CAIMAN

Along with Schneider's dwarf caiman, Cuvier's dwarf caiman *Paleosuchus palpebrosus* is the most heavily armored crocodilian; even its eyelids are protected by bony plates. These two caimans are sometimes called smooth-fronted caimans because they do not have a bony ridge between their eyes like other caimans. They seem to have more terrestrial habits than other crocodilians, with adults spending much of their time away from water.

Characteristics Cuvier's dwarf caimans have a skull that is high, smooth, and doglike, the only

SNAPSHOT

LENGTH Males reach about 5 feet (1.5 m); females reach about 4 feet (1.2 m)

DIET Invertebrates and fish

HABITAT & DISTRIBUTION Lives in gallery forests in savannas or in forests on the margins of large lakes and rivers. It is found in the Amazon, Orinoco, and Sao Francisco river systems and also in the upper reaches of the Parana and Paraguay river systems

crocodilians with this head shape. Unlike most other crocodilians, which have yellowish eyes, the dwarf caimans have rich brown eyes.

Reproduction Mound nests have been found but little else is known about this species in the wild.

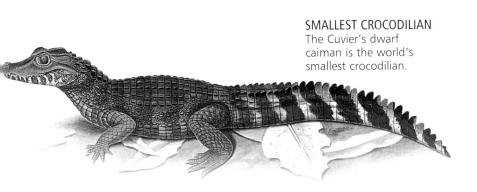

SMALLEST CROCODILIAN
The Cuvier's dwarf caiman is the world's smallest crocodilian.

SNAPSHOT

LENGTH About 8 feet (2.5 m)
DIET Smaller animals eat insects, crabs, and other invertebrates, while larger individuals eat water snails and fish
HABITAT & DISTRIBUTION Found in almost every lowland freshwater habitat from southern Mexico to northern Argentina; large rivers in tropical rainforests, flooded savannas, lakes, permanent swamps and mangroves. Also found in habitats created by humans such as ponds and dams

■ COMMON CAIMAN
Widespread in South America, the common caiman *Caiman crocodilus* is probably the only crocodilian in the world that responds favorably to changes in its habitat.

Characteristics From its outward appearance, the common caiman could easily be mistaken for a small crocodile. It is heavily armored along its back.

Reproduction The common caiman constructs a mound nest out of soil, leaf litter, and fresh vegetation. It is usually hidden among bushes, though some are made in open fields or on the floating grass mats that cover the shallow parts of large lakes. Females lay 15 to 40 eggs, depending on the size of the animal, and stay near the nests to defend them against predators. They remain with the hatchlings at least during the first few weeks of life, but if the level of the water drops markedly, they will abandon the young in search of deeper pools.

A SURVIVOR
The common caiman is the most hunted crocodilian in the world for its skin. Because it can adapt remarkably well to habitat changes, it is still widespread in South America.

Crocodiles

Crocodylidae

2 genera/13 species

■ AMERICAN CROCODILE
Rather than vocalizing, the
American crocodile *Crocodylus
acutus* relies on visual cues
and on a behavior known as
headslapping for communication.
Characteristics Juveniles are light
in color, usually yellowish tan to
gray, with black markings, which
fade as the animal grows older.
Adults are olive-brown or tan with
some populations being darker.
The neck is less heavily armored
than that of most crocodiles.
Reproduction The American
crocodile is the only crocodilian
that builds both mound and hole
nests. Usually it buries its eggs in
holes in sand or riverbanks, but
sometimes it will make a mound

SNAPSHOT

LENGTH Average is about 11½ feet
(3.5 m); can reach up to 23 feet
(7 m)

DIET Hatchlings eat insects and
the juveniles eat fish, aquatic
invertebrates, frogs, turtles, birds,
and small mammals. Adults also
eat larger mammals and birds

HABITAT & DISTRIBUTION Its range
extends from the southern tip of
Florida through the Caribbean
Islands, and along the coasts of
Central America to the northern
coast of South America. It usually
lives in coastal habitats, but can
also be found upstream in rivers
and large lakes; occasionally it
has been sighted far out to sea

of sand or vegetation in which to
place the eggs. The female lays up
to 40 eggs. The adults remain near
the nests, in burrows in the riverbank that are 10–30 feet (3–9 m)
long, and appear to guard them.

HEADSLAPPING
The crocodile lifts its head so the lower
jaw is just above the surface of the
water. It then swiftly opens and closes its
mouth to produce a sound similar to the
slapping of a flat shovel on water.

SNAPSHOT

LENGTH Up to 20 feet (6 m)
DIET The young eat insects,
spiders, and frogs. Adults eat
anything from fish and birds to
antelopes, zebras, and humans.
Large adults have been seen
taking fully grown Cape buffaloes
HABITAT & DISTRIBUTION Live in a
variety of freshwater habitats
including rivers, streams, lagoons,
lakes, swamps—and occasionally
at the mouths of rivers and on
beaches. They are found in Africa
and Madagascar

■ NILE CROCODILE

The Nile crocodile *Crocodylus
niloticus* is the biggest and
strongest freshwater predator
in Africa. When lying motionless
in water, its coloring makes it
difficult to detect. It often
conceals itself even more by
floating next to reeds or under
an overhanging tree. From this
sit-and-wait position, it will
make a powerful lunge at an
unsuspecting animal approaching
the water's edge. If it detects
prey when some distance from
shore, the crocodile will swim
underwater until it is close,
surfacing once or twice to check
the location of the prey. Its final
lunge may take the crocodile
several times its own length up
the riverbank.

POWER AND SPEED
The Nile crocodile kills big
animals by dragging them into
the water and drowning them.

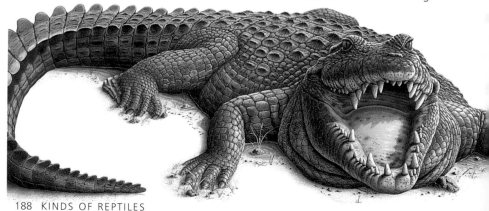

TTLE TO FEAR
he Nile crocodile has no enemies
part from other crocodiles,
umans, and hippopotamuses,
/hich probably only attack in
efense of their calves.

Characteristics It has
a broad, pointed snout
and its skin is shades
of drab green, brown,
and black with adults
being uniformly dark.

Reproduction The
female digs a flask-
shaped hole in the
ground, far enough
from water to avoid
potential flooding.
She lays 50 to 80 eggs
and covers
them with soil.

HOT CROC
If the crocodile becomes too hot it
cools down by opening its mouth
to let moisture evaporate.

CROCODILIA

SNAPSHOT

LENGTH Males can be more than 23 feet (7 m); females reach 13 feet (4 m)

DIET Juveniles eat insects, crabs, shrimps, mudskippers, lizards, and snakes. Adults eat fish, birds, and whatever mammals they can catch

HABITAT & DISTRIBUTION In the sea and in estuaries; in the mouths of large rivers, fresh-water rivers, and lakes. Its range extends from India to northern Australia and the Solomon Islands

■ INDOPACIFIC CROCODILE
There are few more dangerous or formidable predators than a large crocodile, and the largest and probably most feared of them all is the Indopacific or saltwater crocodile *Crocodylus porosus*. The Indopacific, American, and Nile crocodiles commonly enter the sea. The Indopacific has been seen swimming in the ocean 620 miles (1,000 km) from land.
Characteristics The crocodile has a heavy, elongated snout, and its color varies with age. Juveniles are brightly patterned with black blotches or bands. Adults may be dark brown, gray, or golden tan. Some retain the black markings.
Reproduction The females build mound nests during the wet season and lay clutches of 60 to 80 eggs.

PROTECTIVE MOTHER
Female saltwater crocodiles guard their nests by waiting in water-filled wallows near the nest.

HEAVYWEIGHTS
Weights of up to 3 tons (3,000 kg) have been recorded for large adult males.

UP AND AWAY
At the slightest disturbance
the Johnston's crocodile
will gallop back to the
water, dive in, and swim
out to deeper water.

JOHNSTON'S CROCODILE

Although once feared, Johnston's crocodile *Crocodylus johnsoni* of tropical Australia is now usually considered harmless to humans. A slender-snouted crocodile, it is interested in much smaller prey. It is usually sighted basking on the bank or in the shallows at the water's edge where it catches its food.

Characteristics This species is usually brown in color with black bands on the tail and irregular, darker bands on the body.

Reproduction In the dry season, when there is no danger of flooding, the female excavates a hole nest in a somewhat exposed area such as the sand of a dry riverbed. The hole goes down about 20 inches (50 cm) to where the earth is damp. There is relatively little parental defense of the nest and more than half of the dozen or so eggs laid will fall victim to nest robbers, mainly goannas.

SNAPSHOT

LENGTH **Up to 10 feet (3 m)**
DIET **Insects, crustaceans, spiders, fish, frogs, lizards, snakes, birds, and small mammals**
HABITAT & DISTRIBUTION **Upper reaches of rivers, and billabongs and swamps in tropical northern Australia. Habitat size varies with the season—it may be extensive in the wet when large areas are flooded, but limited in the dry to isolated deep pools**

CROCODILIA

■ AFRICAN SLENDER-SNOUTED CROCODILE

The crocodile *Crocodylus cataphractus* has a unique way of catching fish. It swims slowly, parallel to the riverbank with its tail curved toward the bank. Fish in the shallows move ahead of the disturbance and are trapped when the crocodile turns its head toward the bank, seizing the fish with a sideways sweep of its open jaws.

Characteristics The crocodile is quite noisy when vocalizing. It roars repeatedly, sounding like a truck exhaust backfiring.

Reproduction The African slender-snouted crocodile builds a mound nest out of vegetation along the banks of small rainforest streams. The dense canopy prevents sunlight reaching the nest, so heat from the rotting vegetation keeps the eggs warm. About 13 to 27 eggs are laid.

SNAPSHOT

LENGTH Up to 10 feet (3 m)
DIET The slender snout of the crocodile is too fragile to take large prey on land but is equipped with teeth that can subdue quite substantial fish in water. It eats fish, insects, shrimps and other crustaceans, crabs, frogs, and snakes
HABITAT & DISTRIBUTION Inhabits the heavily forested areas of West and Central Africa

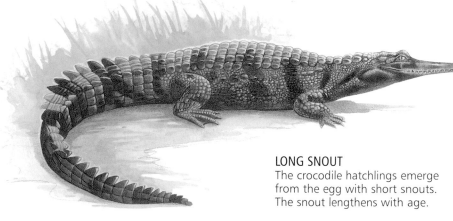

LONG SNOUT
The crocodile hatchlings emerge from the egg with short snouts. The snout lengthens with age.

DWARF CROCODILE

Osteolaemus tetraspis, the dwarf crocodile of West Africa, is a docile, timid, nocturnal creature. It is rarely seen during the day and does not spend long periods basking in the open like many other crocodiles. Little is known of its life history, but because it lives in a similar heavily forested habitat and looks rather like them, it is possible the crocodile has a similar ecology to the dwarf caimans of South America's Amazon basin.

Characteristics It is heavily armored all over its body, even its eyelids, a factor that, along with its small size, has helped to save it from the intense exploitation suffered by the Nile crocodile. Juveniles are dark brown with

ODD ONE OUT
The dwarf crocodile is the only crocodile that does not belong to the genus *Crocodylus*.

black and yellow markings. The adults are uniformly dark. The crocodile has brown eyes.

Reproduction Little is known about the life history of this crocodile but in captivity it builds a mound nest and lays clutches of fewer than 20 eggs.

SNAPSHOT

LENGTH **About 5 feet (1.5 m)**
DIET **Mainly fish, frogs, and crabs**
HABITAT & DISTRIBUTION **Lives in the rainforests and savannas of tropical West and Central Africa. It seems to prefer slow-moving water and avoids major waterways**

Gharials

Gavialidae

2 genera/2 species

■ INDIAN GHARIAL

One of the most distinctive crocodilians, the gharial *Gavialis gangeticus* gets its name from the knob on the tip of the male's snout, called a "ghara," meaning "pot" in Hindi. Air snorted through the nostrils in the knob produces a buzzing noise that warns other males away. The gharial spends more time in water than most other crocodilians and

S N A P S H O T

LENGTH 20 feet (6 m)
DIET Mainly fish, but it also eats insects, frogs, and other small animals
HABITAT & DISTRIBUTION Lives in fast-flowing rivers and hill streams in India, Pakistan, Nepal, Bangladesh, Bhutan, and Burma

its long, narrow snout and many small, pointed teeth are ideal for grasping slippery fish.

Characteristics The thin-snouted head and weak legs of the gharial seem disproportionately small in relation to its large body.

Reproduction The average clutch of a gharial varies from 28 to 43 eggs, depending on the locality. It digs hole nests in sandy riverbanks or on mid-river islands.

HOUSE BOUND
The gharial has heavily webbed feet and relatively weak legs. It does not make the extensive overland journeys of the many other species.

FALSE GHARIAL
Like other slender-snouted
crocodilians, the false or Malayan
gharial *Tomistoma schlegelii*
catches fish with a sweeping
sideways snap. This crocodilian
was called the "false" gharial

because, although it resembled the
Indian gharial, it was considered
to have evolved as part of the
crocodile family. Recent bio-
chemical studies, however, have
placed the false gharial in the
same family as the Indian gharial.

Characteristics This species is
distinctively marked with dark
bands and blotches, and is one
of the few species where the
adults are almost as colorful
as the juveniles.

Reproduction The female builds
a mound nest out of vegetation.
She lays between 20 to 60 eggs in
the dry season and the hatchlings
appear at the beginning of the wet
season 10 or 12 weeks later. Many
of the eggs are eaten by lizards
and wild pigs.

SNAPSHOT

LENGTH 13 feet (4 m) or more

DIET Mainly a fish-eater but it
also feeds on small vertebrates
such as frogs, lizards, snakes,
and water birds

HABITAT & DISTRIBUTION Inhabits
freshwater swamps, lakes, and
rivers. It occurs on the Malay
Peninsula of Thailand and
Malaysia, and on the islands
of Sumatra, Java, Borneo, and
possibly Sulawesi

Tuataras

Tuataras

Sphenodontidae

1 genus/2 species

■ GENERAL

Tuataras are often called "living fossils" but recent research suggests they have much more advanced features than their nearest extinct relatives. Once regarded as a single species, *Sphenodon punctatus*, scientists now believe the tuataras on North Brother Island in the Cook Strait are different enough to be regarded as a separate species, *Sphenodon guntheri*. Tuataras are active mostly at night when they come out to hunt. They spend the day in burrows or, if it is sunny, basking at the burrow entrance. There are no ponds or streams on the islands where the tuataras live, so after dry spells they are particularly active on rainy nights when they may often be found soaking in puddles. For hunting, tuataras usually adopt a sit-and-wait strategy. When small prey come close they are first seized with the tongue. Larger animals are impaled on the tuatara's sharp teeth.

■ CHARACTERISTICS

Tuataras are gray, olive green, or occasionally rusty red. While they

---

SNAPSHOT

LENGTH Males to 2 feet (60 cm); females to 1½ feet (45 cm)

DIET Mainly insects, snails, and earthworms, but they also eat lizards, and small birds and their eggs

HABITAT They live on islands in burrows that have been built by the petrels, which share their habitat. Alternatively, they excavate their own. Some of the islands are forested, others have stunted vegetation

---

resemble lizards, they are quite different. For example, they have no external ears, their teeth are fused to the jaw and they have no penis, whereas lizards have two. Tuataras have a "third eye," part of an organ on top of the brain. It has a lens, retina, and nerve connection to the brain, but early in the growth of the tuatara it is covered by opaque scales. Many lizards also have a third eye that is involved in regulating temperature, but it is not known what function, if any, a tuatara's third eye performs.

■ REPRODUCTION

Tuataras mate by touching cloacae. The females gather in an open, sunny spot to dig nests in the soil where they lay an average of eight eggs. Females guard their nests for about a week to prevent other females digging up the same site. The incubation period of 12 to 15 months is one of the longest of any reptile.

■ DISTRIBUTION

Tuataras are found on 30 small islands off the coast of the North Island of New Zealand.

REDUCED DISTRIBUTION
Tuataras could once be found throughout the North and South islands of New Zealand.

Lizards

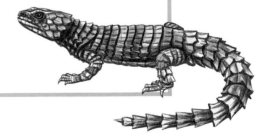

Dragon Lizards

Agamidae

53 genera/about 300 species

SNAPSHOT

LENGTH Body length about 3½ inches (9 cm)
DIET Mainly insects and spiders
HABITAT & DISTRIBUTION Lives almost exclusively in acacia trees. This lizard is found in the hot sandstone plateau regions of northwestern Australia

■ TREE DRAGON

The astonishingly slender tree dragon *Diporiphora superba*, one of the world's most slender agamids, has a tail that is three to four times its body length. When still, its green coloring and thin, almost sticklike body and limbs make it invisible among the narrow leaves of the acacia tree.

Characteristics The tree dragon has a narrow body, and a long tail, limbs, and toes. Its color ranges from pale lime green to a greenish yellow. Although it is agile and fast, it escapes from predators mainly because of its brilliant camouflage. Like most dragon lizards, its tail has no fracture planes and is never shed.

Reproduction The tree dragon lays eggs, probably in a clutch of between two to four. Its preferred egg-laying site is unknown.

RECENT FIND
The tree dragon has been known to science only since 1974. It lives in the foliage of the acacia trees in northwest Australia.

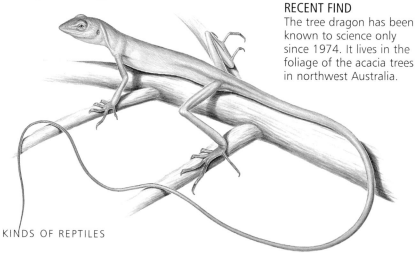

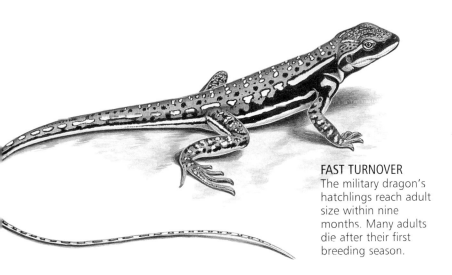

FAST TURNOVER
The military dragon's hatchlings reach adult size within nine months. Many adults die after their first breeding season.

MILITARY DRAGON

The military dragon *Ctenophorus 'solepis* is widespread in the very dry regions of Australia. It can move extremely quickly and if threatened or pursued will run swiftly across open ground, relying on speed to save them rather than seeking cover to escape. During the summer, when temperatures are high, it is active in the cooler periods of the early morning and late afternoon. In winter it is active in the middle of the day.

Characteristics The females of this beautifully marked, rather small species are slightly larger than the males. They have long limbs and a long, slender tail.

Reproduction Two or three clutches of one to six eggs are laid in the spring and summer. The eggs take around two months to hatch.

SQUAMATA
SAURIA

SNAPSHOT

LENGTH 9 inches (23 cm)
DIET Large insects such as beetles and grasshoppers, plus spiders and small mammals, such as mice
HABITAT & DISTRIBUTION Lives in trees where its coloration enables it to blend in with the trunks and boughs on which it rests. It is found in open forests and woodlands across northern Australia

■ FRILLED LIZARD

When threatened, the frilled lizard *Chlamydosaurus kingii* usually tries to escape by running swiftly on its powerful hind legs, its body erect, and its very long tail acting as a counterbalance. However, if the lizard feels cornered, it will resort to a spectacular display of bluff.

Characteristics Colorful areas of red, yellow, and orange are revealed when the lizard's frill is extended, but when folded it disrupts the body's outline and this, along with the lizard's dull gray or brown coloring, provides it with camouflage. There are many blood vessels in the frill, so it is thought that it may also be used to regulate body temperature. Extending the frill in the sun could increase the rate at which the lizard's temperature rises.

Reproduction Between 9 to 12 eggs are laid in a nesting burrow. They hatch in 8 to 12 weeks.

FULL OF BLUFF
Facing its attacker, the frilled lizard raises the front of its body, extends its enormous frill, and hisses loudly through its wide, open mouth.

SAIL-TAILED WATER LIZARD
The large, semi-aquatic sail-tailed lizard *Hydrosaurus amboinensis*, also known as the soasoa or water dragon, basks on rocks and branches at the edge of streams, retreating to the water when in danger. Aided by fringes on the toes of its hind feet, it can run on the surface of the water for some distance before sinking and swimming away.

Characteristics The stocky sail-tailed water lizard is the largest lizard in the agamid family. Its

S N A P S H O T

LENGTH Total length of over 3 feet (1 m)

DIET Ambush predator that preys on a variety of small invertebrates

HABITAT & DISTRIBUTION This semi-arboreal lizard is a tree-dweller, that lives in streams and rivers in Indonesia and New Guinea

strong, compressed tail and toe fringes increase its surface area to increase swimming efficiency. It moves swiftly and effortlessly through the water, using its feet and its flattened, paddle-like tail.

Reproduction Like most agamid lizards, this species is oviparous.

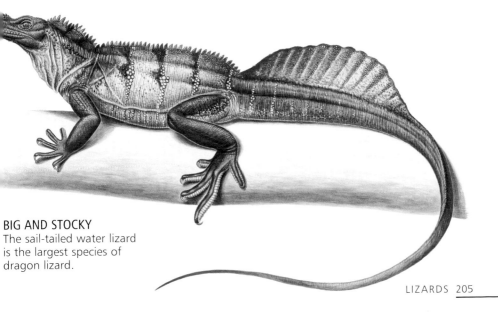

BIG AND STOCKY
The sail-tailed water lizard is the largest species of dragon lizard.

■ AFRICAN AGAMA LIZARDS
There are not many agamid lizards in Africa, but those belonging to the genus *Agama* are the most common and they are very conspicuous. The males of all species are brightly colored, and during the breeding season they intensify or change these colors for courtship and territorial displays. Many have a brightly colored head that they bob up and down rapidly when they are seeking a mate.

Characteristics These spiny lizards vary in length, with the males being larger than the females. The lizards are extremely active during much of the day, darting about the ground looking for ants, or leaping into the air to snap up flying insects. They retreat to cool, shady spots only when the temperature reaches about 100°F (38°C). They come out to hunt again when the temperature drops in the late afternoon.

Reproduction Each brightly colored male has a territory that he defends vigorously

DIFFERENT COLORS
Females and juveniles are less brightly colored than the orange and blue colored males.

ON DISPLAY
These lizards spend much of their time basking in the sun and displaying to other members of their species.

SNAPSHOT

LENGTH 5–12 inches (13–30 cm)
DIET Mostly insects, but also grass, berries, and seeds
HABITAT There are several tree-dwelling African agama lizards, but most species live among rocks and boulders. A few species retreat to burrows to escape from predators or to avoid very high temperatures

against other males, and he mates with a number of females. When a male catches sight of a rival, he will repeatedly raise and lower he front part of his body in a erky, bobbing action, and he may also lash out with his strong tail. Mating and egg-laying take place after the rainy season when the vegetation is lush and the insect populations rise. The female lays a clutch of about 12 eggs.

Distribution The lizards are found all over Africa, south of the Sahara Desert.

A BRIGHT MESSAGE
Only the mature, dominant males like this agama lizard have bright orange and blue coloring. Weak, subordinate males (and juveniles) are various, less conspicuous shades of brown.

Chameleons

Chameleonidae

4 genera/85 species

■ GENERAL
This very distinctive family of lizards is famous for its ability to change color. This trait is shared with many other lizards, but is particularly well developed in the chameleons. Changing color helps these lizards to blend in with their surroundings, a feature that is useful for stalking prey as well

SNAPSHOT

LENGTH **Body length of up to 12 inches (30 cm)**
DIET **Insects, spiders, and scorpions, though the larger species will prey on small birds and mammals**
HABITAT & DISTRIBUTION **See main text**

as for hiding from enemies. Color change is also associated with sexual and territorial displays and with temperature.

■ CHARACTERISTICS
Chameleons, even the ground-dwelling species, are built for living in trees. On each foot

DISTURBED DISPLAY
The Malagasy chameleon is usually dull green in color. When disturbed it takes on this striking disruptive pattern.

THREAT DISPLAY
The Knysna dwarf chameleon is mostly green when at rest. But males develop this bright color as a threat display to other males.

they have two sets of opposed, partly fused toes, used for gripping twigs and narrow branches in a pincer action. Their prehensile tail acts as a fifth limb when climbing and unlike the tail of many other lizards, it is never shed. They have turret-like eyes that can be moved independently of each other, so they have excellent depth perception, necessary for aiming their extremely long, projectile tongue and for judging distance in dense vegetation.

HEAD GEAR
Jackson's chameleon *Chamaeleo jacksonii* of Africa is one of several species in which the males possess horns or other appendages on the head. These play a role in species recognition between the sexes and may be used in intense combat among the males.

◼ REPRODUCTION
Some chameleons, including the dwarf chameleons, give birth to live young several times a year. The young are born in a translucent membrane which they soon struggle out of. Most species

lay eggs, however, with the number per clutch largely dependent on body size. One of the largest, Meller's chameleon, lays up to 70 eggs, and clutches of 30 to 40 are the rule for many species. Females usually bury the eggs in the ground or in rotting logs or other moist, protected spots.

HABITAT AND DISTRIBUTION

Most chameleons live in trees in humid forest areas, and they are especially numerous in the rainforest belt of eastern Madagascar, and the highland forests of East Africa and the Cameroons. However, they are also successful in some Mediterranean climates and even in deserts. Not all are arboreal. The arid-zone species, such as the Namaqua chameleons of southwest Africa, spend most of their time on the ground, as do the stump-tailed chameleons of Madagascar.

WIDE DISTRIBUTION
The flap-necked chameleon *Chamaeleo dilepis* is the most widespread chameleon in southern Africa.

POPULAR REGION
The Fischer's chameleon *Chamaeleo fischeri* is a species from equatorial Africa. The region is home to numerous species.

Iguanas

Iguanidae

10 genera/38 species

■ CHUCKWALLAS

The chuckwallas are stocky, terrestrial lizards that live in American desert regions. When threatened, a chuckwalla will seek refuge in a rocky crevice into which it will wedge itself tightly by inflating its body with gulps of air. These lizards emerge in the early morning and bask in the sun until their optimum body temperature is reached. Then they begin searching for food.

Characteristics Chuckwallas are bulky lizards that have loose folds of skin on their neck and sides. Their thick tail is about the same length as their body. They can change their skin color from dark to light to reflect or absorb heat from the sun.

Reproduction The males use a combination of head-bobbing, push-ups, and mouth displays to attract a mate and to establish their territory. Five to ten eggs are laid in the summer.

SNAPSHOT

LENGTH Body length 8 inches (20 cm)
DIET Chuckwallas are herbivores. They eat flowers, leaves, buds, and fruit, including the fruit of cactus plants
HABITAT & DISTRIBUTION Live on rocky outcrops and hillsides in the deserts of southern USA, Mexico, and the islands of Baja California

EARLY MORNING BASK
The piebald chuckwalla is found on San Estaban Island in the Gulf of California.

GREEN IGUANA

The green, or common, iguana *Iguana iguana* is the largest South American lizard. Never found far from trees, the lizard is an agile climber. If disturbed near water, it can dive under and propel itself through the water with its tail.

Characteristics Under its throat is a folded dewlap that it extends to frighten enemies and that males display to attract a female. The lizard varies from grass green to blue-green in color. In the breeding season, some males develop tinges of orange on their crest and legs. The males claim large territories and warn off intruders by raising their body and nodding their head vigorously. These lizards are fast runners and would rather run than fight. They can throw themselves 40 or 50 feet (12 or 15 m) to the ground and land unhurt. They store fat reserves in their lower jaw and neck.

Reproduction The females build a long burrow in sandy soil where they bury their eggs. The large clutches of between 20 and 70 eggs take about three months to hatch. The hatchlings, which are about 10 inches (25 cm) long, all emerge from the nest together, a strategy that provides safety for individuals against predators.

SNAPSHOT

LENGTH Males are larger than the females, reaching up to 6½ feet (2 m) including the tail

DIET Young eat insects and snails. They become almost totally herbivorous as adults and eat fruit, leaves, flowers, young shoots, and grasses

HABITAT & DISTRIBUTION Tropical forests in Central and South America, and on Trinidad and Tobago and several other smaller West Indian islands

■ MARINE IGUANAS

Found throughout the Galápagos Islands, the marine iguana *Amblyrhynchus cristatus* is the only lizard to venture into the sea, where it feeds on marine algae. Most of the iguanas, including the females and the young, feed in the shallow water close to the rocky shore, but the larger males swim farther out and dive deep down under the water. An average dive lasts for five to ten minutes, though the lizards can stay under for much longer, and they can go to depths of 40 feet (12 m) or more.

Characteristics The iguana has a number of adaptations to suit its marine lifestyle. To rid itself of excess salt ingested when feeding, it excretes concentrated salt crystals from a nasal gland. It does this by sneezing frequently when it is back on land, which is why the iguanas often have salt-encrusted heads. Its flattened, paddle-like tail helps the marine iguana when swimming. They have a blunt snout, a stocky body, and a crest that runs from the neck to the tail.

BLACK BASKER

The cold undercurrent found in the waters of the Galápagos Islands causes the iguana's body temperature to drop while submerged. The lizard's black skin helps it absorb heat more rapidly.

Reproduction After mating, the females travel from the rocky lava reefs to the nesting beaches, a distance of 300 feet (100 m). Here they each scrape out a tunnel in the sand, about 2 feet (60 cm) long, with their feet and lay two or three eggs. The female then covers up the nest and leaves. When the young hatch about 16 weeks later, they are about 9 inches (23 cm) long.

SNAPSHOT

LENGTH About 4 feet (1.2 m)
DIET The marine iguana grazes on the sea bed, feeding almost exclusively on marine algae and seaweed, but it also eats other marine plants, crustaceans, grasshoppers, and, occasionally, the afterbirth of sea lions
HABITAT & DISTRIBUTION Found throughout the Galápagos Islands. When not foraging for food in the sea, the iguanas can be found basking on the rocks and cliffs beside the shore. There may be thousands at one site, often piled up on one another in large heaps to conserve heat

ON GUARD
During the breeding season, the male marine iguana's black skin becomes rusty red and green. Each male claims a territory that he defends vigorously.

Anoles

Polychrotidae

11 genera/about 250 species

■ GENERAL

Popularly known as "false chameleons," anoles are among the most successful lizards. By adapting to and exploiting all the available microhabitats, large numbers can exist in a single area. Although they are all expert climbers, one species may live in the crown of a tree, one on the tree trunk, and another on the ground below. There may even be further divisions based on size, diet, and shade tolerance. In this way the anoles avoid competing with one another for food and other resources.

SNAPSHOT

LENGTH Most are about 8 inches (20 cm), though the giant anoles can reach 2 feet (60 cm). Two-thirds of this length is the tail

DIET The anoles will eat fruit, but they are mostly insectivorous, with different species preferring different insects. Their diet also changes according to the time of the year and the food available

HABITAT Most anoles live in trees, but the water anole lives along the banks of streams, and there are two cave-dwelling species as well

■ CHARACTERISTICS

Anoles have a long, whiplike tail, long legs, and a slender body. Their head is triangular in shape with narrow, elongated jaws. They have climbing pads on their long, delicate toes—similar to those of the geckos, though not as well developed—as well as sharp claws.

LOOK AT ME

Anoles are famous for the colorful sail-like dewlap that the males and the females of some species have on their throat. They display the dewlap to advertise ownership of a territory or to attract a female. The color and shape of the dewlap vary from species to species.

The knight anole *Anolis equestris* from Cuba becomes very defensive when a snake or any form that resembles a snake gets too close.

CHANGE OF DRESS
The green anole *Anolis carolinensis* of North America has the ability to rapidly change color from bright green to dark brown.

■ REPRODUCTION
Nearly all species lay only one egg at a time but most lay a number of times during the breeding season. The female digs a nest in the ground with her feet.

■ DISTRIBUTION
Anoles are found in Central and South America, the West Indies, and in southeastern USA.

S N A P S H O T

LENGTH Up to 19½ inches
(50 cm), including the tail
DIET A variety of small insects
HABITAT & DISTRIBUTION Lives in
shrubs and bushes in South
America. There are several species
of the genus in South America,
but each has a restricted range

■ MULTI-COLORED TREE LIZARD

The multi-colored tree lizard *Polychrus marmoratus* is a slow-moving lizard that relies on its camouflage to escape the notice of predators. Its long tail enables this nocturnal lizard to balance as it climbs and moves in the forest canopy. Extended toes on its hind-limbs help it to grasp branches.

Characteristics The multi-colored tree lizard and others in its genus are South American relatives of the anoles. Several of the species exhibit sexual dimorphism, a marked variation in color between males and females.

Males are uniformly dark green to brownish while the females are distinguished by varying patterns of black, white, and brown. Like the chameleons, they are able to change color quickly when they are excited or threatened.

Reproduction A clutch of 8 to 12 eggs are laid in the ground, where the warmth of the forest litter helps to incubate them.

STILL AND INVISIBLE
When the lizard remains motionless, its mottled colors make it almost invisible among the foliage of the shrubs and bushes where it lives.

Basilisks

Corytophanidae

~ genera/9 species

GENERAL

The ability of these lizards to run on the surface of water is the reason for their common name, Jesus lizards. When threatened or in search of food, a basilisk may run quickly toward the water on its hind legs. This momentary high speed, combined with the fringe of scales on the lizard's toes, which is pushed up when it hits the water, allows it to run on the water for quite some distance before sinking.

SNAPSHOT

LENGTH Up to 3 feet (1 m), including the tail. Females are smaller than males

DIET Invertebrates, especially insects. Juveniles are carnivorous, but adults also eat plant matter such as seeds, berries, and stems

HABITAT & DISTRIBUTION Live in forested areas on the edges of streams, ponds, and lakes. They are found in Central America, from Mexico to Ecuador

■ CHARACTERISTICS

Basilisks are large, green or brown lizards with prominent crests and dewlaps and long, powerful legs. They can run on their hind legs with their long tails providing counterbalance.

■ REPRODUCTION

Basilisks are oviparous, and the number of eggs per clutch varies according to species. Several clutches are laid per season.

BODY PARTS
As well as head ornamentation, the common basilisk *Basiliscus basiliscus* has a finlike crest on its back and tail.

Horned Lizards, Fence Lizards, and Allies

Phrynosomatidae

8 genera/about 40 species

■ HORNED LIZARDS

In the evening, to avoid the cool night air, horned lizards dig themselves into the sand. In the early morning they expose first just their head and then their whole body to the sun. The first few hours of the day are spent basking, often with their body flattened and tilted toward the sun to absorb as much heat as possible. When warm enough,

SNAPSHOT

LENGTH About 6 inches (15 cm)
DIET Feed mainly on ants though they will also eat other slow-moving, ground-dwelling insects and spiders. The lizards sit beside ant trails flicking up the ants with their long, sticky tongue. Because ants are so small, the lizards eat huge numbers of them
HABITAT Live in dry, sandy environments. Some species inhabit scorchingly hot deserts, others live in mountainous areas, as high as 10,000 feet (3,100 m)

they begin to forage for food. If the ground becomes too hot they will seek shade under a bush.

Characteristics Because of their saucer-shaped body, large head, and short tail, these lizards are

MOUNTAIN DWELLER
The short-horned lizard *Phrynosoma douglassi* is about the same size as a human hand. It lives at higher altitudes than other horned lizards and gives birth to live young.

sometimes called horned "toads." Most species have a row of sharp, backward-pointing scales, or "horns," on the back of the head that are used for defense. Most species also have a row of sharp spines along their tail and sides.

Reproduction Most species lay eggs, burying them in the sand where they hatch several weeks later. In some species the eggs are retained, and the young are hatched just before, during, or shortly after laying. The species that live in cooler areas generally give birth to live young.

Distribution These lizards are found in the arid regions of southwestern Canada, western USA, and western Mexico.

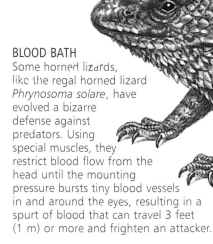

BLOOD BATH
Some horned lizards, like the regal horned lizard *Phrynosoma solare*, have evolved a bizarre defense against predators. Using special muscles, they restrict blood flow from the head until the mounting pressure bursts tiny blood vessels in and around the eyes, resulting in a spurt of blood that can travel 3 feet (1 m) or more and frighten an attacker.

QUIET SITTER
If discovered in the open, the desert horned lizard *Phrynosoma platyrhinos*, which is found in the American western deserts, sits quietly.

SMOOTH EDGES
The round-tailed horned lizard *Phrynosoma modestum* has a short crown of "horns" on its head but lacks the sharp spines along its side and tail.

SQUAMATA

SAURIA

SNAPSHOT

LENGTH Up to 9 inches (22 cm)
DIET Insects, small lizards, and, occasionally, blossoms
HABITAT & DISTRIBUTION Live in the windblown sand dunes and sandy flats in parts of California, Arizona, and other arid areas

■ SAND LIZARDS

The sand lizards are well adapted for their life in the hot, dry deserts of North America. Some are able to withstand body temperatures as high as 116°F (47°C). They have very complex posturing behavior that regulates their body temperature. Some sand lizards bury themselves in the loose sand to avoid high temperatures, and to sleep. They will also dive into the sand to escape from predators.

Characteristics Sand lizards of the genus *Uma* have fringes of enlarged scales on the borders of their toes. These fringes help them to run rapidly across loose sand. These lizards also have valves in their nostrils, flaps over their ears, and an upper jaw that overlaps the lower one to prevent sand entering their bodies. A number of sand lizards, like the zebra-tailed lizard, have black and white bands on the underside of their tail. The waving tail mesmerizes a predator, and when the lizard runs off, the predator is left staring fixedly at the spot where the waving tail once was.

Reproduction Small clutches of up to five eggs are laid in summer, probably more than one clutch per season.

PERKY LIZARD
The zebra-tailed lizard *Callisaurus draconoides* is a fast runner and is often seen running on its hind legs.

FENCE LIZARDS

These widely distributed American lizards are sometimes called spiny lizards because they have pointed scales on their bodies, which give them a spiky appearance. Some, such as the crevice spiny lizard, have a spiny tail that they use to protect themselves when they retreat into a crack or crevice in their rocky habitats.

Characteristics Fence lizards have long tails, sometimes one and a half times that of the head and body length. The females are a drab brown or gray, whereas the males are more brightly colored, especially during the breeding season.

Reproduction About 40 percent of the species, usually those that live at higher altitudes, give birth to live young. Most of the lowland species lay eggs.

BLUE BELLY

The western fence lizard *Sceloporus occidentalis*, commonly called the blue-belly lizard, is found from central Idaho through to Nevada and across to the Pacific coast.

Collared and Leopard Lizards

Crotaphytidae

2 genera/5 species

S N A P S H O T

LENGTH 6–17 inches (15–44 cm)
DIET Small lizards, snakes, and mammals. They also eat insects and spiders
HABITAT Inhabit a range of habitats, from forests to arid or semi-arid areas. They prefer hilly, limestone regions that provide crevices and other hiding places for protection. They live and bask on boulders and take shelter under debris, in crevices, or in animal burrows

■ COLLARED LIZARDS
These lizards are exceptionally fast runners with hearty appetites. When chasing prey, which can be anything from insects to small snakes, collared lizards often run on their hind legs. They are very wary, too, and quick to take cover if startled. They dash across an open space, jump nimbly from rock to rock, or scuttle into a crevice.

Characteristics Collared lizards have large heads, wide mouths, and slender necks. Many have a conspicuous black or black-and-white collar across the back of the neck. The lizards have long, strong limbs and tails. Males and females of the same species are differently colored, with the males often being more vivid during the breeding season.

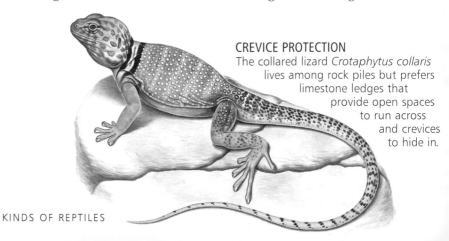

CREVICE PROTECTION
The collared lizard *Crotaphytus collaris* lives among rock piles but prefers limestone ledges that provide open spaces to run across and crevices to hide in.

Changes such as orange spots or bars also appear on the sides of pregnant females.

Reproduction Mating is between April and July. During summer, clutches of eggs are laid in loose sandy soil, in burrows, or under rocks. The young, which take about six to eight weeks to hatch, are marked with bright spots or crossbands that fade as they grow older.

COOLING DOWN
In very hot weather, collared lizards open their mouth to allow them to cool down by evaporation of saliva.

Distribution Their distribution in the United States ranges from Utah and Colorado to Illinois, Texas, and west into Arizona. These lizards are also found in Mexico.

SNAPSHOT

LENGTH 9–15 inches (23–38 cm)
DIET Spiders and insects. Larger lizards also prey on smaller lizards
HABITAT & DISTRIBUTION Live in flat, arid areas with sparse vegetation and loose, sandy or gravelly soil in southwest USA and northern Mexico

■ LEOPARD LIZARDS

The two leopard lizard species live in flat areas with little vegetation, so they need to be fast runners. Some lizards use this vegetation for shelter. Others make use of small mammal burrows, such as abandoned ground squirrel tunnels and abandoned and occupied kangaroo rat tunnels, while some construct their own burrows. In the colder months the lizards hibernate in these burrows.

Characteristics These quick, active lizards have large heads and long limbs and tails. As their common names suggest, the longnose leopard lizard has an elongated head while the endangered blunt-nosed leopard lizard has a blunt snout and a short, broad, triangular head. The females of both species develop red or orange markings on their sides, head, and under their tail just before they lay eggs.

Reproduction The female lays a clutch of two to six eggs once, and occasionally twice, a year in the summer months.

QUICK MOVER
The leopard lizard
Gambelia wislizenii is an agile lizard that often darts from bush to bush in search of insect prey.

Lava Lizards

Tropiduridae

About 13 genera/about 120 species

◼ GENERAL

Lava lizards are a small, agile, and fast-moving species of the genus *Tropidurus*. Although they are popularly associated with the Galápagos Islands, they are also found in South and Central America. Their large numbers and bright colors make them conspicuous on the Galápagos Islands where, as their common name suggests, they scamper over the dark lava formations and rocks in search of prey.

◼ CHARACTERISTICS

Lava lizards are sexually dimorphic—size and color differences between the sexes are quite obvious. During the breeding season the females develop red throats. The lizards have slender bodies, and are shaped rather like a small iguana.

SNAPSHOT

LENGTH Body about 3–5 inches (7–12 cm), tail about one and a half times body length
DIET Insects and other invertebrates such as sand hoppers and spiders
HABITAT & DISTRIBUTION These lizards are found on the mainland of South and Central America and on the Galápagos Islands. They are preyed upon by cats and rats

◼ REPRODUCTION

A clutch of eggs is laid in a nest chamber that has been dug into sandy soil.

BREEDING DISPLAYS

During the breeding season, female lava lizards develop a red throat and males engage in head bobbing and push-ups.

Eyelash Geckos

Eublepharidae

5 genera/22 species

SNAPSHOT

LENGTH About 8 inches (20 cm)
DIET Mainly insects, including crickets, and worms
HABITAT & DISTRIBUTION More terrestrial than most other geckos, the leopard gecko is native to Iran, India, Afghanistan, and Pakistan

■ LEOPARD GECKO

The leopard gecko *Eublepharis macularius* belongs to a family of geckos that have movable eyelids. In most geckos, the eyelids have been replaced by a fixed transparent scale that protects the eyes. Another difference is that the feet of the geckos in the family Eublepharidae do not have the adhesive climbing pads typical of many other geckos.

Characteristics The leopard gecko has a relatively short, fat tail and short limbs. Its slightly flattened body helps it to hide in rock crevices and under dry scrub. Its common name derives from its multitude of black spots and blotches on a yellow background.

Reproduction The female lays a clutch of two to four eggs, which hatch after about two months. The sex of the young may be determined by the temperature experienced by the embryo in its egg.

SEX DETERMINATION

The sex of a leopard gecko is determined by the temperature of its nest—a condition known chiefly in turtles and crocodilians.

■ BANDED GECKO

When hunting for food, the small, banded gecko *Coleonyx variegatus* stalks its victim on straight, stiff legs, and then pounces when it is very close, capturing the prey in its jaws. After eating, the gecko cleans its face with its tongue. The nocturnal banded gecko is inactive for as much as half the year when night temperatures fall below about 73°F (23°C).

Characteristics The banded gecko has large eyes and movable eyelids. It has pointed claws but no climbing pads on its slender toes. Its skin is thin and translucent, and it has a plump tail where fat is stored for times when food is scarce. The tail is waved side to side as it stalks its prey. When protecting its territory against other males, or

NIGHT WALKER

The nocturnal banded gecko is often seen crossing roads at night.

SNAPSHOT

LENGTH Up to 6 inches (15 cm)
DIET Banded geckos eat insects, spiders, baby scorpions, and other small arthropods, often hunting for their prey in rodent burrows
HABITAT & DISTRIBUTION The gecko occupies many habitats, avoiding the heat of the day under logs or debris or in moist rock crevices. It is found in the rocky and sandy desert and semi-desert areas of southwest USA and Mexico

---

when captured, it emits a squeak or chirp.

Reproduction Females lay clutches of two eggs, one to three times during the warmer months.

Austral Geckos

Diplodactylidae

14 genera/about 110 species

SNAPSHOT

LENGTH 3–6 inches (7–15 cm)
DIET Insects, spiders, and other arthropods. Some larger geckos prey on smaller lizards
HABITAT & DISTRIBUTION Some live under rock slabs or outcrops; others prefer tree hollows or under bark in Australian open forests and woodlands

■ GENERAL

The Australian velvet geckos of the genus *Oedura* have tiny, even scales that give their skin a velvety texture, hence their common name. They are secretive, nocturnal creatures. During the day the arboreal species hide behind loose bark or in hollow tree trunks, while the rock-dwellers wedge themselves into crevices or hide under rock slabs or in caves.

■ CHARACTERISTICS

These geckos have plump tails where fat is stored for times when food is scarce. As long as water is available they can survive without food for six months or more. Several species have flattened bodies that help them squeeze into small hiding places. On their toes they have climbing pads with claws at the tips.

■ REPRODUCTION

Two eggs are usually laid in moist, litter-filled rock crevices or under bark.

ROCK LOVER
The southern spotted velvet gecko *Oedura tryoni* is found on granite outcrops on the east coast of Australia.

True Geckos

Gekkonidae

About 75 genera/about 750 species

RING-TAILED GECKO

The ring-tailed gecko *Cyrtodactylus louisiadensis* is one of the largest geckos in Australia. Usually it forages for food on the ground or on rocks or cliff faces, but it is an excellent climber and can sometimes be seen perched on low branches or tree trunks.

SNAPSHOT

LENGTH About 10 inches (25 cm)
DIET Large insects such as tree crickets and beetles, as well as small lizards
HABITAT & DISTRIBUTION Live in woodlands, rocky outcrops, and rainforest areas in the far northeast of Australia and in New Guinea

Characteristics The dark brown and white bands on this gecko's long, slender tail give it its common name. The gecko has no climbing pads, but its long, bent, almost birdlike claws make it an efficient climber.

Reproduction It lays clutches of two eggs, usually in a damp rock crevice or under the bark of a tree.

QUICK RETREAT
If the ring-tailed gecko is disturbed, it will quickly retreat to the safety of a hollow limb, rock crevice, or cave.

SNAPSHOT

LENGTH About 10 inches (25 cm)
DIET In addition to taking arthropod prey such as insects and spiders, day geckos have been known to eat fruit, and the nectar and pollen from flowers
HABITAT Within, and on the fringe of, rainforest and other natural forests. Some species seem to benefit from forestry activities and are common on houses

■ DAY GECKOS

Day geckos—species of the genus *Phelsuma*—are notable for their bright coloring. They are active during the day, when they can be seen scampering through the tropical forests and coconut plantations of Madagascar and their other island homes, or sheltering under rocky outcrops, well camouflaged by their cryptic coloring.

Characteristics Day geckos have greatly reduced claws and rely entirely on their well-developed toe pads when climbing. Most species are a rich green, and are often patterned with red and blue spots. Others, however, are quite plain with drab, dark olive or gray-brown coloring.

DAYTIME GECKO

The blue-tailed day gecko *Phelsuma cepediana* is a colorful gecko from the islands of Réunion and Mauritius. It is active during the daytime and is a tree-dweller.

Reproduction Courtship displays involve head bobbing and tail waving. The females lay one or two eggs, which are often attached to each other and secreted in a rocky hiding place. Unlike most lizards, which produce eggs with leathery shells, the day geckos (and all geckos of the family Gekkonidae) lay eggs with hard, brittle shells. Normally, only one clutch is laid per season, although additional clutches may be laid if environmental conditions are favorable.

TYPICAL DAY GECKO
Like all members of the genus *Phelsuma*, this day gecko from the island of Madagascar has round pupils and greatly reduced claws on its digits, relying solely on its toe pads when climbing.

Distribution Day geckos are distributed in Madagascar and other islands—the Seychelles, Comoros, Andamans, and smaller islands in the Indian Ocean off the coast of East Africa. An endemic species, the Namaqua day gecko, has a restricted range in western South Africa and southern Namibia.

Flap-footed Lizards

Pygopodidae

7 genera/35 species

SNAPSHOT

LENGTH From 6 inches to 2 feet (15–60 cm)

DIET Most species eat insects and other arthropods. The large Burton's snake-lizard eats other lizards, mainly skinks, and snakes

HABITAT & DISTRIBUTION Most prefer semi-arid and arid habitats with low, dense vegetation. They occur in Australia, with two species in New Guinea

■ GENERAL

With their extremely long bodies, tiny hindlimbs, and no forelimbs, flap-footed lizards look remarkably like snakes. Sometimes they use their hindlimbs to move through vegetation and in courtship and defensive behaviors. Some species live underground, while others live on the surface, retreating to the burrows of spiders or other animals, or into clumps of spinifex grass to gain shelter.

■ CHARACTERISTICS

Like their gecko relatives they have a transparent scale over their eyes that they wipe clean with their tongue. Many species have an extremely long tail that can be discarded if the lizard is attacked.

■ REPRODUCTION

All flap-footed lizards lay clutches of two eggs.

LEG FLAPS
The hindlimbs of these lizards are small, flattened flaps that normally lie flat against the sides of the body.

Anguid Lizards

Anguidae

About 10 genera/about 90 species

◾ GLASS LIZARDS

These ground-dwelling lizards are completely legless. Their tails are extremely long. Their common name comes from the tendency of their tail to shatter into several pieces when grabbed by a predator. Most species are secretive animals, hiding under logs, vegetation, or in burrows. During winter, glass lizards hibernate in the deep tunnels made by other animals such as rodents and moles.

Characteristics Glass lizards, like all anguid lizards, have stiff bodies, closable eyelids, and fragile tails.

Reproduction All glass lizards lay eggs and in some species the female stays with the eggs during incubation, though she does not actively defend the nest.

NO LEGS

Reaching total lengths of up to 4½ feet (1.4 m), the sheltopusik *Ophisaurus apodus* of Europe and Asia is the largest glass lizard. Less secretive than other species, it can often be seen basking on the branches of low bushes.

SNAPSHOT

LENGTH **About 12 inches (30 cm)**
DIET **Varies according to size.
They eat insects, scorpions,
spiders, snails, millipedes, birds,
small mammals, and other lizards**
HABITAT & DISTRIBUTION **Occupy
a wide range of habitats from
deserts and tropical lowlands
to heavily forested mountains.
Their distribution ranges from
southwestern Canada to tropical
Central and South America**

■ ALLIGATOR LIZARDS
These slow-moving lizards have
large, rough, squarish scales that
give them their common name.
Their dark brown, mottled skin,
which they shed in one piece like
a snake, increases this likeness to
alligators. Many species live in
the trees in the rainforests of
Central and South America. The
ground dwellers are generally
secretive creatures that hide in
the undergrowth, in rocky
crevices, or down burrows.
Characteristics Alligator lizards
have a flat, wedge-shaped head.
They are slender with small, thin
limbs and a long tail, which in
some species is prehensile.
Reproduction Most species lay
eggs in burrows or other protected
sites. The northern alligator lizard
Elgaria coerulea, which is
adapted to colder conditions,
gives birth to live young three
months after mating.

VERSATILE LIZARD
The southern alligator
lizard *Elgaria
multicarinata* from
North America is a
ground dweller but
it also climbs trees
with the aid of its
partly prehensile tail.

Beaded Lizards

Helodermatidae

1 genus/2 species

GENERAL

The two beaded lizards, the gila monster and the Mexican beaded lizard, are the only venomous lizards. The venom is used to immobilize their prey. They tend to bite and hang on to their prey like a bulldog, to allow the venom to flow into the open wound. Beaded lizards avoid high temperatures, spending much of their time in burrows. Only in the cooler spring months or when the weather is overcast are they active during the day.

CHARACTERISTICS

These large lizards are stocky with broad heads and short tails used for fat storage. Their scales are small and bead-like and do not overlap.

REPRODUCTION

Intense combat between rival males usually precedes mating.

POISONOUS BITE
The gila monster's bite results in localized swelling, severe pain, and may cause vomiting, but is rarely fatal to humans.

The eggs are laid in sandy soil, under rocks or in a burrow. The young hatch about ten months later.

SNAPSHOT

LENGTH Gila monster 2 feet (60 cm); Mexican beaded lizard 3 feet (1 m)

DIET Both species feed on a variety of prey but rely heavily on the nest young of rodents and other small mammals, and bird and reptile eggs

HABITAT & DISTRIBUTION Gila monsters are usually found on rocky slopes in areas of desert scrub, grassland, or oak woods. They occur in southwestern USA and northwestern Mexico. Mexican beaded lizards inhabit desert scrub and tropical woodlands. They occur along the west coast of Mexico and Guatemala

Monitor Lizards

Varanidae

1 genus/about 45 species

■ GENERAL

All monitors have a relatively similar body form, with a long neck, well-developed limbs, strong claws, and a powerful tail. They also have a slender, deeply forked tongue, which they flick like a snake. The largest lizard, the Komodo dragon of Indonesia, is a member of this group. Two-thirds of the monitor species are found in Australia, where they are known as goannas. All monitors are active during the day.

SNAPSHOT

LENGTH 8 inches (20 cm) to 10 feet (3 m)

DIET The prey of monitor lizards relates to their size. They are mostly insectivorous, especially the smaller ones. The medium-sized species eat insects, small lizards, and small mammals. The arboreal species will take young birds from nests and the aquatic ones include fish and frogs in their diet. Large monitors eat small mammals, birds, other lizards, and carrion

HABITAT Live in rocky and sandy deserts, rainforests, open wood-lands, and forests, and along riverbanks and in mangroves

■ CHARACTERISTICS

The Komodo dragon grows to about 10 feet (3 m) in length and can weigh as much as 364 pounds (165 kg). Other "giants" are the perentie, Australia's largest monitor, which grows to 8 feet (2½ m); and the African Nile monitor and the water monitor

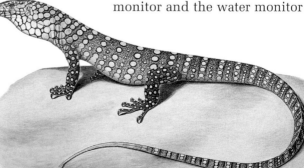

THICK NECK
This perentie *Varanus giganteus* has inflated its neck as part of its impressive threat display.

of Asia, which reach 6½ feet
(2 m). Not all monitors are large,
however. Some Australian
species, such as the short tailed
monitor, measure only 8 inches
(20 cm). Although mainly
terrestrial, many monitors are
proficient tree climbers. The
emerald tree monitor of New
Guinea and northern Australia
is an arboreal specialist with a
prehensile tail. Aquatic species,
like Merten's water monitor,
have a flattened, paddle-like tail,
which is used for swimming.

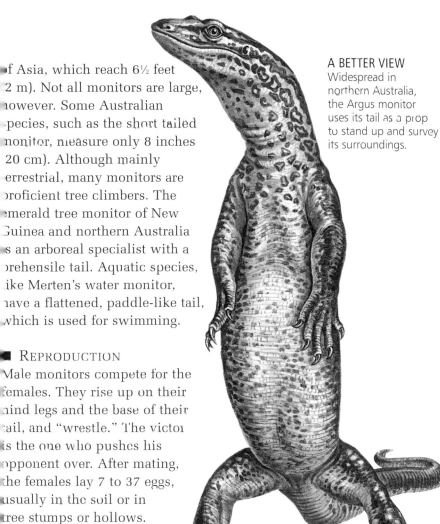

A BETTER VIEW
Widespread in
northern Australia,
the Argus monitor
uses its tail as a prop
to stand up and survey
its surroundings.

■ REPRODUCTION
Male monitors compete for the
females. They rise up on their
hind legs and the base of their
tail, and "wrestle." The victor
is the one who pushes his
opponent over. After mating,
the females lay 7 to 37 eggs,
usually in the soil or in
tree stumps or hollows.

■ DISTRIBUTION
Monitor lizards are found
in Australia, Southeast Asia,
and Africa.

Plated Lizards

Cordylidae

4 genera/about 50 species

■ GIRDLE-TAILED LIZARDS
These heavily armored lizards
have large, rectangular scales
arranged in regular rows around
their body. On the back of their
head and on their tail are rings, or
"girdles," of sharp spines. These
lizards use their tail as a weapon
to defend themselves, or to plug
up a burrow or wedge themselves
into a rocky crevice. Active
during the day, girdle-tails are all
sun-loving, basking lizards.

S N A P S H O T

LENGTH 4–16 inches (10–40 cm)
DIET Feed mainly on insects but
some of the larger species also
eat plant matter such as fallen
fruit, berries, and lichen
HABITAT & DISTRIBUTION These
lizards are mainly rock dwellers
and live in semi-arid to arid
areas. The lizards occur in Africa
and are particularly numerous
in southern Africa

Characteristics The body and
head of these lizards are flattened.
Most species are drab, with
blacks, browns, and straw colors
being dominant.

Reproduction All the girdle-
tailed lizards produce live
young, usually with one to six
young in each litter.

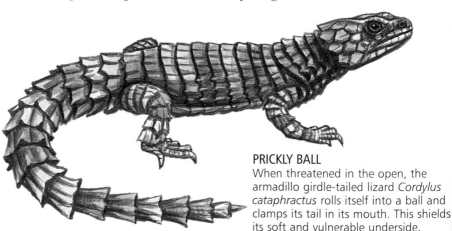

PRICKLY BALL
When threatened in the open, the
armadillo girdle-tailed lizard *Cordylus
cataphractus* rolls itself into a ball and
clamps its tail in its mouth. This shields
its soft and vulnerable underside.

FLAT LIZARDS

These lizards have an amazingly flat head and body that allow them to squeeze into the narrowest of rock crevices. Often large numbers of individuals will be found sheltering together in a thin space beneath a rock flake. In many species the males become vibrantly colored during the breeding season. A common color combination is bright green on top, an orange tail, and electric blue underneath.

Characteristics The females and juveniles do not develop the

bright colors of the males but they do have a striped back.

Reproduction Flat lizards are the only members of the family Cordylidae to lay eggs. Two or so eggs are laid in a deep, damp crack in the rock, and a single site may be shared by ten or more females.

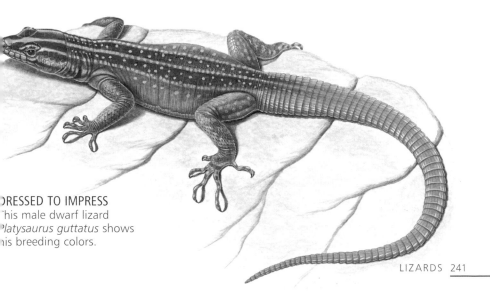

DRESSED TO IMPRESS
This male dwarf lizard *Platysaurus guttatus* shows his breeding colors.

True Lizards

Lacertidae

27 genera/over 230 species

■ WALL LIZARDS

These lizards are very familiar to most Europeans. They prefer open country, but they can often be seen climbing on trees or rocks, or basking on old stone walls. Most species are terrestrial and are active during the day. They prefer high body temperatures so become inactive when weather conditions are unfavorable, and many species spend the winter hibernating among stones or rocks or underground.

Characteristics Wall lizards have a long body with a pointed head, well-developed limbs, and a long,

SNAPSHOT

LENGTH 5½ inches (14 cm)
DIET Mainly insects, their larvae and other small invertebrates, but some species also eat succulent plants and soft fruit
HABITAT & DISTRIBUTION Wall lizards make use of many habitats, such as rocks, the spaces between walls, and old buildings. They are found in the arid regions of central and southern Europe and on the Channel Islands

tapering tail that can be easily shed. The males are often brightly colored, with green being the most common color, but the females and juveniles are more brown or gray.

Reproduction Wall lizards lay small clutches of between three and six eggs in a hole dug in the soil. Those from the warmer regions lay several clutches a year.

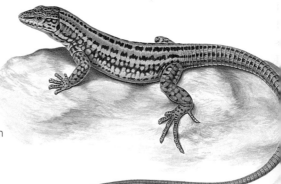

SKIN COLOR
The color of the Italian wall lizard *Podarcis sicula* changes according to the Mediterranean island it lives on.

VIVIPAROUS LIZARD

As its name suggests, the viviparous lizard *Lacerta vivipara* gives birth to live young. It retains the eggs in its body until they hatch. This feature allows the lizard to succeed in harsh climates that could not be colonized by egg-laying species. By retaining the developing embryos within the body, the female can regulate the temperature and moisture more closely than if the eggs were left to develop outside the body.

Characteristics This small, agile lizard has a slender body and strong limbs. The tail accounts for half of its body length. The females are slightly longer and stockier than the males.

Reproduction The litter size of the viviparous lizards is generally four to eleven. The young are born in early summer, giving them time to feed before the winter hibernation.

EGG-LAYING LIZARD
Not all the populations are viviparous. One southern population in a warmer climate lays eggs like other lacertids.

SNAPSHOT

LENGTH 5 inches (13 cm)

DIET Whatever insect happens to be available, as well as spiders, centipedes, slugs, and snails

HABITAT & DISTRIBUTION Lives in a wide range of habitats, including meadows, moors, woodlands, gardens, mountains, and sand dunes. They are widespread and occur in northern Asia and throughout Europe, extending into the Arctic Circle in Scandinavia

Snapshot

Length **Up to 5 inches (12 cm)**
Diet **Small beetles and other insects, but it will also eat windblown seeds when insects are not available**
Habitat & Distribution **Preferred habitat is sparsely vegetated desert sand dunes. It is endemic to the Namib Desert on the west coast of southern Africa**

■ Namib dune lizard

The African Namib dune lizard *Aporosaura anchietae* is a specialized desert dweller. To escape the intense heat of the midday sun, it buries itself in the sand. When moving, the lizard reduces the transfer of heat from the sand by a "thermal dance," alternately lifting two feet while balancing on the other two. The body is sand-colored with a network of black markings.

Characteristics This lizard is also known as the shovel-snouted lizard because when disturbed or pursued, it dives into the dune face, using its flattened snout, which has a sharp cutting edge, and powerful hind legs to "swim" deep into the sand. If it cannot escape, it will raise its body, jump, and bite.

Reproduction One or two large eggs are laid in a chamber dug into firm sand in a dune. There is no fixed breeding season.

DEFINED SPACE
The lizards are territorial particularly during the breeding season. Males will defend choice territories, such as areas where seeds collect.

Night Lizards

Xantusiidae

3 genera/18 species

■ GENERAL

These small lizards have a low preferred body temperature. They are most active at 73°F (23°C), which is 10 degrees lower than most lizards. A few species are active by day, usually in dark, cool hidden places, but most are nocturnal or active at twilight. Night lizards occupy rotting logs, caves, or cracks and crevices in rocks, while others hide under dead leaves or low-lying bushes.

■ CHARACTERISTICS

Like geckos, these lizards have a transparent scale that protects

SNAPSHOT

LENGTH Usually about 4–6 inches (10–15 cm)
DIET Most night lizards eat insects, but a few species include plant matter such as figs, fruit, or seeds
HABITAT & DISTRIBUTION Live in tropical lowland forests and in rocky semi-arid zones in south-western USA, Central America, and the West Indies

their eyes, rather than an eyelid. In color, most are inconspicuous grays or browns, the exception being the granite night lizard that has distinctive markings.

■ REPRODUCTION

All species give birth to between one and eight live young after a gestation period of three months.

DISTINCTIVE MARKINGS
The granite night lizard *Xantusia henshawi* is a rock-dwelling species of the Californian deserts.

Teiid Lizards

Teiidae

9 genera/about 100 species

SNAPSHOT

LENGTH 6–18 inches (15–45 cm)
DIET Mainly insects and other arthropods. Prey such as termites are often excavated by digging
HABITAT & DISTRIBUTION The terrestrial whiptails occupy a variety of habitats, from deserts to tropical forests. They occur from southern USA to Argentina and in the West Indies

■ WHIPTAIL LIZARDS

These slender, agile lizards have a high optimum body temperature. As a result they burn up lots of energy and need plenty of food. They are active foragers, at times moving almost constantly in search of prey. When threatened they can run incredibly fast, which gives rise to their other common name, racerunners. During the cooler parts of the day and throughout the winter, the lizards retreat to burrows.

Characteristics Whiptails are usually brown in color, though some of the tropical species are bright blue or green, and most have some sort of striped pattern. They have large scales on their head and tiny ones on their back, well-developed limbs, and a long tapering tail.

Reproduction Small clutches of one to six eggs are usual, with some species laying twice a year. Several whiptail species are all-female and are able to produce fertile eggs without mating with males.

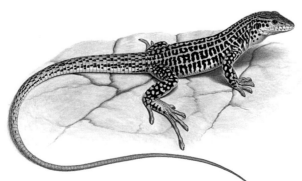

ALL FEMALES
The checkered whiptail
Cnemidophorus tesselatus
of North America is an
all-female species

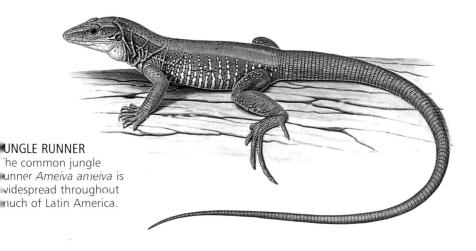

JUNGLE RUNNER
The common jungle
runner *Ameiva ameiva* is
widespread throughout
much of Latin America.

JUNGLE RUNNERS

The jungle runners of tropical Central and South America are efficient predators. As well as snapping up insects with their powerful jaws, they also prey on birds, small mammals, and other reptiles. In behavior and form, the jungle runners resemble the smaller European lizards. The common jungle runner *Ameiva ameiva* is also known as the Surinam lizard; a related species is the South American striped lizard *Ameiva undulatus*.

Characteristics These lizards are essentially larger versions of the whiptails. They are usually brown in color, though in some species the males have bright markings on the back and sides. Their tails are long and their tongues deeply cleft.

Reproduction Females lay small clutches of two to six eggs, which they bury in sand or loose soil.

SNAPSHOT

LENGTH 20 inches (50 cm)
DIET Spiders and insects such as beetles, cockroaches, and caterpillars, as well as small birds, mammals, and reptiles. They also eat small amounts of leaves and fruit
HABITAT & DISTRIBUTION Jungle runners occupy a wide range of habitats but they are often seen along riverbanks or in forest clearings. They are found in tropical Central and South America

SQUAMATA

SAURIA

Skinks

Scincidae

About 85 genera/about 1300 species

■ PINK-TONGUED SKINKS
There are more than 1,300 species of skink, making this the largest of the lizard families. Although it can climb small shrubs and trees, the Australian pink-tongued skink usually forages for its prey among ground litter and low vegetation. When threatened, it usually tries to bolt for cover. It shelters under loose tree bark or rock shelves, or in cracks and crevices.
Characteristics This skink's prehensile tail—which accounts for half its length—along with

S N A P S H O T

LENGTH 17 inches (45 cm)
DIET Mainly slugs and snails, and some insects
HABITAT & DISTRIBUTION Lives in rainforests and other wet forest areas along the coast of eastern Australia from mid-New South Wales to the northern tip of Queensland

its strong claws, is useful for climbing. Like most skinks, it has smooth, overlapping scales. The newborn lizards have blue rather than pink tongues.
Reproduction Like many skinks, the pink-tongued skink gives birth to live young. The litter is usually large, from 12 to 25 young, but the newborn lizards are very small.

SHELL CRUSHERS
The pink-tongued skinks have broad, flattened teeth at the back of the jaws for crushing snail shells.

EMERALD TREE SKINK
This Asian–Pacific skink *Lamprolepis smaragdina* has a long tail, depressed head, and slender snout. Its well-developed limbs assist as it climbs and scuttles along tree trunks.

Characteristics The skink's underside ranges from yellow to greenish white. It is active during the day and is a tree dweller, although it occasionally descends to the ground in search of food. It is swift in movement and very agile as it darts along tree trunks and branches.

Reproduction This is an egg-laying species, laying its two eggs in humus or rotting timber on or above the ground.

COLOR OF THE FOREST
The skink's mottled green color ensures that it is well camouflaged in its tropical forest habitat.

SNAPSHOT

LENGTH 4 inches (10 cm) in body length; tail is equally long
DIET Mainly insects, but it will also eat fruit and flowers if insects are not available
HABITAT & DISTRIBUTION Prefer larger forest trees but have adapted to human settlement. They are found in Asia and the Pacific, from Taiwan and the Philippines through several Pacific islands to Indonesia, New Guinea, and the Solomon Islands

SQUAMATA

SAURIA

■ RED-TAILED SKINK
The small, sun-loving red-tailed skink *Morethia ruficauda* is often most active at midday when temperatures in the north of Australia, where it lives, are high. A terrestrial lizard, it forages among leaf litter and rocks for its food. It is swift and agile, quickly diving under the leaf litter if disturbed. If it is not fast enough, it can discard its bright red tail.
Characteristics The red-tailed skink has smooth, shiny scales, well-developed limbs, and a long, whiplike fragile tail. Individuals, presumably males, have been observed facing one another from

SNAPSHOT

LENGTH Body length 1–1½ inches (3–4 cm)
DIET Arthropods and other small invertebrates found among rocks and leaf litter
HABITAT & DISTRIBUTION Margins of rock outcrops and stony soils in arid and semi-arid rocky areas in northwestern and central Australia

a distance of 4 inches (10 cm) and whipping their tails horizontally, probably as an assertion of sexual or territorial rights. There are two subspecies, distinguished by variations in their color and body markings.
Reproduction Mating occurs in spring and small clutches of eggs are laid in safe hiding places.

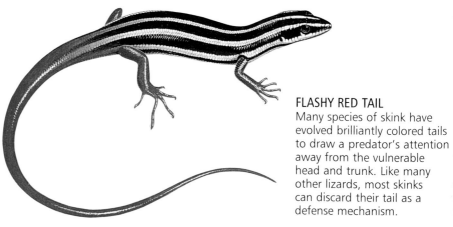

FLASHY RED TAIL
Many species of skink have evolved brilliantly colored tails to draw a predator's attention away from the vulnerable head and trunk. Like many other lizards, most skinks can discard their tail as a defense mechanism.

FIVE-LINED SKINK

The juveniles of the widespread North American five-lined skink *Eumeces fasciatus* have black bodies with white stripes and bright blue tails, making them look remarkably similar to the unrelated Australian red-tailed skink. Tail loss is common and in many populations most of the adults have grown a new one. These skinks are terrestrial and will climb the lower reaches of trees only to bask.

Characteristics The coloring of these skinks changes as they grow. The bright blue disappears, their body becomes brown, and the males lose the striped pattern as well. In the breeding season,

SNAPSHOT

LENGTH 5–8 inches (13–20 cm)
DIET Insects, insect larvae, crustaceans, spiders, earthworms, other lizards, and even small mice
HABITAT & DISTRIBUTION Found in North America, from New England south to Florida, west to Texas, and north to Kansas and Ontario. It prefers damp, wooded areas, decaying leaf litter, rotting stumps and logs but can also be seen in gardens

increased levels of testosterone in the blood cause the males to develop a bright orange head.

Reproduction The skinks mate in April or May. Clutches of 4 to 15 eggs are laid in decaying logs or under rocks. The eggs are guarded by the mother until they hatch in summer.

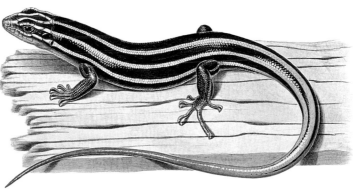

GROWING UP
This striped pattern on the juvenile is retained by adult females, whereas adult males lose both the coloring and the stripes.

Amphisbaenians

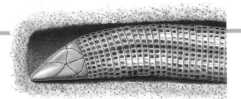

Amphisbaenians

Amphisbaenidae

23 genera/about 140 species

■ GENERAL

Worm lizards spend most of their life underground where they use their hard, strong heads to burrow through the soil. They may emerge at night to feed on the surface, but they are usually only seen if heavy rain floods their burrows. Worm lizards have no external ear openings, but they can sense vibrations in the ground. If they detect an insect crawling through the soil, they can dig very quickly and catch it.

■ CHARACTERISTICS

The skin of a worm lizard is loosely attached to its cylindrical body and is ringed with small scales. Special scales on the face allow it to detect sound vibrations. It has simplified eyes that can barely see movement, and can distinguish only between light and dark. On its snout is a large, reinforced scale, which helps it force its way through the soil. The worm lizard's mouth is deeply recessed under the snout so dirt cannot get in when it is burrowing. They have sharp, interlocking teeth and powerful jaws so they can cut and tear pieces from larger prey. The tail, pointed in some species, rounded in others, is covered in horny scales to provide protection from predators. If grasped by a predator, it can be shed, but a new one does not grow.

TILE PROOFED

Scales arranged like tiles stop the dirt from building up on the body of the shovel-snouted worm lizard.

hard scale on snout

recessed mouth

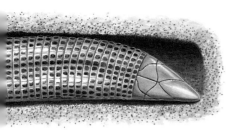

REPRODUCTION

Most species lay eggs, but at least three species are known to retain the eggs inside their body and give birth to live young. Some species lay their eggs in ant or termite nests.

DISTRIBUTION

Amphisbaenians are found in the warmer parts of Africa, the Middle East, southern Europe, and Central and South America.

SNAPSHOT

LENGTH Range from 4–30 inches (10–75 cm), with most being around 6–14 inches (15–35 cm)

DIET Mostly insects, earthworms, and other invertebrates. The larger species also eat small vertebrate animals and carrion

HABITAT Amphisbaenians live in moist and sandy soil. Some inhabit forests, others live in desert areas

WORLDS APART

Keel-snouted worm lizards occur in both South America and Africa but are not closely related.

BURROWING HEADS

Worm lizards are the only true burrowers among reptiles. The way they burrow is reflected in the shape of their head.

Round-headed species push forward into the earth and turn the head in any direction to make the tunnel.

Keel-headed species push the head forward and then to the side.

Shovel-headed species push forward and then up.

Chisel-headed species rotate the head in one direction and then the other.

Snakes

Wormsnakes

Anomalepididae, Leptotyphlopidae, and Typhlopidae

12 genera/about 280 species

■ GENERAL

These burrowing snakes resemble worms in shape and, often, in color. Their eyes are merely small, dark spots that can only tell the difference between light and dark. They rely on scent to locate their food. Their blunt head merges smoothly with the rest of the body, and the tail is short and tipped with a small spine that is used to anchor the snake so that it can move forward more easily as it burrows through soil.

INSECT REPELLENT
The threadsnake *Leptotyphlops humilis* defends itself against the bites and stings of worker ants defending their nest, by secreting chemicals that repel the ants.

S N A P S H O T

LENGTH From less than 4 inches (10 cm) up to 31 inches (80 cm)
DIET Worms or the eggs and larvae of ants and termites
HABITAT & DISTRIBUTION
Wormsnakes prefer moist habitats, and shelter in burrows in sand and soil, or under logs and rocks. The blindsnakes are found in Africa, Asia, Australia, and Central America. The threadsnakes inhabit the USA, Central America, the West Indies, Africa, Arabia, and Pakistan. The blind wormsnakes occur in Central and South America

■ CHARACTERISTICS

The blindsnakes (family Typhlopidae) have teeth only on their upper jaw, while the very slender threadsnakes (family Leptotyphlopidae) have teeth only on their lower jaw. The third family, the blind wormsnakes (family Anomalepididae), have teeth on their upper jaw, with rarely more than a single tooth on the lower jaw. All the wormsnakes are non-venomous.

■ REPRODUCTION

Although a few African blindsnakes produce live young, most wormsnakes lay eggs.

Filesnakes

Acrochordidae

1 genus/3 species

GENERAL

The three totally aquatic filesnakes are among the most unusual of snakes. Their skin is loose and baggy. When underwater the skin straightens out beneath the underside of the snakes and allows them to swim more efficiently.

CHARACTERISTICS

The skin of the filesnakes is covered with small, granular scales like the surface of a file, which allows them to hang on to and squeeze slippery fish. They have lost the large scales on their belly that characterize most snakes and have trouble moving

FOOD FROM THE SEA
The little filesnake *Acrochordus granulatus* hunts for fish, crabs, and other crustaceans in intertidal areas.

SNAPSHOT

LENGTH 3–7 feet (1–2 m)
DIET Mainly fish
HABITAT & DISTRIBUTION The filesnake lives in rivers and freshwater billabongs in Australia and New Guinea. The elephant's trunk snake, also a freshwater species, inhabits rivers in Southeast Asia. The third species, the little filesnake, can be found in estuaries and coastal waters in the Indian and Pacific oceans

about on land. These snakes have a flap in the roof of their mouth that can be used to close their nostrils, and they have salt glands under their tongue. Filesnakes are mainly nocturnal and they often exist on low rates of energy. They eat rarely and are mostly sluggish.

REPRODUCTION

The females may reproduce only once every few years. They retain the eggs in their body until they are ready to hatch. The largest snakes give birth to 25 to 35 live young in a single litter.

Pipe Snakes

Aniliidae

3 genera/about 10 species

■ GENERAL

The pipe snakes are a small group of burrowing snakes that use their head to force their way through the damp soil and mud of the rice fields and swamps they inhabit. Although the Asian pipe snakes are usually quite dull in color, some species have brightly patterned undersides, especially of the tail. If threatened, these snakes hide their head and wave their tail to distract the predator.

SNAPSHOT

LENGTH Up to 3 feet (1 m)
DIET The coral pipe snake eats small mammals such as mice, caecilians, amphisbaenians, and small lizards and snakes. The Asian pipe snakes feed on eels and other snakes, sometimes catching and eating prey that exceeds their own body length
HABITAT & DISTRIBUTION See main text

■ CHARACTERISTICS

The bones in the skull of the burrowing pipe snakes are solidly united, unlike those of most other snakes. Another unusual feature of the group is the presence of rudimentary hind legs in the form of small spurs on either side of the vent. The only South American pipe snake, the coral

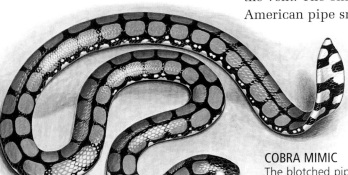

COBRA MIMIC
The blotched pipe snake *Cylindrophus maculatus* from Sri Lanka raises its brightly colored tail in mimicry of a cobra's head and hood.

pipe snake, is a red and black banded snake with a blunt snout. It has small eyes, each covered by a transparent scale. The Asian pipe snakes are not as brightly colored. Most are dark brown with few, if any, markings on their back.

REPRODUCTION

The coral pipe snake gives birth to between four and ten live young. The Asian pipe snakes include both egg-laying and live-bearing species.

■ HABITAT AND DISTRIBUTION

The South American coral pipe snake lives in swampy and marshy areas in the forests of the Amazon Basin. The Asian pipe snakes occur in lowland marshy areas and paddy fields. They are found in eastern Asia from Sri Lanka to Indonesia. The smallest of the group, the elegantly marked blotched pipe snake, inhabits forested (and formerly forested) areas of Sri Lanka.

DECEPTIVE COLORING
The close resemblance of the brightly patterned coral pipe snake *Anilius scytale* to the venomous coral snake has resulted in its South American common name "coral falsa." Completely non-venomous, its main defense tactic is to hide its head and present its blunt tail as an alternative "head."

Boas and Pythons

Boidae

20 genera/about 90 species

SNAPSHOT

LENGTH Up to 6½ feet (2 m), but more commonly about half this length
DIET Mainly birds and sometimes small mammals such as rats and mice. The young also eat tree frogs
HABITAT Inhabits tropical rainforests, monsoon forests, and bamboo thickets

■ GREEN TREE PYTHON

The green tree python *Chondropython viridis* is a tree-dwelling snake whose brilliant green coloration camouflages it among the ferns and other epiphytic plants of its rainforest habitat. The snake hunts by night, rarely coming down to the ground to search for its prey. The python sometimes lures prey by wriggling the thin tip of its tail. When the prey comes to investigate, the python seizes it. The day is spent basking, draped in coils over a branch or vine. Sometimes it shelters in a tree hollow or among the large leaves of a fern.

Characteristics This solidly built tree-dweller has a large, broad head, which is distinct from the neck. An adept climber, it has a prehensile tail that it uses to grasp branches and to suspend

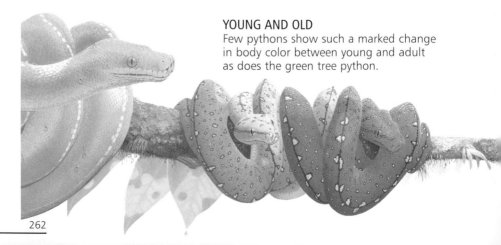

YOUNG AND OLD
Few pythons show such a marked change in body color between young and adult as does the green tree python.

itself from a height. The adult python is emerald green with a yellow belly and sometimes a stripe of white scales down its back. A nocturnal snake, it has large eyes with long, vertical pupils that open up in the dark, and pale irises.

Reproduction The green tree python lays between 10 and 25 eggs in a clutch. When they first hatch, green tree pythons are either bright yellow or a rich, brick red. They stay this way for two or three years. Then, in a period of a few weeks, they change to the adult coloration. The skin is not shed at this time. Rather, in the center of each scale, a green speck appears that expands until the snake is green all over.

Distribution The green tree python is found in Papua New Guinea and in the far northern tip of eastern Australia.

WATER CONTAINER
It has been reported that the green tree python drinks rainwater collected in its coils.

■ CARPET PYTHON

There are many pythons in Australia, but the most widespread and familiar species is the carpet python *Morelia spilota*. A good climber, it can be found on tree branches and in hollows of trees, but it also shelters in animal burrows, caves, rock crevices, and below boulders. It is mainly nocturnal though sometimes basks and forages for food during the day. Like all pythons, it throws a series of coils around its prey as soon as it is caught, and suffocates it by tightening the coils each time the trapped animal exhales.

Characteristics Carpet pythons come in many colors and patterns.

SNAPSHOT

LENGTH **Grow to 6½ feet (2 m), but some are nearly twice this length**

DIET **Birds, mammals, and sometimes lizards**

HABITAT & DISTRIBUTION **The carpet python occupies almost all possible habitats wherever it occurs, from wet, tropical rainforests to semi-arid deserts. It is found over much of southern, eastern, and northern Australia and also occurs in New Guinea**

Reproduction The female lays her eggs in a sheltered place such as a tree hollow or abandoned burrow. She coils around the eggs, shivering to warm them, staying in this position until they hatch. Sometimes she will leave the eggs to bask, returning when she has raised her body temperature.

LIMITED DISTRIBUTION
The jungle carpet *Morela spilota cheynei* is a small, brightly colored subspecies of carpet python restricted to rainforest habitats in northeast Queensland.

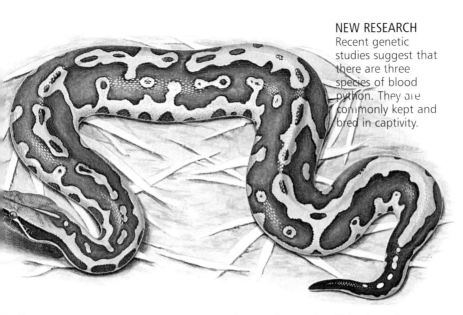

NEW RESEARCH
Recent genetic studies suggest that there are three species of blood python. They are commonly kept and bred in captivity.

◼ BLOOD PYTHON

The blood python *Python curtus* is a short, semi-aquatic snake from Southeast Asia where it inhabits swamps, marshes, and slow-moving rainforest streams. It is a nocturnal predator, lying in wait for prey while partially submerged in ditches, pools, or on the banks of rivers. Its common name is derived from the deep red coloring of some individuals. Because of its thick and stumpy tail, the blood python is also known as the short-tailed python.

Characteristics The color of this species' broad head ranges from red to yellowish or even gray, and the snake's overall body color is similarly variable, ranging from yellow to brick red with yellowish or brown blotches.

Reproduction The female lays from 10 to 15 eggs and coils around them to protect them until they hatch three months later.

SNAPSHOT

LENGTH **Almost 10 feet (3 m)**
DIET **Feeds almost wholly on birds and small mammals**
HABITAT & DISTRIBUTION **Inhabits swamps or rainforests through southern Indochina, Malaya, Sumatra, and Borneo**

SNAPSHOT

LENGTH Up to 33 feet (10 m)
DIET The reticulated python has been known to attack and feed on mammals and domestic fowl
HABITAT & DISTRIBUTION Lives in the forests of Southeast Asia, India, Bangladesh, Indochina, and the Philippines

■ RETICULATED PYTHON

The record for the "longest snake in the world" belongs either to the reticulated python *Python reticulatus* of Asia, or to the South American anaconda. Both have been measured at about 33 feet (10 m), but the anaconda is a much heavier, thicker-bodied snake than the more slender reticulated python.

Characteristics Like many nocturnal snakes, the reticulated python has narrow, vertical pupils. Its color varies from purplish brown to tan, with a chain of darker markings. The head is yellowish, with a darker line. This python is largely a tree-dweller but commonly descends to the ground in search of food. It kills its prey by constriction.

Reproduction Reticulated pythons usually lay large clutches of about 50 eggs, but clutches of up to 100 have been recorded. When the young hatch they are already about 2 feet (60 cm) long.

NIGHT HUNTER
The pits on the scales along the lips are heat-sensing organs, useful in locating warm-blooded prey at night.

BOA CONSTRICTOR

Boas are similar in many ways to pythons except that they bear live young instead of laying eggs. The best known of the boas is the large boa constrictor *Boa constrictor.*

Characteristics A boa's colors and markings vary, but most are gray or silver with numerous large brown or deep red blotches along the back. It is virtually harmless to humans and, like most snakes, its first reaction to danger is to flee. If threatened it may hiss very loudly, a sound that can be heard over 100 feet (30 m) away. Boas have small teeth that slant toward the throat and prevent prey from slipping out of the mouth. After the boa has eaten, it will lie motionless for many days while the food is digested.

Reproduction The female boa constrictor retains the unshelled eggs within her body, and gives birth to between 20 and 50 young, which are about 12 inches (30 cm) long. The growth rate of the young snakes depends on the temperature of the environment and the availability of food, but they may double their length in the first year, maturing when they are two or three years old.

TIGHT SQUEEZE
The Madagascan boa constrictor *Boa madagascariensis*, like other boas, kills its prey by constriction.

SNAPSHOT

LENGTH About 10 feet (3 m) with some reaching 20 feet (6 m)
DIET A variety of animals including birds, bats, opossums, squirrels, rats, and large lizards
HABITAT & DISTRIBUTION The boa constrictor is both terrestrial and arboreal and it lives in many different habitats, including semi-desert regions, open savanna, cultivated fields, and wet tropical forests. It is found in Central and South America from southern Mexico to Paraguay and Argentina

SNAPSHOT

LENGTH Up to 33 feet (10 m)
DIET Turtles, caimans, birds, and fish, and small mammals such as deer, peccaries, and large rodents
HABITAT & DISTRIBUTION Lives near large rivers, swamps, and lakes in tropical South America, mainly in the Amazon Basin

■ ANACONDA

The reticulated python may be as long, but the giant, semi-aquatic, green anaconda *Eunectes murinus* is without doubt the largest and heaviest of snakes, sometimes weighing more than 550 pounds (250 kg). It spends most of its time lying in wait at the water's edge for unwary mammals and caimans. During the day it basks on low branches overhanging a stream or rests in shallow water.

Characteristics The anaconda's dull coloring and black markings allow it to blend in well with the thick vegetation of its habitat. The nostrils are on top of its snout so it can breathe while it is swimming or lying submerged.

Reproduction Like other boas, the anaconda gives birth to live young. The 20 to 40 young are 2 to 3 feet (60 cm to 1 m) long when they are born.

LARGE TO SMALL
This green anaconda is the largest of the anacondas. Further south, it is replaced by the much smaller yellow anaconda.

COOK'S TREE BOA

Cook's tree boa *Corallus enydris cookii* is one of three species of South American tree boas. All are specialized for their arboreal life, with long, slender bodies and large, well-defined heads. The most spectacular of the three species is the emerald green tree boa, which is a brilliant green above with white or yellow blotches. Cook's tree boa and the garden tree boa are much duller in color.

Characteristics Within the Cook's tree boa species there is considerable variation in color

SNAPSHOT

LENGTH Grows to 6½ feet (2 m)

DIET Mainly birds and small mammals such as bats, but lizards are also taken when possible

HABITAT & DISTRIBUTION Cook's tree boa is one of two subspecies of garden tree boas that occur in South America. This species is more common in the northern part of the range

and skin pattern, ranging from dark orange, through brown to almost black. In some cases the body is distinctly patterned; other individuals have a uniform color. The underside is white, spotted with gray. This boa has an unusual technique for climbing trees. It stretches upward, wraps the front of its body around the trunk and gradually pulls the rest of its body along the tree trunk.

Reproduction Like other boas, this species bears live young. Between 7 and 30 offspring are born about 6 months after mating.

GRIPPING TEETH
The tree boas have very long teeth to allow them to firmly grip fast-moving prey.

SQUAMATA

SERPENTES

■ Brazilian rainbow boa
Named because of the iridescent patterned sheen of its scales, the Brazilian rainbow boa *Epicrates cenchria cenchria* spends part of its time in trees, but feeds on the ground. It is often found near village outskirts where there is a steady supply of rodents and other food. A nocturnal snake, it rests during the day in trees or on rafters in buildings.

Characteristics Although there are nine subspecies of rainbow boas, only the five subspecies of Brazilian rainbow boas have the bright patterning that justifies the group's common name. Between

S N A P S H O T

LENGTH Up to 5 feet (1.5 m)
DIET A variety of small mammals, lizards, and birds
HABITAT & DISTRIBUTION Rainbow boas are widespread through continental South America and the southern part of Central America

the scales bordering the upper lip, the Brazilian rainbow boa has heat-sensitive pits that are used to detect warm-blooded prey.

Reproduction Like other boas, this is a viviparous snake. The female retains the developing eggs within her oviduct until they are fully formed and gives birth to live young.

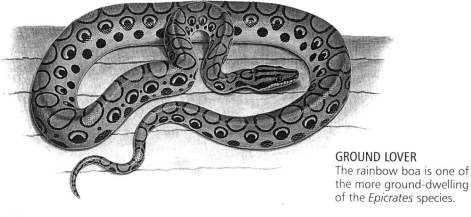

GROUND LOVER
The rainbow boa is one of the more ground-dwelling of the *Epicrates* species.

SAND BOAS

The ten species of African and Asian sand boas of the genus *Eryx* are burrowing snakes that are rarely seen above ground during the daytime. They are well adapted for their burrowing habits. They dig their way through sand or loose soil with their blunt, shovel-shaped snout. In some species the eyes are on top of the head so they can still see when they are partially buried.

Characteristics Sand boas have thick, cylindrical bodies and a blunt tail. The snake's main

SNAPSHOT

LENGTH 16–35 inches (40–90 cm)
DIET Small rodents, birds, and lizards
HABITAT & DISTRIBUTION Found in the arid regions of Africa and western Asia with one species, the javelin sand boa, in southeastern Europe

method of defense is to raise its tail so it looks like a head. This distracts a predator's attention away from the real head. Sand boas can be quick to seize and kill prey.

Reproduction Like all boas, the sand boas give birth to live young.

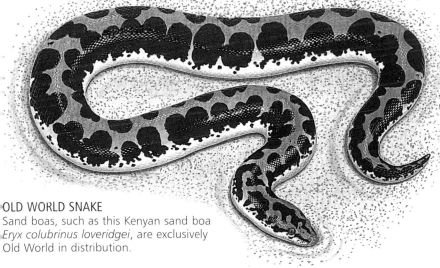

OLD WORLD SNAKE
Sand boas, such as this Kenyan sand boa *Eryx colubrinus loveridgei*, are exclusively Old World in distribution.

Colubrid Snakes

Colubridae

about 300 genera/about 1,600 species

SNAPSHOT

LENGTH Average is 12–16 inches (30–40 cm); maximum recorded is 22 inches (55 cm)

DIET Feeds on blindsnakes, legless lizards, and other snakes, but rarely feeds in captivity

HABITAT & DISTRIBUTION Lives in varied habitats, from semi-desert to savanna and coastal bushland in southern Africa

■ SPOTTED HARLEQUIN SNAKE The spotted harlequin snake *Homoroselaps lacteus* of South Africa is a venomous snake often found in old termite mounds, under stones, or in other secure hiding places. While its venom is toxic to humans, few bites have been recorded because of its small gape and reluctance to attack without provocation.

Characteristics This small, slender snake varies in its color phases. The back can be yellowish with numerous broken black bands and orange or yellow stripes, or it may be black with irregular yellow-white crossbars and red to orange spots.

Reproduction Up to 16 eggs are laid in a single clutch in December.

MYSTERY SNAKE
This snake is a puzzle to taxonomists. It has fixed front fangs like an elapid and yet has been classified with both the vipers and the colubrids.

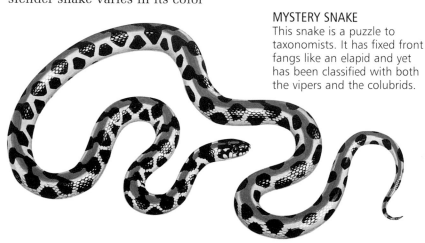

SLUG-EATING SNAKES

The common name of these Asian snakes comes from the fact that they feed on snails and slugs. They have an elongated lower jaw that can be inserted into the opening of a snail's shell. The long front teeth then hook into the snail's soft body, which the snake drags out with twisting movements. The snake does not consume the snail's shell, which it probably could not digest anyway.

Characteristics Slug-eating snakes are quite small and an undistinguished color of gray to brown, sometimes with darker crossbars.

Reproduction Although we know they are oviparous, little more is known of the breeding habits of these snakes.

SNAPSHOT

LENGTH 18–20 inches (45–50 cm)
DIET These snakes eat only snails and slugs of varying kinds
HABITAT & DISTRIBUTION Common in parts of Asia and occupy habitats from sea level to mountains. They can be found in gardens and around cultivated areas as well as more remote areas, where isolation makes them difficult to study

A TASTE FOR SNAILS
Pareas formosensis is one of several specialized slug-eating snakes found in the Asian region.

■ VINE SNAKES

These long, thin snakes are called vine snakes because, when draped over a branch, that's just what they look like. This provides them with excellent camouflage but their length also helps them to bridge the gaps when moving from branch to branch. They are amazing climbers and can go up a vertical tree trunk without coiling around it. They simply utilize crevices in the bark for grip. There are two groups of vine snakes: one in Latin America (genus *Oxybelis*) and another, sometimes called the twig snakes, in Africa (genus *Thelotornis*).

Characteristics Vine snakes are superbly adapted to their arboreal habitat, with narrow, pointed heads, large eyes, and long, slender bodies.

Both groups are rear-fanged snakes. The twig snakes are highly venomous and have caused human fatalities. When threatened by a predator, a twig snake will inflate the loose skin on its chin and throat to make itself look bigger.

Reproduction Vine snakes are all egg-layers, but there is considerable variety between species in the number of eggs, nesting preferences, and gestation times.

BIRD TRAP
It is thought that the twig snake *Thelotornis capensis* uses its black-tipped, red tongue to lure birds.

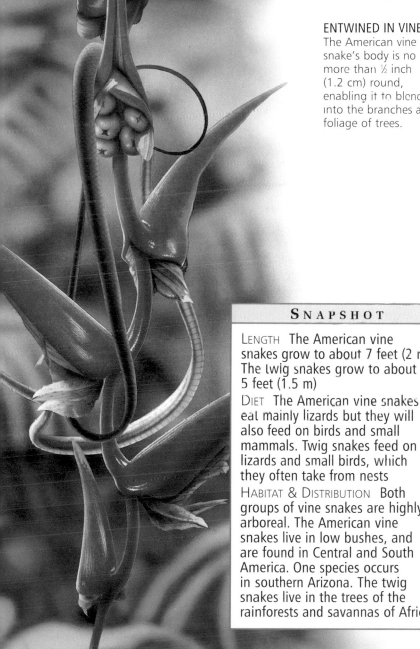

ENTWINED IN VINES
The American vine snake's body is no more than ½ inch (1.2 cm) round, enabling it to blend into the branches and foliage of trees.

SNAPSHOT

LENGTH The American vine snakes grow to about 7 feet (2 m). The twig snakes grow to about 5 feet (1.5 m)

DIET The American vine snakes eat mainly lizards but they will also feed on birds and small mammals. Twig snakes feed on lizards and small birds, which they often take from nests

HABITAT & DISTRIBUTION Both groups of vine snakes are highly arboreal. The American vine snakes live in low bushes, and are found in Central and South America. One species occurs in southern Arizona. The twig snakes live in the trees of the rainforests and savannas of Africa

SQUAMATA

SERPENTES

■ HOUSE SNAKES
These nocturnal snakes earned their common name from their habit of entering houses to search for food, usually rodents or other reptiles. There are 13 species in the genus *Lamprophis*, all of which are found in Africa.

Characteristics As with other nocturnal snakes, the eyes of house snakes are small and their pupils vertical. Their scales are smooth, and the number of scales varies according to species. The most common species is the brown house snake *Lamprophis fuliginosus*, which is found throughout most of Africa.

SNAPSHOT

LENGTH Up to 3 feet (1 m)
DIET Mice and rats are the preferred food, although smaller reptiles are also taken. Some species even forage for bats
HABITAT & DISTRIBUTION Most are terrestrial, although some live underground in abandoned termite nests and others forage in rock crevices. Thirteen species are found in Africa, with two species isolated in Arabia and on the Seychelles Islands

Reproduction House snakes are oviparous and lay clutches of oval, white eggs. The number and gestation period vary.

CONFINED HOME
Lamprophis guttatus, the spotted house snake, is endemic to the arid regions of the inland mountains of the Cape. Its blotched color varies according to the region.

WHITE-BELLIED MANGROVE SNAKE

On the mangrove mudflats at night, the white-bellied mangrove snake *Fordonia leucobalia* stalks crabs left behind by the receding tide. When the snake is close enough, it strikes the crab from above, pushing it into the soft mud with its forebody. Here the snake immobilizes the crab with its venom, then proceeds to eat it, biting off its legs and claws before consuming the rest of the crab.

Characteristics This mildly venomous, rear-fanged snake has

SNAPSHOT

LENGTH About 2 feet (60 cm)
DIET Crustaceans, especially crabs and sometimes fish
HABITAT & DISTRIBUTION This semi-aquatic snake lives in coastal mangroves. It shelters in crab burrows and among the root tangles of the mangroves. It is found around tidal creeks and estuaries in northern Australia, New Guinea, and Southeast Asia

a broad head with a round snout and a thin neck.

Reproduction The white-bellied mangrove snake gives birth to live young. There are usually between five and ten in a litter.

PURE WHITE BELLY
The color of these snakes varies between individuals, ranging from black and dark brown to reddish brown and cream, though the belly is always pure white. Some have blotches, spots, or bands on their back; others do not.

SQUAMATA

SERPENTES

SNAPSHOT

LENGTH About 2½–3 feet
(76 cm –1 m)
DIET Mainly fish, frogs, and
newts. They will also eat lizards,
birds, and small mammals. The
young prefer tadpoles
HABITAT & DISTRIBUTION Live near
ponds and streams, or in marshy
areas or damp woodlands. Some
extend into drier areas. They are
found in most of Europe, except
for Ireland, the Balearics, Malta,
Crete, and some of the Cyclades

■ COMMON GRASS SNAKE
The common grass snake *Natrix natrix* is widespread over much of Europe, even at high latitudes. Like many species from temperate regions, it spends the winter hibernating in holes in the ground. In the warmer months, it is active during the day and may often be seen basking on logs or the bank of a stream. It is never far from water and is an excellent swimmer. It can also climb, and sometimes goes up into the branches of shrubs or low trees.

Characteristics The common grass snake is brown, gray, or olive green in color with black bars along its sides. Around its neck is a broken collar of orange, yellow, pink, or white. If a predator cannot be put off by hissing and mock-striking, the grass snake defends itself by giving off a foul smell or, as a last resort, playing dead.

Reproduction The grass snake lays an average clutch of 30 to 40 eggs. Egg-laying snakes are not usually able to survive severely cold regions because the eggs need high temperatures to develop. Female grass snakes overcome this problem by migrating long distances to find suitable incubation sites.

NURSERY PATCH

The snakes in areas as far north as Sweden lay their eggs in cow manure piles on farms. The heat caused by decomposition allows the eggs to complete their development before the first frosts of winter.

WATER SNAKES

The water snakes of North America are often seen basking on logs or rocks at the water's edge, or in branches overhanging a stream. All are good swimmers, though some prefer slow-moving water. They search for their prey in the vegetation along the shoreline or hunt for it in the water.

Characteristics These snakes are usually dark brown, gray, or black with lighter undersides. Escape is their main method of defense, but if cornered they will bite, or emit foul smells or excrement.

Reproduction All water snakes give birth to between 20 and 40 live young. They have a placenta to nourish the embryos.

LUNCHTIME
This unlucky carpenter frog is a meal for a northern water snake *Nerodia sipedon*, which is active during the day and night.

DEFENSE TACTICS
If frightened when resting, the brown water snake *Nerodia taxispilota* drops into the water. However, it readily bites when confronted.

SNAPSHOT

LENGTH 15 inches (38 cm) to over 4 feet (1.2 m)

DIET Fish, frogs, tadpoles, salamanders, young turtles, and crustaceans

HABITAT & DISTRIBUTION Found in or near most aquatic habitats: rivers, streams, lakes, swamps, ponds, marshes, ditches, bogs, and canals. They are common and widely distributed throughout North America

SQUAMATA

SERPENTES

■ RIBBON SNAKES

The semi-aquatic ribbon snakes are rarely found far from water. They like to bask in the bushes on the shoreline, but if startled will take to the water. Unlike water snakes which dive, ribbon snakes glide swiftly across the water's surface. Ribbon snakes are almost always found in low, wet places like swamps and marshes, or the weedy margins of lakes, ponds, and quiet streams and rivers. They prefer shallow water.

Characteristics Ribbon snakes are active during the day, and have a slender, streamlined body with large eyes and round pupils.

SNAPSHOT

LENGTH Range from 18 inches (45 cm) to 4 feet (1.2 m) of which a third is a thin tail
DIET Small fish, frogs, tadpoles, salamanders, and earthworms
HABITAT & DISTRIBUTION Live on the margins of streams, swamps, ditches, and lakes in North and Central America

Reproduction Ribbon snakes give birth to live young, with litter sizes varying between 3 and 27. The newborn young are about 10 inches (25 cm) long.

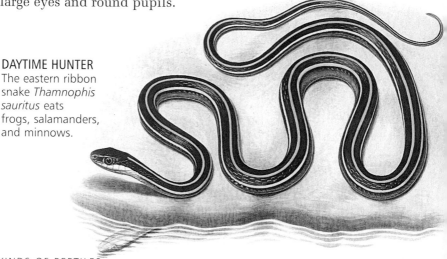

DAYTIME HUNTER
The eastern ribbon snake *Thamnophis sauritus* eats frogs, salamanders, and minnows.

GARTER SNAKES

Garter snakes are common throughout North America. The most widely distributed species, the common garter snake *Thamnophis sirtalis*, is found from warm regions in the south where it is active all year through to severely cold areas in Canada. Here, huge groups gather together to spend the winter in the few sites where underground crevices are deep enough for them to escape the winter freeze.

Characteristics Most garter snakes have light stripes on a dark background running the length of their bodies. Many also have some spots, usually on or around the head. Garter snakes are active during the day when they bask and hunt for food.

SNAPSHOT

LENGTH **About 22–57 inches (56–145 cm)**

DIET **A wide range of food is eaten, including small fish, frogs, leeches, earthworms, insects, birds, and small rodents**

HABITAT & DISTRIBUTION **Live on the margins of lakes, streams, ponds, marshes, swamps, drainage ditches, and irrigation canals. They are common and widely distributed throughout North America, from Costa Rica to southern Canada**

When cornered, some species will bite and emit foul smells.

Reproduction The females retain the eggs inside their body and give birth to live young. At the time of birth, some may still be covered in a thin membrane, which they soon burst. Litter sizes vary enormously, from four or five up to 85.

CLOSE TO WATER

Garter snakes inhabit all sorts of environments, from deserts to forests, from mountain slopes to the coast, but they are semi-aquatic and are always found near water.

SQUAMATA

SERPENTES

■ HOGNOSE SNAKES

These heavily built snakes have a remarkable defense display. When threatened, they flatten their neck and head in a cobra-like pose, inflate their body, and hiss and strike vigorously. If this formidable display fails to deter the attacker, the snake turns onto its back and feigns death with its mouth open and its tongue hanging out. The snakes are active in the daytime and burrow deep into loose earth in the winter.

Characteristics Hognose snakes have a stout body, broad head, wide neck, and a slightly up-turned, pointed, and shovel-shaped snout.

SNAPSHOT

LENGTH About 15–33 inches (38–84 cm)
DIET Mainly toads
HABITAT & DISTRIBUTION Live in a wide variety of habitats, including open sandy areas, grasslands, thinly wooded areas, and rocky, semi-arid lands. They are found in southern Canada, the USA, and Mexico

Reproduction Hognose snakes lay clutches of between 4 and 60 eggs, with 15 to 25 being more typical.

DIGS FOR FOOD

The eastern hognose snake *Heterodon platyrhinos* is sometimes called a puff adder. It uses its broad snout to dig its prey out of burrows.

FALSE VIPERS

The markings and behavior of this group of Latin American snakes are similar to those of several terrestrial pit vipers that live in the same area. They are fairly sedentary snakes and feed mainly on toads. False vipers and hognose snakes have enlarged teeth at the back of their mouth that they use to puncture the toads when they inflate themselves. If threatened, false vipers flatten their neck and body so they look more intimidating.

Characteristics Active day or night, the false vipers have large eyes with round pupils.

Reproduction False vipers lay clutches of 15 to 25 eggs.

FALSE PIT VIPER
The toad-eater snake *Xenodon rabdocephalus* from Costa Rica is sometimes called the false fer-de-lance, because it resembles that species of pit viper.

SNAPSHOT

LENGTH 22–28 inches (55–70 cm)
DIET Mainly toads and frogs
HABITAT & DISTRIBUTION Usually found near water, false vipers live on the banks of rivers in rainforests from Mexico to Argentina

SNAPSHOT

LENGTH Up to 51 inches (130 cm) in the USA and larger in Central America

DIET A variety of prey including rodents, birds, lizards, other snakes, and occasionally frogs, fish, earthworms, and insects

HABITAT & DISTRIBUTION Milk snakes inhabit many areas including forests, woodlands, cultivated land, prairies, sand dunes, even vacant lots in urban areas. They are found in the USA, Mexico, and Central and northern South America

■ MILK SNAKE

One of the most colorful snakes in the king snake genus is the milk snake. Its common name comes from the myth that it enters barns and sucks the milk from cows.
A secretive snake, it is usually not seen in the open in daylight hours as it hides away under rotting logs or stumps or in damp rubbish piles. When threatened, it will either coil up and hide its head, or vibrate its tail and strike. Milk snakes enter mammal burrows, where they take the young from their nest.

Characteristics There are several subspecies of this snake with varied colors and markings.

Some have bright red, black, and yellow bands.

Reproduction In the summer the female lays a clutch of between 2 and 17 eggs. She will often lay the eggs in a rotten log.

ALBINO SNAKE
This eastern milk snake *Lampropeltis triangulum triangulum* is an albino without the usual black bands of the species.

PINE-GOPHER SNAKES

The pine-gopher snakes of North America are large, powerful snakes that kill their prey by constriction. When threatened, they try to intimidate their attacker by raising and shaking their tail and hissing loudly. They have a specially modified epiglottis, which increases the volume of the hiss. Because of their coloring, the pine-gopher snakes are sometimes mistaken for rattlesnakes.

Characteristics These snakes usually have cream or yellow skin

SNAPSHOT

LENGTH 4–8 feet (1.2–2.5 m)
DIET Rodents, rabbits, lizards, birds and their eggs, and insects
HABITAT & DISTRIBUTION There are 15 subspecies occupying a wide range of habitats in the USA and through to Mexico and Baja California

with black patches on their back. They have a small head with a rather pointed snout (unlike the larger, more triangular head of a rattlesnake).

Reproduction These snakes mate in spring and lay clutches of between 3 and 24 cream to white eggs.

NATURAL COLORS
The Florida pine snake *Pituophis melanoleucus mugitus* is grayish to rusty brown with indistinct blotches.

SQUAMATA

SERPENTES

■ RAT SNAKES

The rat snakes are powerful, non-venomous constrictors that feed on warm-blooded prey, particularly rodents, giving the group their common name. The snakes are mostly terrestrial, spending much of their time in burrows looking for food. The most common North American rat snakes—the six subspecies of *Elaphe obsoleta*—are skillful climbers and will go up into trees or the rafters of abandoned buildings looking for

SNAPSHOT

LENGTH 24 inches (60 cm) to 8½ feet (2.6 m)

DIET As well as rats and mice, rat snakes eat other small mammals, lizards, frogs, birds and their eggs

HABITAT & DISTRIBUTION A variety of habitats from rocky deserts to swamps and marshes, from coastal plains to mountains, and from forests to farmland and barnyards. They are found in the USA, Mexico, Europe, and Asia

mice, and birds and their eggs. When threatened, rat snakes will coil up and strike, with their tail vibrating rapidly.

MOUNTAIN DWELLER
The Mandarin rat snake *Elaphe mandarina* is a brilliantly colored snake from high-altitude regions in China.

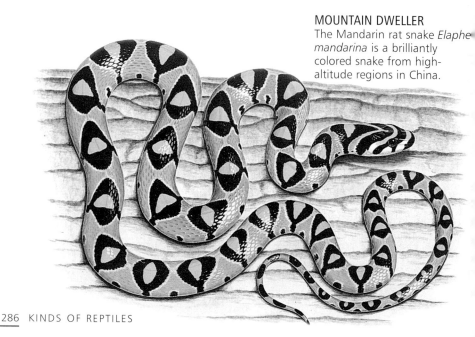

Characteristics The color and pattern of many rat snakes change as they grow and mature. Young rat snakes are often marked with large, dark blotches that gradually disappear and give way to longitudinal stripes as the animal gets older. Sometimes the areas between the blotches become darker with each slough until the snake is eventually a uniform color. The snakes tend to hunt in the early morning or at dusk. They

BRILLIANT ORANGE
The Everglades rat snake *Elaphe obsoleta rossalleni*, one of six subspecies of rat snake in the southern and eastern parts of the USA, has a red tongue and its skin is a distinctive red-orange with faint stripes.

become more nocturnal on warm, summer nights.

Reproduction Rat snakes lay eggs in the summer months in places such as rotten logs and stumps, in leaf litter, or under rocks.

SNAPSHOT

LENGTH **Nearly 8 feet (2.5 m)**
DIET **Birds, bats, lizards, and other snakes**
HABITAT & DISTRIBUTION **This snake inhabits lowland jungles and mangrove swamps. It is found in Indonesia, Malaysia, Singapore, Thailand, the Philippines, and Vietnam**

■ MANGROVE SNAKE

The strikingly marked mangrove snake *Boiga dendrophila* of Southeast Asia is a nocturnal, tree-dwelling snake. The *Boiga* species are known as "cat snakes" because of the vertical slit in their eyes, which resembles that of a cat.

Characteristics The mangrove snake has a long, slender body that is compressed from side to side, an adaptation that suits its highly arboreal existence. At the back of its mouth it has enlarged teeth that break the skin of prey, allowing venom from the snake's salivary glands to enter the animal's bloodstream. Like many rear-fanged snakes, its head is short and broad. Most rear-fanged snakes are not harmful to humans, but because of this snake's size, it can be dangerous.

Reproduction The mangrove snake lays eggs, but little is known about its reproductive biology.

QUICK SWOOP
The mangrove snake is a remarkably adept climber and pursues its prey swiftly and efficiently, swooping from its tree vantage point.

BLUNT-HEADED TREE SNAKE
The blunt-headed tree snake *Imantodes cenchoa* is a nocturnal tree-dwelling snake with an incredibly long and slender body that is compressed from side to side. It forages for its "cold-blooded" prey—lizards and frogs—among the tree branches and subdues it with venom delivered from the fangs at the back of its mouth.

Characteristics The blunt head is clearly distinct from the narrow neck. Although they are largely

S NAPSHOT

LENGTH 31 inches (80 cm), half of which is tail

DIET Lizards and frogs

HABITAT & DISTRIBUTION Lives in trees and shrubs in the rainforest, especially trees with many epiphytes. It is distributed through Central America and northern South America

tree-dwellers, they sometimes descend to the ground in search of prey.

Reproduction The blunt-headed tree snake is oviparous, laying small clutches of between one and three eggs.

BRIDGING THE GAP
This arboreal species crosses wide gaps between branches by straightening and stiffening its body, flattening it from side to side as it bridges the gap.

Snapshot

LENGTH **Nearly 4½ feet (1.4 m), half of which is tail**
DIET **Arboreal lizards, and occasionally frogs, young birds, eggs, and small mammals**
HABITAT & DISTRIBUTION **Occurs in tropical rainforests and is distributed in parts of Asia from India south to Thailand**

■ LONG-NOSED TREE SNAKE
The long-nosed tree snake *Dryophis nasuta* is one of a small number of species that have horizontal pupils and are able to focus their eyes in a forward direction. This binocular vision allows them to see better than other snakes.

Characteristics This incredibly long and slender snake has large grooves that run from its eyes to its snout. These grooves allow both eyes to look forward. In color, it ranges from light green through to gray-brown, sometimes with light stripes on both sides.

This rear-fanged snake is active during the day, and can move swiftly over ground as well as in the trees.

Reproduction The long-nosed tree snake is an egg-laying species, laying clutches of between 2 and 12 eggs.

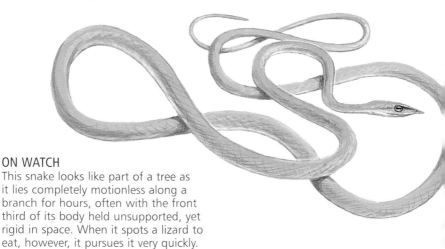

ON WATCH
This snake looks like part of a tree as it lies completely motionless along a branch for hours, often with the front third of its body held unsupported, yet rigid in space. When it spots a lizard to eat, however, it pursues it very quickly.

HIDEAWAY
Ringneck snakes
shelter under
shrubs, flat rocks,
logs, or the loose
bark of dead trees.

RINGNECK SNAKE

The ringneck snake *Diadophis punctatus* gets its common name from the golden ring around its neck. While its upper surface is dull, to match its surroundings, it has bright red or orange scales on its tail and sometimes along the length of its belly. When the snake feels threatened it will coil its tail tightly and lift it up. The sudden appearance of the bright underside startles the predator, and gives the snake time to seek cover.

Characteristics The dorsal coloring of this small, slender snake varies according to where it is found and can be gray, olive, brown, or black. In some snakes the neck ring is either broken up or missing altogether.

Reproduction Clutches of one to ten eggs are laid in the summer months. The females often lay their eggs in communal nesting sites and may return to the same sites, year after year.

SNAPSHOT

LENGTH 10–18 inches (25–45 cm)
DIET Earthworms, slugs, frogs, lizards, small salamanders, and newborn snakes
HABITAT & DISTRIBUTION Ringneck snakes prefer moist areas and live in forests, woodlands, grasslands, or near the edges of streams. They are widespread throughout the USA and much of Mexico

---

SQUAMATA

SERPENTES

■ RACER

The racer *Coluber constrictor* is an agile snake that actively seeks its prey. When it spots an animal, it moves swiftly through the undergrowth toward it. Despite its scientific name, the racer does not kill its prey by constriction but by pressing it to the ground. When threatened, the racer may try to intimidate its attacker by vibrating its tail against the ground or among dead leaves to produce a sound.

Characteristics Like many other fast-moving, diurnal species, the racer has large eyes with prominent pupils. It has a slender,

SNAPSHOT

LENGTH 34–77 inches (86–195 cm)
DIET Small rodents and other mammals, insects, birds, lizards, and frogs
HABITAT & DISTRIBUTION Lives in the brushy undergrowth of grassy areas. It is found in southern Canada, the USA, Mexico, and Guatemala

streamlined, and agile body with a rather large, angular head.

Reproduction In the summer, the female racer lays clutches averaging between 5 and 28 eggs. The eggs are laid in rotting logs or tree stumps, in loose soil, or leaf litter, or they may be laid in the burrows of small mammals such as gophers and ground squirrels.

LET ME GO!
If the racer is grabbed, it will bite repeatedly and thrash its body about violently.

Elapid Snakes

Elapidae

about 45 genera/about 250 species

■ RED-BELLIED BLACK SNAKE
The red-bellied black snake
Pseudechis porphyriacus is one
of eastern Australia's best-known
snakes. It shelters in abandoned
burrows, in hollow logs, or under
rocks. It hunts during the day
and can often be seen basking at
the edge of a creek or on the side
of a road.

Characteristics This large snake
has a thick body and a small
head. It is always a glossy
purplish black on top, but its

SNAPSHOT

LENGTH 5–6 feet (1.5–1.8 m),
with some reaching 8 feet (2.5 m)
DIET Mainly frogs, but also small
lizards, other snakes, birds, mice,
rats, and occasionally fish,
including eels
HABITAT & DISTRIBUTION It prefers
moist habitats such as swamps,
riverbanks, or the edges of wet
forests. It is widespread along
the coast of eastern Australia,
though the cane toad has
depleted its numbers

belly scales vary from pink to
red. The snake is very venomous,
but only one human fatality has
been recorded.

Reproduction The female retains
the eggs in her body, giving birth
to between 5 and 40 young.
When they are born, the young
are enclosed in a membrane from
which they emerge soon after birth.

STAGES OF DEFENSE
The snake will flee if it feels
threatened, but if cornered it
will hiss loudly, flatten its
neck and raise its head
and upper body,
cobra-like, so it looks
as big as possible to
an attacker.

DEATH ADDERS

These slow-moving, terrestrial snakes have a very unusual way of catching food. With its body in a loose coil and the tip of its tail near its snout, the death adder lies motionless and half-buried in sand or leaf litter. When prey approaches, the snake wriggles the tip of its tail. As a bird or lizard moves closer to investigate the wriggling "worm" or "caterpillar," the snake strikes with lightning speed.

Characteristics With their broad, triangular head, stocky body, and thin tail, the three Australian death adders look similar to the unrelated vipers. They are highly venomous, and capable of injecting large quantities of venom with their long fangs. Death adders are usually active at night, especially during the warmer part of the year.

Reproduction Death adders give birth to live young, about once every two years. The litters vary from a couple of young to more than thirty.

SNAPSHOT

LENGTH 26–30 inches (65–75 cm)
DIET Lizards, mice, frogs, and birds
HABITAT & DISTRIBUTION These snakes occupy a wide range of habitats from deserts to rainforests. They are found in New Guinea and in Australia except Tasmania and Victoria

AMBUSH PREDATOR
A stocky, ambush predator, the common death adder *Acanthophis antarcticus* is the most widespread of the three Australian death adders.

COBRAS

These African and Asian snakes are famous for the pose they adopt when they are threatened or disturbed. They rear up and spread the loose skin on their neck into a "hood." This is done by extending the thin neck ribs behind the head. Most cobras are not aggressive and will merely lunge at their attacker.

Characteristics Cobras vary in color, from yellow to brown and black. They have quite short fangs attached to their upper jaws through which their venom is delivered.

SNAPSHOT

LENGTH From 2 feet (60 cm) up to 16 feet (5 m), which is the world's largest venomous snake

DIET Frogs, lizards, rats, birds and their eggs, and fish

HABITAT & DISTRIBUTION With the exception of the forest cobra, which lives in African rainforests, cobras prefer open habitats like savannas and grasslands. They are often found near areas of human habitation. Cobras are found in Africa, the Middle East, and Asia

Reproduction With the exception of the African spitting cobra, which gives birth to live young, all cobras lay eggs. Asian cobras guard the eggs. The king cobra builds the most complex nest of all the snakes. The female scrapes together a large pile of grass, leaves, and soil, and makes a cavity in the top of the pile where she lays the eggs. She then covers the clutch with more leaves and guards the eggs until they hatch.

SPITTING FROM AFAR
Unlike other non-aggressive cobras, there are several spitting cobras that spray venom at the eyes of intruders. They can hit targets nearly 10 feet (3 m) away.

SNAPSHOT

LENGTH 5–14 feet (1.5–4.3 m)
DIET Small mammals, especially rodents; lizards and birds
HABITAT & DISTRIBUTION The mainly terrestrial black mamba usually inhabits rocky or open bush country. The three tree-dwelling species live in thick bush or forest or rainforest. Mambas are found only in Africa

■ MAMBAS

While tales of their speed and aggressiveness are highly exaggerated, there is no doubt that the black mamba is among the most dangerous of all the snakes. The threat display of an angry mamba—head and neck held high, black mouth gaping open—is a truly terrifying sight. It is also probably the swiftest of snakes when chasing its prey through the undergrowth. The mamba differs from most snakes in that it strikes its prey and then waits for it to die before eating it.

Characteristics The color of the black mamba varies from olive brown to a dark pewter or gunmetal gray. The three other mamba species are all arboreal snakes, and are predominantly green in color. All four species have long, slender bodies and coffin-shaped heads.

Reproduction Mambas lay an average of about 12 eggs. The black mamba usually lays her eggs in a moist, unused mammal burrow.

LARGE AND DANGEROUS
The black mamba *Dendroaspis polylepis* is the largest mamba, reaching lengths of 14 feet (4.3 m).

CORAL SNAKES

These brightly colored snakes have extremely potent venom. Their startling bands of red, black, yellow, and white warn predators to stay away, and some predatory birds have an innate fear of the colors. Some coral snakes defend themselves by hiding their head and waving their tail in the air like a head. Any predator seizing this "head" is likely to receive an unpleasant surprise when the real one appears.

Characteristics The coral snakes are small and slender. They have short fangs, fixed to their upper jaw, and small heads.

SNAPSHOT

LENGTH 14–63 inches (36–160 cm)

DIET Lizards and other snakes are their main food, but some species also take mammals, birds, frogs, and invertebrates

HABITAT & DISTRIBUTION Some species are aquatic but most are secretive, terrestrial snakes that spend much of their time in tunnels below the ground or under rocks and logs. They are found mainly in the tropical regions of South America as well as in Central America and southern USA

Reproduction Coral snakes usually lay 1 to 15 eggs but little else is known about their reproductive biology.

WARNING COLORS
If the warning colors of the Arizona coral snake fail to deter a predator, it will hide its head, raise its tail, and make a popping sound by turning its cloacal lining outward.

Sea Kraits

Laticaudidae

1 genus/6 species

■ GENERAL

The sea kraits are brightly banded marine snakes of the Indopacific region. One sea krait, *Laticauda crockeri*, is restricted to a land-locked lake in the Solomon Islands, but the other five species are truly marine. They have highly toxic venom but are extremely reluctant to bite, even in self-defense. They spend much of their time ashore on small coral islands where they seek shelter, bask in the sun, and lay their eggs.

SNAPSHOT

LENGTH About 5 feet (1.5 m)
DIET Some species feed almost exclusively on eels, but others eat a variety of fish species
HABITAT & DISTRIBUTION Found in the shallow waters around reefs in the warm tropical areas of the Indian and Pacific oceans. One species is restricted to a lake in the Solomon Islands

■ CHARACTERISTICS

Sea kraits have a specialized, flattened, paddle-like tail for swimming, but have retained their cylindrical shape and enlarged belly scales for crawling on land. They can close their nostrils with fleshy valves when they are underwater. Sea kraits have fixed front fangs.

■ REPRODUCTION

Sea kraits lay their eggs on coral islands, often in caves above the tideline.

COASTAL SWIMMER
The yellow-lipped sea krait *Laticauda colubrina*, found from the Bay of Bengal and the South China Sea to the islands of the western Pacific, basks on rocks or mangrove roots.

Sea Snakes

Hydrophiidae

16 genera/55 species

SNAPSHOT

LENGTH 16 inches (40 cm) to 9 feet (2.7 m)
DIET Fish and their eggs
HABITAT & DISTRIBUTION Except for the yellow-bellied sea snake, these snakes are found from the Persian Gulf to the Western Pacific

GENERAL

These snakes are more aquatic than the sea kraits as they do not need to return to land to breed. In fact they have become so specialized for movement in the water that most are almost helpless on land. Most species are restricted to shallow coastal water, but the yellow-bellied sea snake is found far out to sea, drifting across the open oceans apparently at the mercy of the winds and currents.

CHARACTERISTICS

The body and tail are flattened from side to side to help them swim and their belly scales are usually very narrow. Their nostrils are on top of the snout, so they can breathe when most of the head is under the water, and they can be sealed by valves when the snake dives. The lung is much longer than in terrestrial snakes, and some species can take in oxygen from the water through the skin. Glands at the base of the tongue excrete excess salt from the snake's bloodstream. Sea snakes are highly venomous.

REPRODUCTION

The embryos remain in the female's body and she gives birth to live young.

OCEAN SWIMMER
The yellow-bellied sea snake *Pelamis platurus* is the most widespread sea snake, from East Africa through the Pacific and Indian oceans to Central America.

True Vipers

Viperidae

12 genera/about 70 species

■ GENERAL

Coiled beside a mammal trail, or in the branches of a fruiting tree where birds gather, or beside a desert shrub where lizards will come seeking shade, a viper is almost invisible because of its superb camouflage. Here it will wait for its prey to come within range. Some vipers actually lure prey within striking range by wriggling the insect-shaped tip of their tail. To kill their prey, vipers

inject venom with one quick strike and then wait. Even if the animal runs away to die, the viper can follow its scent trail.

■ CHARACTERISTICS

Most vipers are heavy-bodied, muscular snakes, with large heads. They have a single pair of very long, hollow fangs that are attached to a small bone on the upper jaw. This bone can rotate so that the fangs lie back along the length of the upper jaw when the snake's mouth is closed, but can swing forward into

SNAPSHOT

LENGTH 8–70 inches (20–170 cm)
DIET Frogs, lizards, birds, and small mammals
HABITAT True vipers are found in an extremely wide range of habitats, from swamps and lake shores to deserts, from tropical rainforests to cold Arctic tundra

SPOT THE SNAKE
The rhinoceros viper *Bitis nasicornis* from Africa is one of the most colorful vipers, but its disruptive pattern makes it almost invisible in leaf litter.

striking position when the mouth
is opened. Large jaw muscles
squeeze the viper's very toxic
venom from glands on either
side of its head into the fangs,
which penetrate deep into the
victim's body.

REPRODUCTION

Only a few vipers are egg-layers.
Most give birth to live young.
Pregnant females of species in very
cold areas spend most of their
time basking so the live young
can develop quickly in the short
warm period. These females do
not feed during this time and may

LEAF-LIKE VIPER
The Usambara mountain viper
Atheris ceratophorus of central
Africa is one of eight species in
its genus. They are commonly
called leaf or bush vipers. Six of
these are arboreal, with strong,
prehensile tails, large, prominent
heads, and slender bodies. They
are quite small, growing to
about 2 feet (60 cm).

become so emaciated that many
die after they have given birth.

■ DISTRIBUTION
True vipers are widely distributed
in Asia, Africa, the Middle East,
and Europe.

Pit Vipers

Crotalidae

14 genera/about 150 species

■ GENERAL

The pit vipers are so named because of the deep pit between the eye and the nostril on each side of the head. Here there are sensory organs that detect heat. These organs are incredibly sensitive and can detect minute differences in temperature. They allow the pit vipers to locate warm-blooded prey, even on pitch-black nights.

■ CHARACTERISTICS

Like the true vipers, pit vipers are heavy-bodied, muscular snakes, with large heads and long, hollow

SNAPSHOT

LENGTH 15 inches (38 cm) up to 13 feet (4 m)
DIET Warm-blooded animals such as rabbits, muskrats, ground squirrels, rats, mice, and birds, but some eat a wide range of food
HABITAT Most pit vipers live in forested regions and plantations, though some inhabit dry areas. Most species are terrestrial, some are tree-dwellers, and a few, such as the cottonmouth that lives in swamps and beside lakes and streams, are semi-aquatic

fangs. The best known are the 30 species of rattlesnake (genera *Crotalus* and *Sistrurus*) of North America, famous for the warning device on the tip of their tail. Another North American pit viper, the cottonmouth or water moccasin *Agkistrodon piscivorus*, derives its common name from the white interior of its mouth, which gapes widely when threatened. The largest viper is the bushmaster *Lachesis muta* of

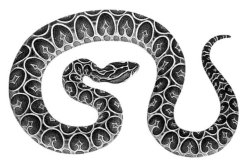

LIVE YOUNG
The urutu *Bothrops alternatus* is a large, terrestrial South American pit viper that gives birth to live young.

Central and South America which grows to almost 13 feet (4 m) in length. The arboreal temple vipers (genus *Trimeresurus*) of Asia are mainly green in color and have prehensile tails.

REPRODUCTION

Most pit vipers give birth to live young with only a few laying eggs. One species, the mountain viper *Trimeresurus monticola* of Southeast Asia, remains coiled around or near the eggs until they hatch.

DISTRIBUTION

Pit vipers are widely distributed throughout the Americas, Africa, and Asia.

PREY DETECTOR
The eyelash pit viper *Bothriechis schlegeli* of Central and South America uses the heat-sensitive pits near its eyes to detect prey.

YOUNG LITTER
The massasauga rattlesnake *Sistrurus catenatus* has a litter of 2 to 19 young between July and early September.

ENCYCLOPEDIA *of* DISCOVERY

Insects &
Spiders

CONSULTANT EDITOR
Dan Bickel

FOG CITY PRESS

CONTENTS

KINDS OF ARACHNIDS 564

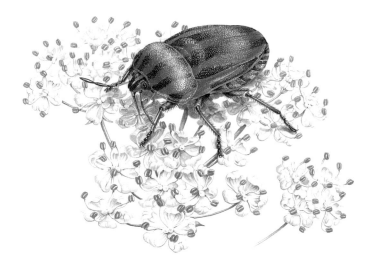

A WORLD
OF INSECTS
AND SPIDERS

*An insight into the secret lives
of these extraordinary creatures.*

Understanding Insects and Spiders

INSECT AND SPIDER ORIGINS

Insects and spiders first appeared on the Earth during the early Devonian period, but no one is really sure how they evolved. This is because there are relatively few fossilized specimens. We do know, however, that they had begun to colonize the continents long before vertebrates struggled onto land.

DELICATE LEGACY

Despite their abundance, insects and spiders rarely became fossils because of the delicate nature of their exoskeleton and muscle tissue. The fossilized insect specimens that have been found are very often badly crushed. But the study of early fossil arthropods has allowed scientists to draw some conclusions. The first insects may have evolved from centipede-like ancestors. There is evidence that the earliest fossil scorpions, which are related to spiders, date back about 425 million years. Some were amphibious "giants," measuring more than 3 feet (1 m) long. Fossils do confirm that land-based insects were flourishing about 395 million years ago.

Age of flowers During the Carboniferous Period, about 360 to 285 million years ago, many new species of arthropod emerged to exploit every inch of the humid forests. By 300 million years ago, diverse groups had developed new equipment and techniques to feed on different plant parts.

Insects continued to adapt to environmental forces. One force was the evolution of flowering plants, or angiosperms. This food supply enhanced the chances of survival of any creature that could exploit it. Many insects developed the ability to see wavelengths of light invisible to other animals, enabling them to find pollen and nectar more easily.

On the wing By far, the most important development for insects was the ability to fly. Insects could move to new and varied environments and to the new and sometimes abundant food sources that angiosperms provided. The plants also took advantage of this mobility, rewarding insects with nectar to spread their pollen over great distances.

AMBER AND STONE

Amber, or fossilized tree resin, contains the best examples of ancient insects and spiders. Delicate insect hairs and even DNA fragments are preserved (above). Fine-grain shale can yield beautiful specimens, such as this snakefly (right).

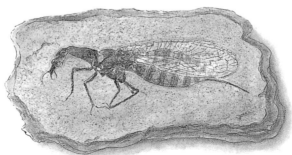

Hard Cases

Insects and spiders belong to a group of animals called arthropods (from the Greek word *arthropoda*, meaning "jointed legs"), which also includes scorpions, ticks, crabs, and centipedes. One thing that all these creatures have in common is a tough outer skeleton covering the whole body. This is called an exoskeleton, or cuticle, and it is made from a material called chitin. This substance is remarkably light yet incredibly strong. Insect and spider muscles are attached to the appendages and the body wall in such a way that great strength in relation to size results. Ants, for example, can carry many times their own body weight in their mandibles.

Shedding skin In order to grow to adult size and shape, and because their cuticle is relatively inflexible, arthropods shed their old exoskeleton and replace it with a new, larger one at regular intervals. Some insects molt only twice in their lifetime, whereas others molt more than 25 times.

NEW SKIN Spiders molt their old skin to grow to a new size. Timing is important; if the weather is too dry, the spider gets stuck in the old exoskeleton and dies.

1 A spider hangs from its web as its old exoskeleton splits along the edge of the cephalothorax.

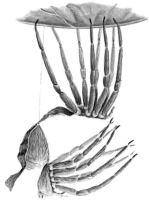

2 The old skin covering its abdomen comes away as it tries to pull its legs free.

3 The spider expands to its new size while its exoskeleton is soft. The new skin takes 20 minutes to dry.

ICADA EMERGING All the arthropods hown here have an exoskeleton. The icada's new exoskeleton (above) has lready formed beneath the old one.

Centipede

Scorpion

Tick

CLASSIFYING INSECTS

All insects have certain characteristics in common, the most obvious of these being a body divided into three parts and usually three pairs of jointed legs. But with more than 1 million species of insect identified by scientists, and the possibility that there might be 30 million in total, a method for identifying and classifying species is essential.

TAXONOMIC SYSTEM

Zoologists classify animals on the basis of structure. Animals with features in common are placed together in a group. Those with other characteristics are placed

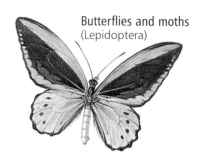

Butterflies and moths
(Lepidoptera)

in other groups. These groups are divided and divided again, until there is a taxonomic group with many characteristics in common.
All class Insects are classified under the Phylum Arthropoda, Class Insecta. Insects have bodies that are usually divided into three parts: the head, the thorax, and

CLASSIFYING CHARACTERISTICS

This green scarab beetle belongs to the largest order of insects, the Coleoptera, which has more than 350,000 species. All species in this order have armored bodies and hardened wing cases, called elytra. Scarabs belong to the Family Scarabaeidae. Scientists assign a unique name to each species and place it within this structure.

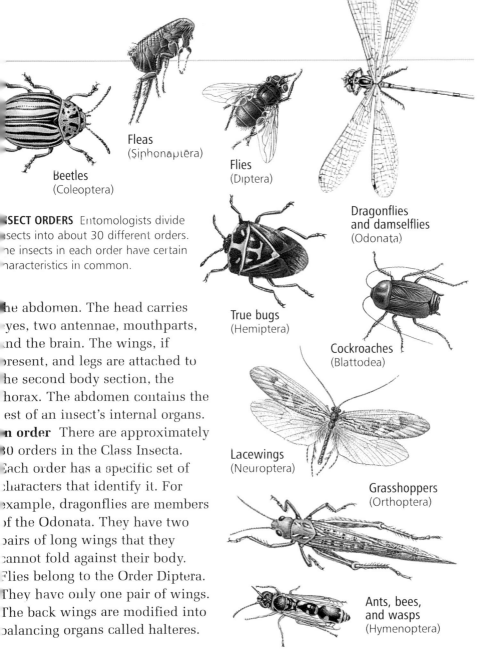

Fleas
(Siphonaptera)

Beetles
(Coleoptera)

Flies
(Diptera)

Dragonflies
and damselflies
(Odonata)

INSECT ORDERS Entomologists divide
insects into about 30 different orders.
The insects in each order have certain
characteristics in common.

the abdomen. The head carries
eyes, two antennae, mouthparts,
and the brain. The wings, if
present, and legs are attached to
the second body section, the
thorax. The abdomen contains the
rest of an insect's internal organs.

In order There are approximately
30 orders in the Class Insecta.
Each order has a specific set of
characters that identify it. For
example, dragonflies are members
of the Odonata. They have two
pairs of long wings that they
cannot fold against their body.
Flies belong to the Order Diptera.
They have only one pair of wings.
The back wings are modified into
balancing organs called halteres.

True bugs
(Hemiptera)

Cockroaches
(Blattodea)

Lacewings
(Neuroptera)

Grasshoppers
(Orthoptera)

Ants, bees,
and wasps
(Hymenoptera)

INSECT COVER STORY

Insects and their relatives have adapted to living on Earth more successfully than any other type of animal. In fact, today, they make up more than half of all the species on Earth. The basic insect body plan has become modified through the process of evolution, resulting in a group of animals superbly adapted to their habitats.

DRESS FOR SUCCESS

Insects have many features that have contributed to their phenomenal success. Their exoskeleton helps to protect them from environmental stresses and from predation. Many have developed protective coloration, mimicry, and defensive chemicals to deter predators. Their small size and energy-efficient physiology have helped them survive in virtually every habitat. Adaptable wings, legs, and mouthparts have allowed them to exploit many food sources. An advanced sensory system allows most insects to sense danger, send signals to mates, find prey, and to survive in hot or dry habitats.

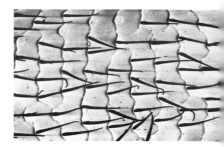

HAIR SENSE An ant's leg is covered with tiny, sensitive hairs that send information about motion, temperature, and chemicals to the insect's brain.

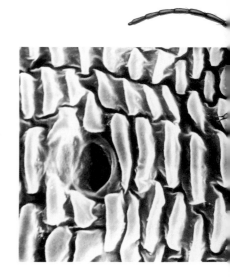

HOLE STORY This electron micrograph shows a spiracle, the opening to an insect's respiratory system. Rows of spiracles are on the thorax or abdomen.

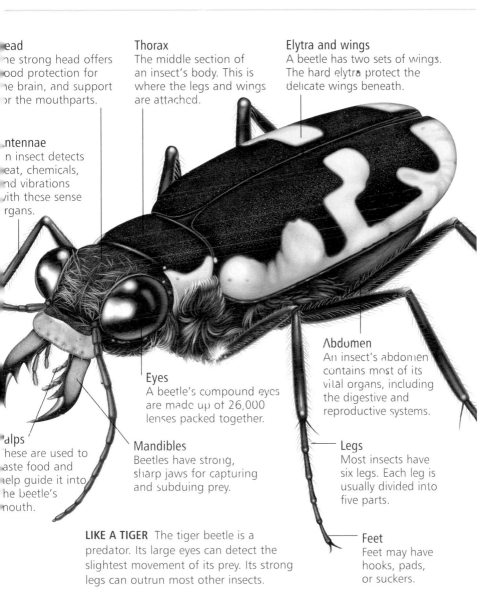

ead
he strong head offers
ood protection for
he brain, and support
or the mouthparts.

ntennae
n insect detects
eat, chemicals,
nd vibrations
ith these sense
rgans.

Thorax
The middle section of
an insect's body. This is
where the legs and wings
are attached.

Elytra and wings
A beetle has two sets of wings.
The hard elytra protect the
delicate wings beneath.

Eyes
A beetle's compound eyes
are made up of 26,000
lenses packed together.

Abdomen
An insect's abdomen
contains most of its
vital organs, including
the digestive and
reproductive systems.

alps
hese are used to
aste food and
elp guide it into
he beetle's
nouth.

Mandibles
Beetles have strong,
sharp jaws for capturing
and subduing prey.

Legs
Most insects have
six legs. Each leg is
usually divided into
five parts.

LIKE A TIGER The tiger beetle is a
predator. Its large eyes can detect the
slightest movement of its prey. Its strong
legs can outrun most other insects.

Feet
Feet may have
hooks, pads,
or suckers.

Inside an Insect

Inside an insect's body, many different systems are at work. Like most animals, insects eat, breathe, move, and reproduce. Blood, usually yellow or green in color, carries nutrients to the body parts and removes wastes, and is pumped by a long, thin heart that stretches through the body.

Breathe in Insects have no lungs. Instead, they get oxygen through openings along the sides of their bodies, called spiracles. Spiracles are connected to tracheae, which branch into smaller tubes. These carry oxygen to every part of the insect. Each spiracle can open or shut, depending on how much oxygen is required.

Nerve center All bodily functions are controlled by the large brain, which is connected to all nerves by a long nerve cord. Clusters of nerve cells along the nerve cord, called ganglia, collect signals from the sense organs and carry messages from one part of the body to another.

Burning energy To keep all these systems running, an insect needs energy from food. In the case of this wasp (right), the food is mixed with saliva in the mouth. It passes down the throat to the crop, where it is broken down by more saliva. It then passes to the stomach, where special enzymes churn up the food further, making it ready for the insect to use.

DOWN THE TUBE Some water-dwelling insects, such as this water scorpion, breathe oxygen at the surface through a tiny tube attached to their abdomen.

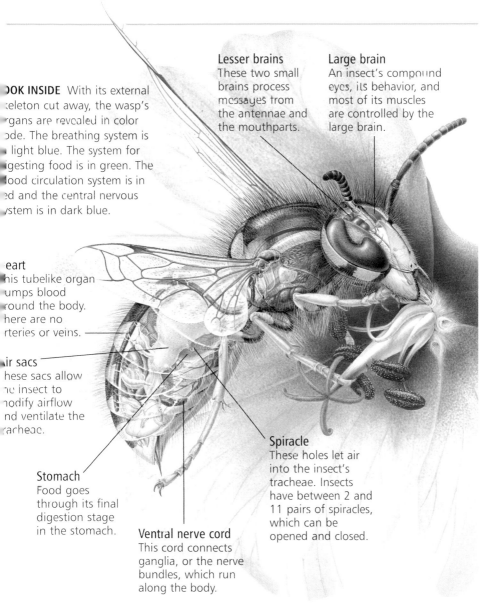

Lesser brains
These two small brains process messages from the antennae and the mouthparts.

Large brain
An insect's compound eyes, its behavior, and most of its muscles are controlled by the large brain.

OOK INSIDE With its external ce128eleton cut away, the wasp's rgans are revealed in color ode. The breathing system is light blue. The system for igesting food is in green. The lood circulation system is in ed and the central nervous ystem is in dark blue.

eart
his tubelike organ umps blood round the body. here are no rteries or veins.

ir sacs
hese sacs allow he insect to nodify airflow nd ventilate the racheae.

Stomach
Food goes through its final digestion stage in the stomach.

Ventral nerve cord
This cord connects ganglia, or the nerve bundles, which run along the body.

Spiracle
These holes let air into the insect's tracheae. Insects have between 2 and 11 pairs of spiracles, which can be opened and closed.

CLASSIFYING ARACHNIDS

Like insects, spiders and their relatives are arthropods. They have jointed legs and a hard exoskeleton, or carapace.

TWO-PART BODIES

Spiders and their allies are in the Class Arachnida, which includes scorpions, mites, and ticks. They differ from insects in having two rather than three body segments and four pairs of jointed legs.

A diverse group Arachnids are a diverse group of eight orders. They vary in size from tiny mites, smaller than a pinhead, to tarantulas the size of a plate.

The sting Spiders have powerful jaws equipped with fangs that can deliver venom to paralyze prey.

Scientists differentiate spiders into two groups, according to the way they move their fangs to stab prey (see opposite).

Top and tail Scorpions differ from spiders in having an abdomen that is divided into 12 segments. The last five segments make up the upturned tail, or telson, which has a poisonous stinger on its tip.

Mites and ticks have an unsegmented abdomen. Most species are less than $\frac{1}{32}$ inch (1 mm) long. Both eat liquid food with their piercing mouthparts.

MITE AND POWER Mites (above) appear to have one body part, but they have two. Scorpions (left) have a segmented abdomen, eight legs, pedipalps, and a venomous tail stinger.

SPURRED ON The shape is unusual, but this *Micrathena* spider still displays the characteristics common to the order Aranea—spiders.

Mygalomorph

Araneomorph

FANGS DIVIDE Spiders are classified into two main types by the way they use their fangs. Mygalomorph fangs hinge downwards and araneomorph fangs hinge together and sideways.

ARACHNID ANATOMY

Arachnids vary greatly in appearance, but the major groups have characteristics that are relatively easy to identify.

HEAD AND LEGS

Arachnid bodies are divided into two parts: a fused head and thorax, called a cephalothorax or prosoma, and an abdomen, or opisthosoma. All arachnids have eight walking legs and never have antennae or wings. Arachnids have a pair of chelicerae, which in the case of spiders, have fangs attached. Pedipalps are modified legs that carry out many functions, including the manipulation of food and the capturing of prey. In scorpions, the pedipalps are

SILK SPINNERS Most spiders have three or four pairs of spinnerets. These deliver the liquid silk to the outside. As the spider tugs on it with its legs, the silk hardens.

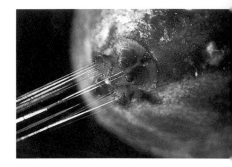

enlarged and bear a large, pincer-like claw.

Eyes have it Spiders have a group of six to twelve simple eyes. One pair of eyes forms the image, while the surrounding eyes detect movement. Most species have poor vision and rely on sensing movement through body hairs. They also have slits in their exoskeleton that are sensitive to vibrations.

FATAL FANGS A spider's venom is stored in glands at the base of its fangs. When the spider bites, venom flows through a small hole at the tip of the fang.

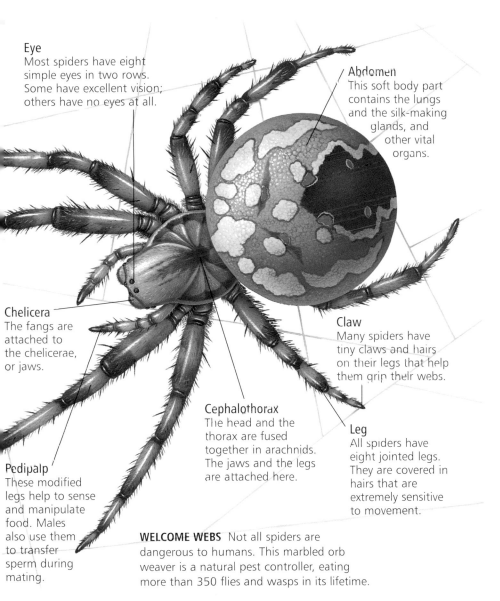

Eye
Most spiders have eight simple eyes in two rows. Some have excellent vision; others have no eyes at all.

Abdomen
This soft body part contains the lungs and the silk-making glands, and other vital organs.

Chelicera
The fangs are attached to the chelicerae, or jaws.

Claw
Many spiders have tiny claws and hairs on their legs that help them grip their webs.

Cephalothorax
The head and the thorax are fused together in arachnids. The jaws and the legs are attached here.

Leg
All spiders have eight jointed legs. They are covered in hairs that are extremely sensitive to movement.

Pedipalp
These modified legs help to sense and manipulate food. Males also use them to transfer sperm during mating.

WELCOME WEBS Not all spiders are dangerous to humans. This marbled orb weaver is a natural pest controller, eating more than 350 flies and wasps in its lifetime.

Inside a Spider

■ A spider's internal body systems are similar to those of other arachnids and insects. The cephalothorax houses the sensory organs, poison glands, sucking stomach, and the brain. The remainder of its vital organs—heart, lung, digestive gland, reproductive organs, and silk gland—are found in the abdomen.

INSIDE OUT

A spider's nervous system consists of a brain—the main control center—and a series of nerve bundles, or ganglia.

Life blood Spiders have a long, tubular heart that pumps nutrient-rich blood to its organs.

Book to breathe Most spiders obtain oxygen through a book lung, so named because it contains many flat sheets like a book. These sheets increase the surface area of the lung.

Liquid lunch Spiders must partially digest their food before they eat it. Most inject their prey with paralyzing venom and digestive enzymes to dissolve the victim's tissues.

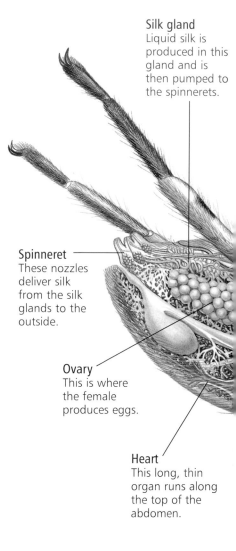

Silk gland
Liquid silk is produced in this gland and is then pumped to the spinnerets.

Spinneret
These nozzles deliver silk from the silk glands to the outside.

Ovary
This is where the female produces eggs.

Heart
This long, thin organ runs along the top of the abdomen.

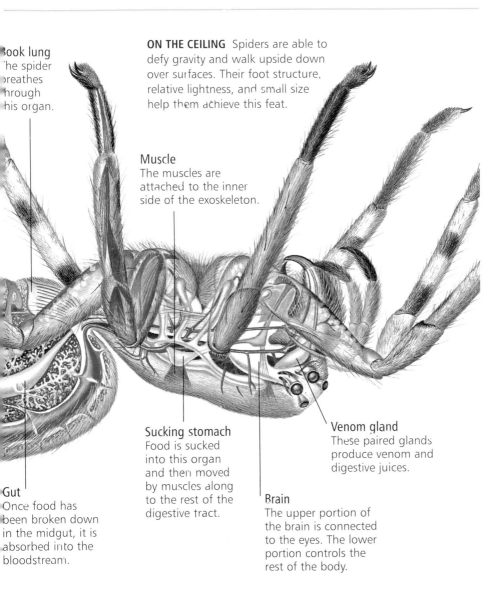

Book lung
The spider breathes through this organ.

ON THE CEILING Spiders are able to defy gravity and walk upside down over surfaces. Their foot structure, relative lightness, and small size help them achieve this feat.

Muscle
The muscles are attached to the inner side of the exoskeleton.

Sucking stomach
Food is sucked into this organ and then moved by muscles along to the rest of the digestive tract.

Venom gland
These paired glands produce venom and digestive juices.

Gut
Once food has been broken down in the midgut, it is absorbed into the bloodstream.

Brain
The upper portion of the brain is connected to the eyes. The lower portion controls the rest of the body.

The Life of Insects and Spiders

HOMES AND HABITATS

Insects and spiders are found almost everywhere on Earth, from freezing mountain peaks to dry, inhospitable deserts. Some live in highly urbanized areas and others thrive living on the bodies of other animals. Certain alpine species can survive at temperatures below -40°F (-40°C), while some desert insects are able to withstand temperatures in excess of 104°F (40°C). Many insects cope with the extreme temperatures by becoming dormant, re-emerging when

HIDDEN JEWELS Flower mantids live in most tropical habitats around the world. Their superb camouflage allows them to pounce on unsuspecting insect prey.

conditions have normalized. Survival strategies such as this, teamed with their small size, their protective casing, and speedy reproductive methods, have afforded insects the largest range of all animal species.

HABITAT DIVERSITY

Insect diversity is low in polar regions, but numbers may be great, especially in summer. The variety and number of species are greater near the equator, especially in tropical rainforests.
Vital role Insects and spiders play an essential role in the maintenance of the Earth's food chains and ecosystems. They pollinate flowers and help to recycle and return nutrients to the soil by eating decomposing plant and animal material. Protecting insect habitat from destruction is of paramount importance if these ecosystems are to be maintained.

FRAGILE SILVER This silver scarab lives in the cloud forests of Costa Rica. These forests are at risk from deforestation.

Deserts and Grasslands

■ There are many contrasts between arid deserts and vast areas of swaying grassland, but insect and spider species flourish in these dry environments.

HEAT HAZE

Desert-dwellers live with little moisture and in extremes of temperature. Most species avoid the day's heat by being active in the cooler dawn or dusk. Giant desert scorpions and tarantulas venture out at this time to search for mates and food. Ants seem to thrive in temperatures that would be fatal to other species. After rainfall, many desert plants produce masses of flowers, which provide an abundance of food for insects, as well as pollination opportunities for the plant.

Tall grass Tropical and temperate grasslands provide rich habitats for many species, especially ants and termites. Moths, hover flies, and bees feed on the flowering plants, grasshoppers chew seeds, and spiders spin webs between the grass stalks to capture prey.

IN THE GROOVE

This darkling beetle lives in Africa's Namib Desert. The only regular moisture available in this dry habitat is the fog that comes rolling in from the coast. In order to utilize this resource, the beetle points its abdomen into the wind and collects the moisture that condenses on its body. The water droplets pool in a groove on the beetle's body and trickle down to its mouth.

HOT SPOTS To survive the dry desert environment, honey ants (above) store nectar and water in their abdomens. Many scorpion species (right) have adapted to the desert extremes

Woodlands and Rainforests

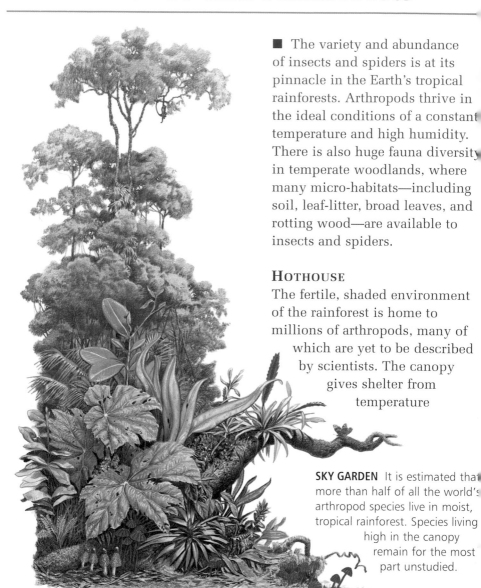

■ The variety and abundance of insects and spiders is at its pinnacle in the Earth's tropical rainforests. Arthropods thrive in the ideal conditions of a constant temperature and high humidity. There is also huge fauna diversity in temperate woodlands, where many micro-habitats—including soil, leaf-litter, broad leaves, and rotting wood—are available to insects and spiders.

HOTHOUSE

The fertile, shaded environment of the rainforest is home to millions of arthropods, many of which are yet to be described by scientists. The canopy gives shelter from temperature

SKY GARDEN It is estimated that more than half of all the world's arthropod species live in moist, tropical rainforest. Species living high in the canopy remain for the most part unstudied.

luctuations, and flowers and oliage provide year-round food supplies for adults and larvae. Mantids, beetles, ants, butterflies, and spiders use camouflage to avoid being eaten. Often, the most bizarre examples of camouflage are found in rainforests. Some species mimic unpalatable animals to discourage predators.

Wooded wonderland Temperate old-growth forests have extremely fertile soil because of the constant vegetation decay. The thick layer of leaf litter and lush understory of shrubs houses a myriad of arthropod species. Ants, termites, beetles, scorpions, and spiders all thrive in these conditions, where there are plenty of small invertebrates available as food.

Underwater and Underground

Many insects and spiders have aquatic or fossorial (underground) habits. They display unique specializations to ensure survival in these environments.

WATER WORLD

Aquatic insects are streamlined to help them move swiftly through water to escape predators and find food. **Holding breath** Whirligig beetles live on pond surfaces. They have divided compound eyes that can see above and below water at the same time. Water boatmen and diving beetles trap air under their wing cases as oxygen reserves. The European water spider constructs a diving bell out of silk, filling it with air bubbles it drags from the surface.

The seashore offers another niche for insects, including beetles and flies that feed on decaying seaweed.

GONE TO GROUND

Underground or cave-dwelling insects must adapt to low light or total darkness. Many have eyes reduced to light-sensitive patches. Some are wingless, while others have extremely long antennae for detecting prey in low light.

THE GOOD OIL

Some insects live in extremely harsh habitats and conditions. The petroleum fly lives in puddles of crude oil. It feeds on other insects that fall into the oil and get stuck.

WATER SENSE Whirligigs locate food by creating ripples and sensing how they bounce back.

GILL FANS This damselfly nymph can extract oxygen from the water through its fanlike gills.

TTLE DIGGER The nocturnal
rusalem cricket lives its life
ostly underground. It has
rong legs for digging but unlike
her crickets, it is wingless.

OND LIFE The bodies of aquatic insects
e often streamlined to help them glide
rough water. Water boatmen paddle
rough the water with oarlike legs.
/ater striders use surface tension to
ate across the water's surface.

Animal Hosts

■ Parasitic arthropods, such as ticks, mites, and lice, feed on the living tissue or blood of a host animal. Although most will not kill the host, they cause blood loss and may carry diseases.

GIANT LEAP A flea springs from host to host using specialized muscles in its thorax. It can jump up to 100 times its own height.

LIVING TOGETHER
Parasitic arthropods have mouthparts or appendages specially adapted for feeding on their host's tissues. Some also have flattened bodies for burrowing through skin layers.

Fleas have heat-sensitive antennae to sense the body heat of a passing mammal, or the presence of carbon dioxide exhaled by the potential host.

Cling-ons Human head and body lice have legs equipped with strong claws for gripping. The head louse lives its entire life in hair, gluing its eggs, called nits, to the base of hair shafts. The micro-organism that causes typhus is carried by body lice and is transmitted to the host through contact. Some lice live on sea mammals. These lice can survive long periods in salt water, an unusual feat for insects.

Skin deep Scabies mites feed on the skin and hair of mammals, including humans. They burrow into the epidermis, leaving visible tunnels in the skin's surface. The host's scratching often results in a secondary infection. Mites penetrate the exoskeleton of many insects, usually at the body joints, where the cuticle is thinnest.

FULL BLOWN After two days of sucking blood, a female tick expands up to 200 times its own weight.

BEDBUG BITE Bedbugs use their piercing mouthparts to feed on human blood. They are active at night, but hide away in bedding and clothes during the day. They find their host by sensing body heat.

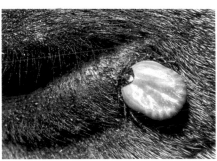

TICK OFF Ticks often feed in clusters on their hosts, using chelicerae adapted for piercing and sucking. They are significant carriers of human and animal disease.

FORM AND FUNCTION

The basic insect and arachnid body plans have been modified in a variety of ways through the process of evolution. These specializations mean insects and spiders increase their chances of survival and pass this success to their future progeny.

WINGS AND THINGS

Because insects are small they can inhabit a wide range of micro-habitats—for example, a decaying log may be home to hundreds of different species. Fast reproductive rates allow a high rate of evolution and adaptation to environmental conditions. As a result, insect adaptations are many and varied.

Good sense An insect's antennae can sense sound and vibration, but can also detect chemical messages from a potential mate or pass on information about food. **Leg up** Insect legs have been modified for digging, swimming, jumping, and even hearing. An insect's wings are used for flight, but they may also have a protective function. Mouthparts are modified to bite, slice, or suck nectar or blood. An insect's coloration can be used for camouflage, to attract a mate, or confuse a potential predator.

Spider forms Although the arachnid body plan displays greater uniformity, spiders in particular have developed sensory specializations associated with hunting and web-spinning. The development of cryptic coloration and mimicry has served not only to protect spiders from predators, but has also helped disguise them from their victims.

STEALTH AND SPEED The front legs of a praying mantis (above) are modified for catching prey. Wasps (right) are superbly adapted as flying predators.

Focus on Flight

■ Insects were the first animals to fly. It is the key to their immense success and incredible diversity. Today, they are still the most numerous fliers in the animal world. Flying allows insects to escape from danger, and find new habitats. It also makes it easier for them to find mates and establish new colonies. One of flight's most important benefits is that insects can reach and exploit a huge variety of food sources.

FLYING SUCCESS

Insects have been flying for more than 300 million years, since wings evolved from the gills on aquatic nymphs. The first fliers probably did little more than glide, but as wing design improved through the process of evolution, flying became more reliable and sophisticated. The earliest fliers were not able to fold their wings back alongside their bodies, but as this ability developed, the radiation and success of insects began in earnest. The only insects today unable to fold their wings are the dragonflies and mayflies.

Places to go Modern insects vary greatly in the distances they fly. Some insects manage only a few yards, while others embark on journeys of thousands of miles.

WING BEATS All the insects shown below are strong fliers. They achieve this through beating their wings at vastly different speeds.

Dragonfly
35 beats/sec

Housefly
170 beats/sec

Honeybee
130 beats/sec

Butterfly
10 beats/sec

Mosquito
600 beats/sec

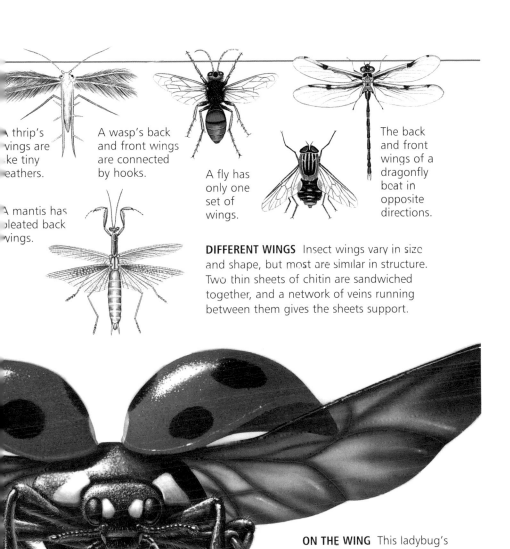

A thrip's wings are like tiny feathers.

A wasp's back and front wings are connected by hooks.

A fly has only one set of wings.

The back and front wings of a dragonfly beat in opposite directions.

A mantis has pleated back wings.

DIFFERENT WINGS Insect wings vary in size and shape, but most are similar in structure. Two thin sheets of chitin are sandwiched together, and a network of veins running between them gives the sheets support.

ON THE WING This ladybug's tough forewings, or elytra, act as covers for its delicate hindwings. During flight, elytra also keep the beetle stable, while giving extra lift.

Taking to the Air

■ Although most insects have wings, not all are accomplished fliers. Many species, such as scorpion flies, need to launch themselves from a high point to gain enough lift for them to take off. By contrast, the two-winged flies are strong and fast fliers, displaying impressive maneuverability in the air.

LIFT-OFF POWER

An insect's wings are powered by strong muscles in the thorax. Unlike birds and bats, the flight muscles of insects are not directly attached to the wings. Instead, the muscles change the shape of the thorax and the wings move in response. Each wing is connected to the thorax by a tiny plate or joint called a sclerite. This joint allows the wing to move up or down, backward or forward, giving it extra control in the air.

More than a beat To fly, an insect must tilt its wings and beat them. This pushes air backward, which gives the insect thrust. When the wings are at the top of the upstroke, their front edges are

WIND POWER

Some insects, such as thrips (below) and some aphids, are too small and slow to get very far under their own wing power. Instead, they rely on the power of wind currents to blow them from one place to another.

FAST FLIGHT Dragonflies are the fastest fliers in the insect world. During flight, they can reach speeds of more than 31 miles (50 km) per hour.

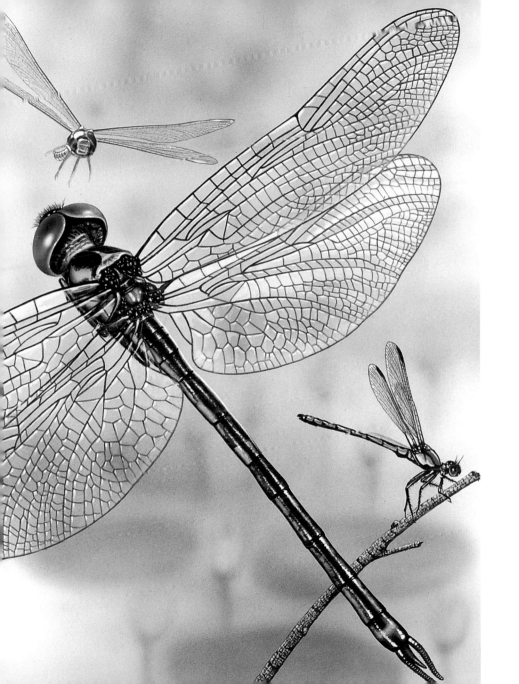

raised. As the downstroke begins, the front edges start to dip. The greater the angle of the edges, the stronger the thrust, and the faster the insect travels.

WING WATCHING

Flying insects have two pairs of wings attached to their thorax. Wings are made from chitin, the same hard material that covers the rest of the body. Butterflies and dragonflies use both pairs of wings to fly. In some insects, wings are covered by minute hairs. In butterflies and moths, the wings are made up of tiny, overlapping scales, each reflecting light to produce the brilliant colors. In some species, such as honeybees, the larger forewings are joined to the hindwings by a row of hooks, so that the two pairs beat in unison.
Flying aces Flies are the aviation experts of the insect world. Unlike almost all other flying insects, they have only a single pair of wings, which gives them great speed and agility in the air. Their hindwings have been modified into small, club-like balancing organs called halteres.

FLIGHT INSTRUMENTS The crane fly's halteres vibrate at high speeds during flight to keep its body balanced and level. Modern ships use a similar technique to stabilize them during a storm.

These organs monitor the insect's movements while it is in the air. Hover flies display such precision in flight that they can slow down, change direction suddenly, hover in the same spot, and even fly backwards. Houseflies flip themselves over in midair, ready to land upside down on a ceiling.

Flight check Unlike warm-blooded birds and bats, insects must warm up their flight muscles before they become airborne. To achieve this, they vibrate their wings for a time before a flight or they simply bask in the sun until the correct muscle temperature is reached.

TAKEOFF Prior to takeoff, this ladybug opens its front wings (far left) and unfolds its back wings. The front wings swing outward (left), and when the back wings are beating fast enough, liftoff is achieved.

SENSING SURROUNDINGS

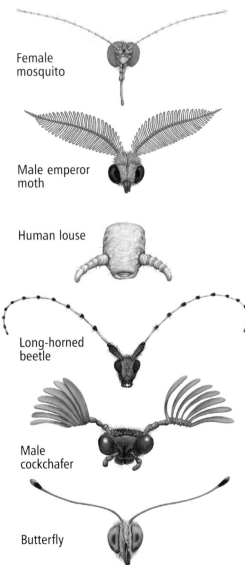

Female mosquito

Male emperor moth

Human louse

Long-horned beetle

Male cockchafer

Butterfly

Insects have five main senses—sight, smell, touch, taste, and hearing—which they use to monitor their surroundings, find a mate, and avoid predators. Each insect type specializes in using some senses more than others.

TUNING IN

Much of the information an insect receives is filtered through its antennae, which enable it to smell, touch, and hear. The shape of antennae varies greatly among insects and sometimes even between males and females of the same species (see left).

Sight Most insects have compound eyes, which are made of many smaller eyes, called eyelets, packed tightly together. Some eyes may have as many as 56,000 lenses, each recording a different view. Many insects also have simple eyes on the top of their heads, called ocelli, to help with flight and light detection.

Good taste Insects taste food using sense organs clustered around the mouth, the most important being the palps.

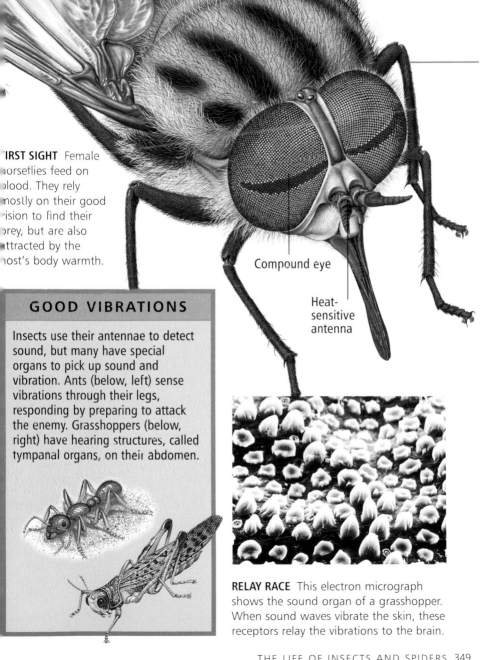

FIRST SIGHT Female horseflies feed on blood. They rely mostly on their good vision to find their prey, but are also attracted by the host's body warmth.

Compound eye

Heat-sensitive antenna

GOOD VIBRATIONS

Insects use their antennae to detect sound, but many have special organs to pick up sound and vibration. Ants (below, left) sense vibrations through their legs, responding by preparing to attack the enemy. Grasshoppers (below, right) have hearing structures, called tympanal organs, on their abdomen.

RELAY RACE This electron micrograph shows the sound organ of a grasshopper. When sound waves vibrate the skin, these receptors relay the vibrations to the brain.

SPIDER SENSE

All spiders are predators. Most species trap their food in silken webs, but many actively hunt for food or wait in ambush for it. These different methods require specialized sensory organs. Because most spiders are solitary, they must also rely on their senses to detect the signals that will guide them to a mate.

EYES ON MOVEMENT

A spider sees the world through a group of eyes along the front of its cephalothorax. One pair of eyes forms images, while the ancillary eyes detect movement. Although hunting spiders, such as wolf and jumping spiders, have excellent vision, spiders for the most part have poor eyesight.

NET CAPTURE A spider senses struggling prey ensnared in its web using slits in its exoskeleton that can detect vibration.

Spider sensitivity Because many spiders have poor vision, they rely instead on sensitive body hairs to convey information about prey. Each hair is anchored in a tiny pit surrounded by nerve endings. A vibration from any direction will move the hair. Some spiders also have tiny slits in their exoskeletons that are sensitive to vibrations. Web-spinning spiders use these sense organs to detect if prey is trapped in their web.

Fine sensory hairs are abundant on the pedipalps and legs of arachnids. These are used for smelling and tasting.

LEGS AND EYES Sensitive hairs on spiders' legs (left) detect prey caught in their web. The ogre-faced spider's large eyes (right) see in near total darkness. Crab spiders (right) rely on vibration sensors, only seeing with their eyes as prey approaches.

Ogre-faced spider
Night vision

Crab spider
Sit and wait

Insect and Spider Behavior

STAYING IN TOUCH

Insects have sophisticated sensory systems for such small creatures. They are able to respond to a range of physical, chemical, and visual stimuli. Many can sense infra-red radiation or ultraviolet light, magnetic fields, or humidity fluctuations. Insects communicate with one another using sight, sound, touch, and taste—and even light. Many have bright colors or patterns to identify themselves to others. Most butterflies and dragonflies recognize each other's markings, with males often being the most colorful partners.

Light show Fireflies and other organisms can produce cold light—called bioluminescence—by mixing chemicals together in the body. Males and females

NIGHT LIGHTS This female firefly communicates by flashing a code on her glowing abdomen to males performing a special dance in the sky above her.

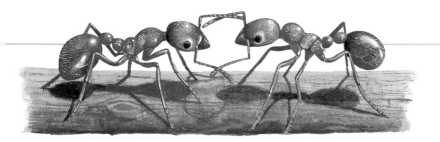

lash coded signals to one another through the darkness.

Sounding off For crickets, cicadas, and some smaller insects, sound provides a way to contact a mate. Unlike sight, sound works during the day and night, and allows an insect to stay hidden while it broadcasts its call.

Touch and taste Insects often use touch and taste to communicate, but they can also make contact by smell. Some of their scents, or pheromones, waft considerable distances through the air. Others mark the ground with scent to show where they have been.

DIFFERENT WAYS

Insects employ many other ways of communicating. Lacewings and treehoppers stamp messages on the branches they sit on. Aquatic insects such as water striders and backswimmers sense vibrations in the water with their feet.

SMELL CHECK Some insects use chemicals called pheromones to communicate. Red ants touch with their antennae to check smells and see if they are from the same nest. Invaders are quickly expelled.

DISTANT CALLS

The Y-shaped burrow of the male mole cricket helps to amplify his call. He produces his sound by scraping his left front wing against his right—much like a fingernail against a comb. In fact, it is one of the loudest calls in the insect world, and in still air it can be heard more than half a mile (800 m) away.

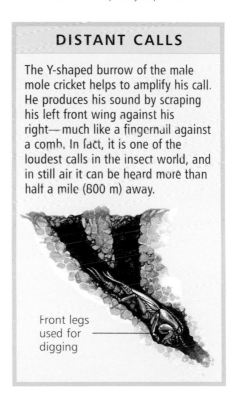

Front legs used for digging

Spider Communication

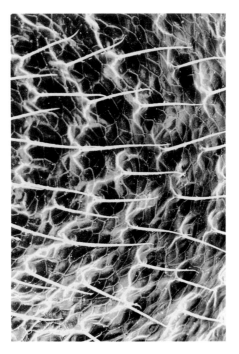

FEEL THE BREEZE The sensory hairs on a spider's body are crucial for detecting stimuli from the surroundings and for communicating with its own species.

■ As solitary predators, most spiders communicate only when they come together to mate. Communication strategies depend largely on the sensory capabilities of the species; those with good eyesight use visual signals and those with poor eyesight use touch and vibration. Some web-spinning spiders prefer to use scent messages, coating their silk with pheromones.

COURTSHIP DISPLAYS

Most spiders live alone and treat approaches by others as a threat. Males often have elaborate courtship displays that are designed to signal their intentions to mate with a female, therefore avoiding attack, and possible death, by the female.

Dance recital Spiders with good eyesight usually display to females by waving their legs or pedipalps in a special, sometimes

MORSE CODE A male spider sends signals to a potential mate by tapping a specific code on her web as he approaches. In this way, he avoids being attacked.

MATING DANCE A male jumping spider signals a female by waving his front legs in the air and maneuvering his body to display his colors and patterns. The female recognizes him as one of her species and a potential mate. He moves closer, stroking her and then mating with her.

ntricate sequence. Once recognized as one of her own species and not a rival, the female will allow the male to approach and mate with her.

Web song Male web-spinning spiders avoid being eaten when courting a female by signaling to her using a species-specific code. He tugs on the female's web in a particular sequence as he tentatively moves toward her. If the approach is accepted, the pair will mate.

Grating sounds Some male spiders have stridulating organs that they use to produce a high-pitched grating sound while they are in the female's web. In one species, the male has minute bristles on his legs that are

rubbed on the surface of his book lung to produce a vibration.

Ripple soles Male nursery-web spiders live on the water's edge. They send ripple messages across the water when courting. Sensory slit organs on the female's feet detect the ripples on the surface.

FROM EGG TO ADULT

Virtually all insects start out life as eggs. Adults come together to mate and females lay fertilized eggs that eventually develop into adults. One notable exception to this sequence is female aphids, which may produce thousands of offspring by parthenogenesis, a process whereby eggs develop without fertilization. In the insect world, the development of an egg into an adult requires periods of growth and the shedding of the exoskeleton to increase size. Arachnids molt throughout their lives, and the young look like small versions of the adults.

TRANSFORMATIONS

With the exception of silverfish and bristletails, all insects change their appearance on their journey to adulthood. For dragonflies, damselflies, grasshoppers, termites, mantids, and cockroaches, this process is a gradual one. It is usually termed "incomplete" metamorphosis. In more advanced insects, the immature stage, called a larva, looks completely different from the adult. Instead of many gradual changes, the larva reorganizes its immature tissues during pupation and makes one dramatic transformation to adulthood. This is called "complete" metamorphosis. The larvae focus on feeding and growth, and the adults complete the lifecycle with reproduction and dispersal.

BODY CHANGES Sawfly larvae (left) eat voraciously before they transform into adults. A dragonfly (right) emerges from its final nymphal skin as a winged adult.

Passing on the Genes

■ In most arthropod species, males and females come together to mate before the female lays her eggs. Mating may occur when individuals are gathered together at a food or water source. For other species, sophisticated sensory and physical signals are used to court a mate, including the use of odors, sounds, or displays. Sometimes males fight with rivals for the right to mate.

NEW GENERATION

Males deliver their sperm to females in a packet called a spermatophore. This packet is either deposited into the female's genital pore or is picked up by the female herself. Females often store sperm in special organs

GETTING TOGETHER Sperm transfer to a female may take only a few minutes, but some males clasp the female to ensure she does not mate with other males.

inside the body for use when conditions are optimal. Male spiders transfer sperm to their pedipalps using a specially woven sperm web. The palps draw up drops of sperm when they are dipped into the web and this is then transferred to the female's genital opening.

Bearing gifts Copulation may last from a few seconds to many hours. In some species, mating is preceded by an elaborate courtship ritual or by the presentation of food offerings from the male to his mate.

RULE OF CLAW Male hercules beetles use their enlarged mandibles to fight for the right to mate with a female.

Eggs

■ Almost all insects and arachnids lay eggs. The eggs develop outside the female's body and are usually laid near a suitable food source. Many plant-eating species must lay their eggs on plants that are suitable for their hatched larvae.

COMPLETE PACKAGE

A female sometimes lays single eggs, but more often eggs are laid in clusters of hundreds or even thousands. During her lifetime, a queen termite can lay more than 10 million eggs.

Horsefly eggs

Eucalyptus tip bug eggs

Female insects lay eggs through a specialized tube on their abdomen called the ovipositor. Some eggs hatch soon after being laid, but others stay inactive during months of cold or dry weather, during which all the adults may die. Some eggs hatch inside the mother's body, with live young emerging from the genital pore.

Young and alone Most females make no attempt to care for their eggs. However, the giant water bug and some shield bugs will protect their young from danger.

MOTHER LOVE In what is unusual behavior in insects, the female shield bug protects her eggs and young. She will try to scare predators away if they threaten.

BORING DETAILS The female ichneumon wasp (right) drills into wood with her modified ovipositor. She stings the larva of a wood wasp and deposits her eggs into it. When the eggs hatch, they will feed on the host.

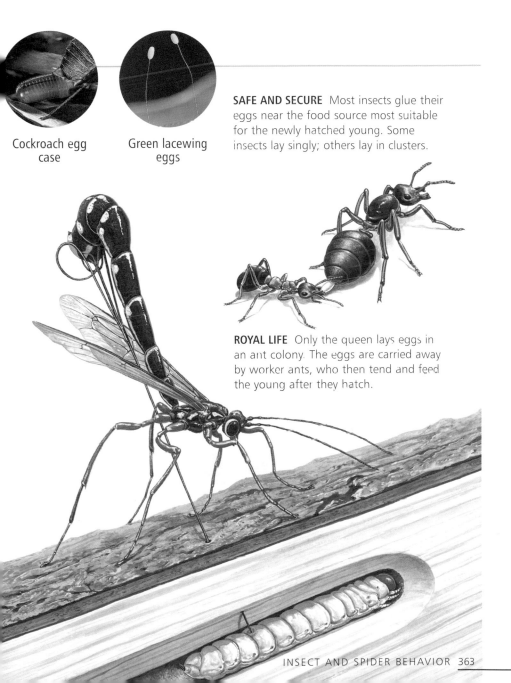

Cockroach egg
case

Green lacewing
eggs

SAFE AND SECURE Most insects glue their eggs near the food source most suitable for the newly hatched young. Some insects lay singly; others lay in clusters.

ROYAL LIFE Only the queen lays eggs in an ant colony. The eggs are carried away by worker ants, who then tend and feed the young after they hatch.

Nests and Shelters

■ Insects are among the most experienced of nature's builders. They construct many different structures to house and protect their families.

BUILDING PROJECTS

Some insects work alone to build simple shelters just for themselves or for their young. Others—the termites, ants, social bees, and wasps—work in family groups. Their nests are far more ambitious, and many are large

IN THE POT The female potter wasp places a caterpillar in a mud nest, lays an egg, and seals the pot. After the grub hatches, it eats the caterpillar.

enough to house millions of individuals. Social insects use a range of building materials, from leaves and dead plants to wood fibers, mud, and wax. They chew up the material to form a paste and spread the paste where it is needed. Termite mounds range in size from tiny nests to enormous above- and below-ground structures (see opposite). Weaver ants make nests by pulling together leaves and gluing them with a sticky fluid secreted by their larvae. Honeybees use wax secretions to construct hives of hexagonal cells. These intricate building tasks are all guided by instinctual behavior.

SPIDER NESTS

Spiders produce silk cocoons to protect their developing young. In some cases, the sacs are placed in a safe location and then deserted. Some species guard their eggs and young, and may even carry them on their bodies. The water spider places her silk-cocooned eggs in the top of her submerged home.

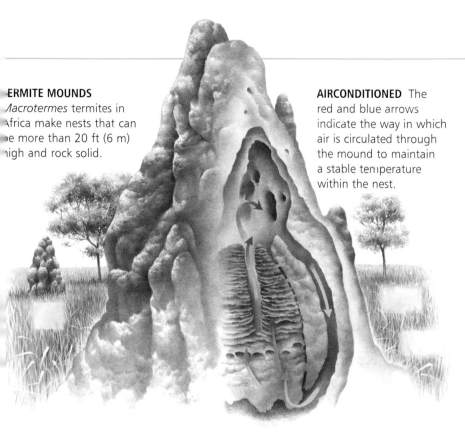

TERMITE MOUNDS
Macrotermes termites in Africa make nests that can be more than 20 ft (6 m) high and rock solid.

AIRCONDITIONED The red and blue arrows indicate the way in which air is circulated through the mound to maintain a stable temperature within the nest.

1 The queen starts the nest by building a hanging cup from chewed wood fibers.

2 She makes cells inside the cup in which she lays her eggs.

3 The eggs hatch into worker wasps, which work to expand the nest.

COMMUNAL LIVING When the nest of the common wasp is completed, it may contain more than 10,000 cells.

Journey to Adulthood

■ Insects such as earwigs, dragonflies, grasshoppers, true bugs, and mantids undergo an incomplete metamorphosis. This process involves the gradual transformation of a larva into an adult through a succession of molts and physical changes. The immature stages of this process are called nymphs. Nymphs look similar to the adult, but they are wingless, different in color, and lack any reproductive structures. Wings grow gradually on the outside of a nymph's body. During the final molt, the nymph emerges from its old exoskeleton as an adult with functional wings.

MAYFLY LIFE

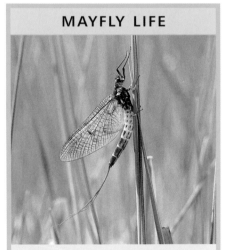

A female mayfly spends up to three years as a nymph, but will live for just one day as an adult. She cannot eat or drink, because she has no mouthparts. Her only purpose is to mate with a male and lay eggs to ensure the next generation.

NYMPH TO ADULT Dragonfly nymphs spend up to five years developing underwater before climbing up a plant stem, molting their skin for the last time, and emerging as adults, able to fly.

An adult female inserts eggs into a water plant.

Each tiny nymph chews its way out of its egg case.

Some cicada species take up to 17 years to mature underground. Millions of adults emerge together. The cicadas mate and lay eggs and the cycle is repeated. Nymphs often live in similar habitats and feed on similar food to the adult insect. Damselfly and dragonfly nymphs are less like the adult they transform into. They live in ponds and use gills on their tail to take in oxygen.

The nymph bursts its old skin and emerges as an adult.

A male and female mate.

The nymph climbs out of the water.

The nymph catches tadpoles and worms.

Life Changes

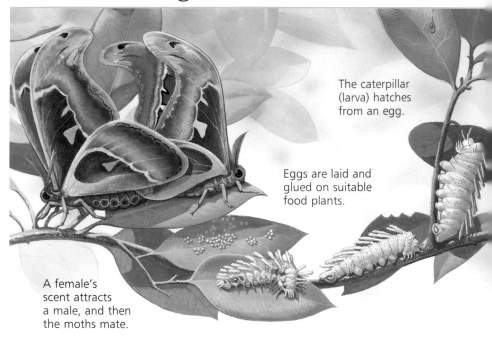

The caterpillar (larva) hatches from an egg.

Eggs are laid and glued on suitable food plants.

A female's scent attracts a male, and then the moths mate.

■ Eighty-five percent of all insect species alive today develop through a process of complete metamorphosis. The larvae look very different from the adult and they go through a single, dramatic transformation to adulthood.

EATING MACHINES

When the larvae hatch from eggs, they are soft-bodied, wingless, and often legless. The larvae of butterflies and moths are called caterpillars; those of beetles are called grubs; and the larvae of flies are called maggots. Larvae eat constantly. Their first meal is often their eggshell, which may contain chemicals to stimulate larval feeding. When fully grown (which may involve a series of molts), the larva stops eating in preparation for pupation. Many insects form pupal cases, and some build silk or earth cocoons for protection. During pupation,

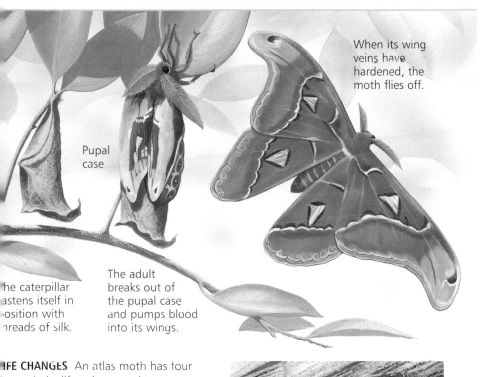

When its wing veins have hardened, the moth flies off.

Pupal case

The caterpillar fastens itself in position with threads of silk.

The adult breaks out of the pupal case and pumps blood into its wings.

LIFE CHANGES An atlas moth has four stages in its lifecycle— egg, larva, pupa and adult. Larvae put all effort into feeding, while adults mate and lay eggs.

the juvenile body starts to take on adult features. The fully mature adult emerges, complete with wings and reproductive organs. Adults look vastly different from their larval stages. They often eat different foods and live in completely different habitats.

LONG WAIT Jewel beetle larvae spend up to seven years burrowing through oak trees. They form a chamber in which to pupate and then emerge as adults.

Spider Young

■ Like insects, many spiders produce thousands of eggs, but very few survive through to adulthood. All spiders wrap their eggs in silk bundles called egg sacs or brood chambers. Many species can be identified by the color and design of their egg sac. The young break out of these sacs soon after they hatch, often clinging to each other or to their

SILK PURSE The black widow's eggs are wrapped in a silk case and attached to the web. She may lay up to 20 eggs.

mother's body. Young spiders, called spiderlings, are miniature versions of their parents. The majority molt for the first time safely inside the egg sac. Many leave the sac by using threads of silk as sails to launch themselves into the wind.

Maternal care Some spiders, scorpions, and some harvestmen and ticks guard their eggs and young from predators.

FIRST MEAL

Many female spiders die soon after they have laid their eggs. For some spiderlings, their mother's body is the first food they eat before they have to catch it for themselves. Their mother ensures them a safe meal, and an increased chance of survival at a vulnerable stage of life.

SECURE RIDE The egg sac of a female wolf spider is attached to her spinnerets. After hatching, the spiderlings climb up on their mother's abdomen and stay with her until their first molt.

CAMOUFLAGE

There are many examples of camouflage in all the major animal groups, but the insect and spider world provides some of the most spectacular. Camouflage is one of the simplest means of defense—but it can also be used as a tool in the deception and capture of prey.

DIFFERENT HUES
Simple camouflage relies on an animal's color (through a

HIDDEN AWAY The yucca moth's close association with the yucca plant is reflected in a body shape and color that help to conceal it from predators.

process of natural selection and evolution) blending in with the colors of its surroundings. Many bugs and spiders that live on flowers display colors that are a close match with their chosen vegetation. It can be difficult to spot them against a backdrop of similar color or texture.

Warning colors Insects not only use color to help conceal them, but many use vibrant hues to broadcast to a potential predator that they are dangerous to eat. Large numbers of beetles and butterflies sport bright warning colors to advertise that they are poisonous. Some non-poisonous species mimic these patterns and colors and, therefore, derive their mimic's defensive benefits.

SHAPES AND FORMS
An animal's shape or body form can betray it to a predator. Many insects and spiders have conquered this problem with specialized shapes, spines, and appendages that help them mimic dead leaves, thorns, seed pods, sticks, stones, and bird droppings.

LEAFY DISGUISE The upper side of this butterfly's wings are colorful and brightly patterned. But when it comes to rest on a branch, it folds its wings to reveal the dull, brownish underside that looks not unlike a dead leaf.

NEW LEAF The long-legged leaf katydid's body shape and coloration help to camouflage it from predators. Stillness is an important component of the disguise.

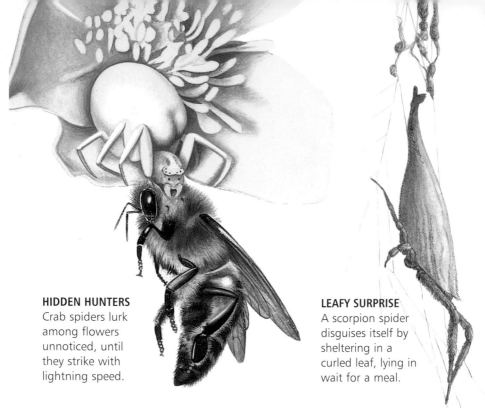

HIDDEN HUNTERS
Crab spiders lurk among flowers unnoticed, until they strike with lightning speed.

LEAFY SURPRISE
A scorpion spider disguises itself by sheltering in a curled leaf, lying in wait for a meal.

They carry this deception further by also copying the posture and other characteristics of the species or object they mimic. Many adult mantids resemble either green or dry leaves. When this is coupled with a to-and-fro movement similar to a leaf swaying in the wind, the mantid creates a formidable disguise. Insects may also mimic the body forms and postures of insects that are considered dangerous, particularly stinging insects, such as bees, ants, and wasps. Some beetle species hold their wings in a similar way to wasps, as well as walking in the same fashion.

Cover up Many insects, especially young beetles and bugs, camouflage themselves by covering their bodies with sand, soil, or even their own excrement. Their body surface is often covered with hooks or bristles to help hold the materials in place.

Some species flatten themselves out against their background, using fringes of hairs to prevent them casting a shadow.

Group benefit Some butterfly, bee, wasp, and dragonfly species assemble in groups for resting. They cling to twigs or straws with their legs or mandibles, looking to a predator like a cluster of flowers on a plant.

Spider disguise

Although most spiders can bite and inject venom, many employ camouflage to protect themselves from predators and to help them

STILL HIDING A significant part of this lichen spider's disguise is stillness. Many spiders also camouflage their egg sacs, with moss, leaves, and twigs.

catch prey. During the day, the female bird-dung spider looks, as its name suggests, like a bird's dropping. At night, it releases a chemical that mimics a female moth's scent, thus luring male moths and then eating them. Some Asian jumping spiders are nearly perfect mimics of a dangerous wasp species, complete with long spinnerets that look just like an wasp's antennae.

CAPTURING FOOD

Speed, good vision, strong jaws, stingers, and sometimes stealth and camouflage are the weapons used by predacious insects. Predators catch their prey by hunting actively, or by lying in wait until their victim comes within reach.

SPEED AND STEALTH
On the ground, active hunters include fast-moving beetles, as well as many ants and wasps. Tiger beetles have large, strong jaws, often armed with serrations to help them subdue prey. They are also among the fastest sprinters in the animal world.

GLOWING SUCCESS

The larvae of fungus gnats, a small fly found in caves in Australia and New Zealand, catch flying insects using light and sticky threads. Each luminescent larva produces a thread of sticky mucus that it suspends from the cave rock. This thread traps insects as they fly toward the glowing light. The larva then eats the insect and the trap.

Moving at more than 1½ feet (0.5 m) per second, they chase, grab, and crush ants in their jaws.

In the air, dragonflies swoop down and snatch up other flying insects with their long legs. Many other insects wait for prey to come to them, often by hiding in flowers or disguising themselves in foliage or leaf litter. Assassin bugs lurk among flowers, using their sharp proboscis to stab their victims and then suck out their body fluids.

Downhill run A few of these stationary hunters build special traps to catch their food. Antlion larvae dig steep-sided pits in loose soil and then wait for ants to tumble in.

Vision splendid Excellent eyesight is especially important for aerial predators, such as horseflies and dragonflies. The eyes of these groups are often larger and equipped with more acute vision than those of ground-dwellers. This is probably the result of the fine adjustments that must be made when flying and hunting simultaneously.

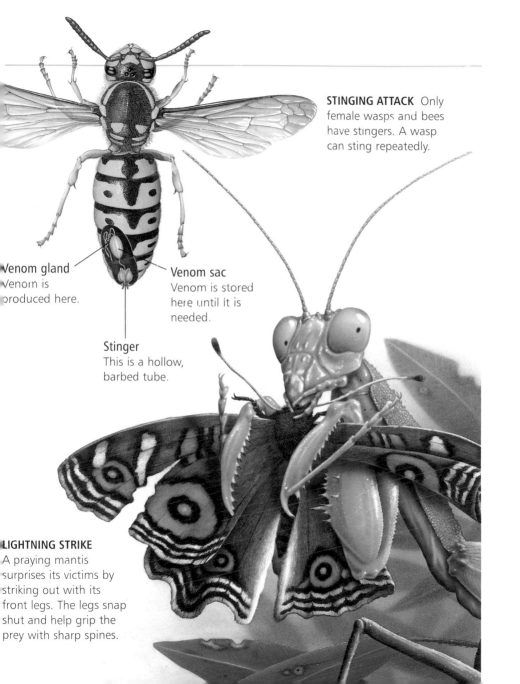

STINGING ATTACK Only female wasps and bees have stingers. A wasp can sting repeatedly.

Venom gland
Venom is produced here.

Venom sac
Venom is stored here until it is needed.

Stinger
This is a hollow, barbed tube.

LIGHTNING STRIKE
A praying mantis surprises its victims by striking out with its front legs. The legs snap shut and help grip the prey with sharp spines.

Weaving Webs

■ Spiders are the most versatile silk-makers in the world, and they are capable of making silk that has many uses. A spider's silk may be used to wrap prey and eggs, to line burrows, to make draglines for traveling, to produce sticky lines for prey capture, and to weave webs.

STRONG AS SILK

Spider silk is a liquid protein made in the silk glands. It is secreted from spigots on the spinnerets. The spider pulls out several strands at once and under tension the silk hardens. Spider silk is incredibly strong and elastic. Some giant orb-weaving spiders make webs strong enough to catch small birds.

Sticky traps Once a web is complete, spiders usually lie in wait, either on the web itself or close enough to touch it with their legs, and to sense vibrations.

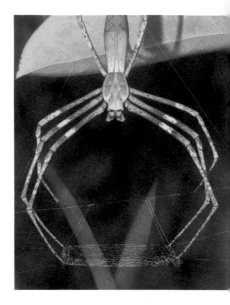

WEB DESIGN A net-throwing spider (above) holds its web with its legs, casting it over the prey. Spiders may wrap their prey to store it (opposite).

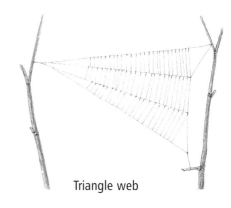

Triangle web

TAKING SHAPE Spiders' webs vary from extremely precise structures to untidy tangles. The shape of the web (right) can help to identify the owner.

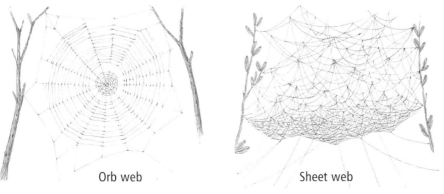

Orb web   Sheet web

HUNTING FOR FOOD

Not all spiders catch their prey using webs. Many use traps of different kinds, while others actively seek their prey, pouncing on it when it comes into range.

STALKING SPIDERS

Spiders that search for food operate either by day or night. Because they are solitary hunters, most stake out their territory and defend the boundaries. Some wolf spiders chase off any intruder that tries to move in on their territory. Jumping spiders hunt mostly during the day. They are more free-roaming and leap after prey, trailing their silk drag lines behind them.

Ambushers Some spiders ambush their prey. Trapdoor spiders wait in their tunnels, just beneath a trapdoor made of silk, ready to pounce as soon as they detect vibrations in their trip wires. Others use camouflage to blend in with their surroundings, biding their time until an insect wanders into range. Some

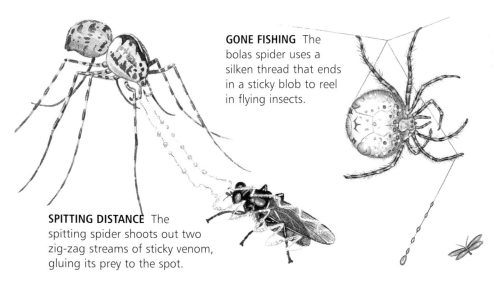

GONE FISHING The bolas spider uses a silken thread that ends in a sticky blob to reel in flying insects.

SPITTING DISTANCE The spitting spider shoots out two zig-zag streams of sticky venom, gluing its prey to the spot.

tarantulas use both sit-and-wait tactics or active hunting methods. Many tarantulas have poor eyesight. Instead, they use sense organs in their legs to pick up the vibrations of passing prey. When prey is detected, the spider rears up, ready to strike faster than the eye can see.

Raft spiders hunt in water by sensing ripples made by prey in the water. After stabbing the prey with its fangs, the spider hauls its catch ashore. Some spiders are specialized ant predators. They run among the swarm, attacking and injecting poison before the ants can defend themselves.

DEADLY BITE Hunting spiders are often armed with robust fangs, like this funnel-web spider. It raises its cephalothorax to attack and stabs its prey by moving its head down, with the fangs pointed downward. Venom flows into the victim through holes in the tips of the fangs.

EAT OR BE EATEN

Insects are under constant threat of being preyed upon by birds, lizards, spiders, and other insects. Many defend themselves by retreating from danger or by staying still and well hidden. They hide in soil or rotting wood, or make themselves look like the objects around them. Some harmless insects imitate those that are unpalatable or mimic those with dangerous stings.

LINES OF DEFENSE

If all other defenses fail, some insects stand their ground and attack. Some have armored bodies, sharp jaws, or toxic chemicals to deter a predator just long enough to make an escape.

Bush crickets exude droplets of foul-smelling liquid from their thorax to repel attackers. The bombardier beetle blasts hot, caustic substances at predators from a chamber in its abdomen. The bloody-nosed beetle breaks thin membranes in its mouth and forces out a droplet of its own blood. The blood of this beetle contains chemicals that make its attacker very ill.

Copycats Monarch butterflies are poisonous and their bright orange colors advertise this well. The harmless viceroy butterfly mimics the monarch's colors and patterns, hoodwinking predators into believing it to be toxic also.

Startling flash Some bugs and katydids startle intruders by flashing normally concealed eyespots or brilliant colors, giving them a chance to make a getaway.

EYES AND SPOTS Many moths sport large eyespots on their wings (left). These may startle a predator by making the moth appear to have a large, threatening face. Ladybugs (right) warn enemies of their bitter taste with bright colors and spots.

ON GUARD The puss moth caterpillar raises its head and flicks two rear whips from side to side when it is disturbed. As a last resort, it sprays formic acid.

Five-spotted ladybug

Ten-spotted ladybug

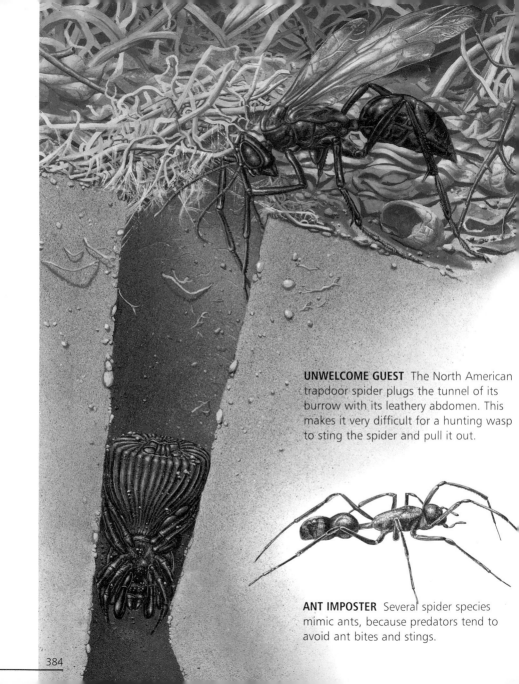

UNWELCOME GUEST The North American trapdoor spider plugs the tunnel of its burrow with its leathery abdomen. This makes it very difficult for a hunting wasp to sting the spider and pull it out.

ANT IMPOSTER Several spider species mimic ants, because predators tend to avoid ant bites and stings.

SPIDER DEFENSE

Spiders are vulnerable to attack from many different animals, mostly birds, lizards, toads, and small mammals. They may also be attacked by parasitic insects, such as the ichneumon wasp, and from members of their own species.

Out of sight Many spiders have developed strategies to avoid being eaten. Some conceal themselves by lurking in burrows or burying themselves in sand. A few will suddenly drop out of their web, dangling from a safety line. Others escape notice by camouflaging themselves or by mimicking a more dangerous animal.

Spiny-backed spiders have unusually hard and spiky abdomens. This is thought to be a defense against predation by birds. Some spiders display their toxicity by having bright red markings to warn off potential predators. Large South American tarantulas are known to flick microscopic barbed hairs, which irritate the skin of their attackers.

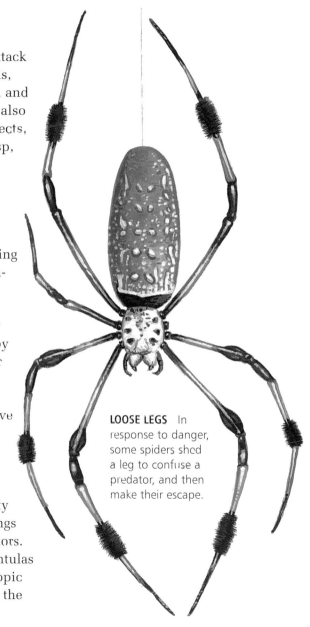

LOOSE LEGS In response to danger, some spiders shed a leg to confuse a predator, and then make their escape.

FOOD AND FEEDING

As a group, insects devour a vast range of different foods. Individual species may have highly specialized requirements, and specially adapted mouthparts for procuring and eating food. Often larval stages have very different food requirements and feeding habits to the adults. In some species, adults may not feed at all, depending on the reserves stored in the larval stage.

DIFFERENT FOOD

Many insects are predators, killing and eating other animals to survive. Predators do not require as much food as plant-eaters because their meals provide significantly more protein and nutrition. The mouthparts of these insects are often equipped with strong, sharp mandibles.

Vegetarians and bloodsuckers
Plant-eating insects have mouthparts ideal for cutting, tearing, shredding, or drilling into their food. Many species feed exclusively on sap, nectar, or other plant liquids. These insects have mouthparts that can suck or sponge up liquid. Parasites, such as fleas and some flies, have specialized mouthparts for drinking blood from their hosts.

GNAWING HUNGER An acorn weevil has the perfect proboscis for boring through tough nuts. Jaws on the tip of the snout can gnaw on the seed inside the acorn.

NECTAR SIPPER
The hairy bee fly
has long, needlelike
mouthparts, which it
uses to drink nectar
from flowers.

MOUTHPARTS
A grasshopper's strong
jaws have sharp edges for
cutting tough grasses.
Carnivorous tiger beetles
have toothed jaws to catch,
subdue, and cut up prey.

Grasshopper
Herbivore

Tiger beetle
Carnivore

DANGEROUS MEAL

The larvae and adults of monarch
butterflies are poisonous to eat
and are avoided by most predators.
The larvae feed on a highly toxic
plant called milkweed, with no
ill-effects. In fact, the larvae
incorporate the milkweed's poisons
into their own body tissues, which
also makes their flesh poisonous.
During metamorphosis, this chemical
defense is passed on to the adult.
Most insects that store plant poisons
have bright colors and patterns to
warn predators of this peril.

LIQUID LUNCH This close-up of a
housefly's tongue shows the structures
that help them mop up their liquid food.

Arachnid food

Arachnids cannot ingest solid food. To be able to eat their prey, they begin to break it down before it reaches their digestive system.

Deadly bite Most hunting spiders bite and inject poison and digestive juices into their prey simultaneously. Web-making spiders usually wrap their prey first, to help immobilize it before they deliver the deadly bite. Spider families with stabbing fangs (mygalomorphs) inject digestive juice into their prey by

SLOW EATERS After this *Dysdera* spider has immobilized its prey with venom, it may take twelve hours to digest it. It may store its catch until it is ready to feed.

piercing through the skin of their prey, and suck the body fluids out through the same holes. As a consequence, their prey looks outwardly undamaged. Spider families with laterally moveable fangs (araneomorphs) tear their food while they pour in digestive juice. The remains of their prey are totally unrecognizable.

Scorpions Scorpions use their modified pedipalps to catch prey, and then subdue it by injecting poison from their tail stinger. Some have powerful venom that can cause respiratory and muscle paralysis. Once the prey is dead, they digest it in a similar way to spiders, breaking it down before it enters the digestive system.

Ticks and mites Ticks and mites use their specialized chelicerae to feed on skin, blood, and body tissues. Some ticks feed on a host for as little as an hour; others may

SUCKING UP Scorpions digest their prey by reducing the victim's tissues to a soupy consistency. They then suck up the liquid into their mouth.

feed for up to six months. They inject an anti-coagulant to help the blood flow freely. When fully engorged, they simply drop off the host. In most cases, the initial bite and penetration of the tick is not felt by the victim. Some mites have chelicerae that are adapted for cutting through skin or for eating body tissue or lymph.

LIVING TOGETHER

The majority of insects and spiders live solitary lives, only coming together to mate, or to feed at a common food source. Truly "social" species—termites, ants, and some wasps and bees—cooperate to find food, build the nest, take care of young, and defend the colony from attack. Many generations may exist in the same nest at the same time.

LABOR DIVIDED

Members of colonies are divided into strictly defined "castes"—usually a queen, drones, workers, and soldiers—each with a specific role. Male drones mate with the queen, who produces all the eggs. The workers collect food and care for the eggs and young. Ant and termite colonies have soldiers to protect them from intruders. All this behavior is instinctively led—no one individual directs the others. Together, their efforts add up to a better chance of survival for the colony as a whole.

Building together Most social insects construct special nests to protect their young. In social bees

PAPER HOME Social insects cooperate to build shelters for their developing young, and for the rest of the colony. Social wasps construct layered, paper nests.

and wasps, nests consist of many hexagonal cells. The ingenious hexagonal shape allows for the maximum number of cells to be packed into the smallest area. Ants and termites construct a nest above or under the ground, often made up of a maze of tunnels and chambers. Here, the eggs are laid, the young are fed and protected, and in some cases, food is cultivated for the colony.

TOTAL CONTROL

Within the nest, the queen controls the reproductive status of her workers by exuding pheromones to prevent them from breeding. Queen ants, wasps, and bees can also determine the sex of their offspring. They withhold sperm stored in their body if male offspring are preferred, because males are produced from unfertilized eggs. Fertilized eggs become females.

Bees and Wasps

■ Some of the best-known wasps and bees, such as hornets, bumblebees, and honeybees, are social insects. They are vital to most ecosystems as pollinators, parasites, and predators. These social species collaborate to build sometimes elaborate nests in which to raise their young.

HIGH SOCIETY

Social bees live in colonies consisting of a queen, female workers, and male drones. They nest in hollow trees or human-made hives, constructing a

water-resistant, waxen comb made up of a matrix of hexagonal cells. The cells provide a chamber for the developing larvae, as well as storage bins for honey that can feed the colony when nectar and flowers are scarce.

The reproductive female, or queen, is the head of the colony, and she produces all the larvae—sometimes more than 50,000 in her 5 years of life. The purpose of the short-lived drones, which develop from unfertilized eggs, is to mate with the queen. Worker bees build the nest, attend to the young, and gather food for the whole hive.

Wasps Most social wasps have similar social structures to bees. Many build nests using layers of chewed wood "paper." Hornets make their nests in hollow trees. Their colonies consist of only a few hundred workers.

NEW DIRECTION Honeybees communicate information to nestmates using a special dance. A fast abdomen waggle means plenty of nectar, and the direction of the dance tells nestmates where to locate it.

BEE YOUNG Worker bees bring food to the larvae as they mature inside their wax cells. These larvae are transforming into pupae, and will then emerge as adults.

COMMUNITY WORK Social bee larvae are fed bee bread —a mixture of honey and pollen—by the workers. Royal jelly is reserved for the queen's daughter.

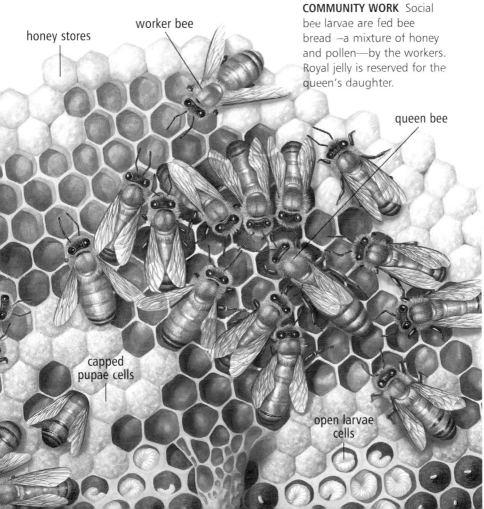

honey stores

worker bee

queen bee

capped pupae cells

open larvae cells

Termites

■ Termites live in permanent social colonies and have distinct castes: the queen, the king, soldiers, and workers. Workers build the nest, forage for food, and tend the young. Soldiers have larger heads than the workers, and they produce repellent secretions to ward off attackers.

ROYAL SWARM

Winged reproductive termites spend their life in the cool of the nest, eating the food collected by the workers. Thousands leave their nests on warm evenings, swarming in the air in search of a partner. After landing, a king and queen break off their wings and mate. Depending on the species, they excavate a cell below the soil's surface in which the first worker nymphs are hatched. These workers undergo an incomplete metamorphosis, and then begin extending the nest by constructing a network of tunnels and chambers. Unlike the workers of social bees and ants, which are all female, worker termites can be sterile males and females.

WOOD DIGESTION Termites and their young eat wood fibers. Their digestive tracts contain bacteria that secrete enzymes capable of digesting cellulose.

Good foundations The royal cell is the foundation of a termite nest. The only fertile male in the colony, the king lives beside the queen, who can lay an egg every few seconds. The king and queen may live for more than ten years and produce millions of eggs. Radiating out from the royal cell are the larval chambers, where the eggs and nymphs are cared for by the workers.

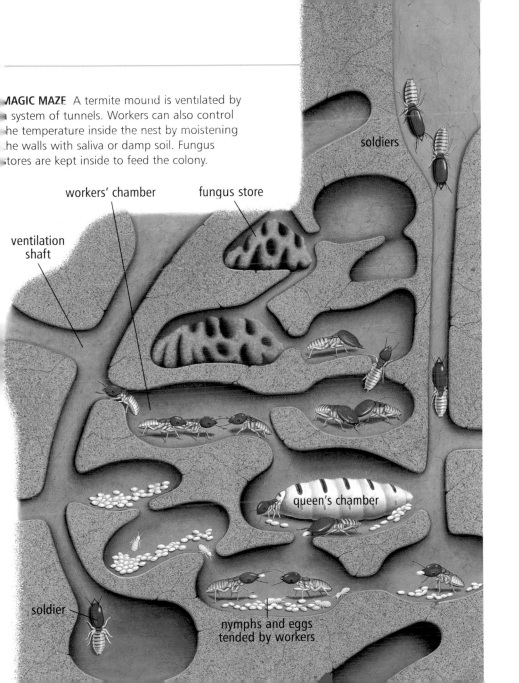

MAGIC MAZE A termite mound is ventilated by a system of tunnels. Workers can also control the temperature inside the nest by moistening the walls with saliva or damp soil. Fungus stores are kept inside to feed the colony.

soldiers

workers' chamber

fungus store

ventilation shaft

queen's chamber

soldier

nymphs and eggs tended by workers

Ants

■ All 9,000 species of ant are social insects. They live in colonies divided into castes and are controlled by a queen. Most ants build their nests in wood or plants, or out of soil.

CASTE OUT

There are two castes of ants within most colonies—the queen and the workers, who are all female. The few males in the colony exist only to mate with a new queen in order to start a new nest. The young winged queen flies from her old nest and mates once with a winged male. After biting off her wings, she starts a nest that is then extended by her female offspring.

Scent trails Like social bees, ants use pheromones to identify themselves, and to communicate with each other. Pheromones are used by the queen to sterilize the workers, and workers leave pheromone trails to guide other ants to food or to the nest.

On guard When a nest is attacked, workers rush to defend it. They attack in great numbers, biting the enemy with their powerful jaws.

COMPOST FACTORY Leaf-cutter ants snip fragments from leaves and carry them back to their nest. There, the fragments are chewed and inserted into mounds of fungus. The fungus breaks down the leaf fibers into food for the ants.

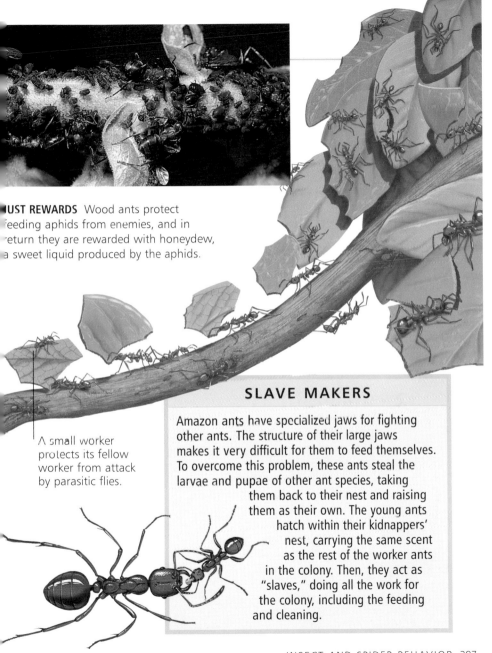

JUST REWARDS Wood ants protect feeding aphids from enemies, and in return they are rewarded with honeydew, a sweet liquid produced by the aphids.

A small worker protects its fellow worker from attack by parasitic flies.

SLAVE MAKERS

Amazon ants have specialized jaws for fighting other ants. The structure of their large jaws makes it very difficult for them to feed themselves. To overcome this problem, these ants steal the larvae and pupae of other ant species, taking them back to their nest and raising them as their own. The young ants hatch within their kidnappers' nest, carrying the same scent as the rest of the worker ants in the colony. Then, they act as "slaves," doing all the work for the colony, including the feeding and cleaning.

Fantastic Journeys

■ At certain times of the year, the air may be teeming with insects on the move. Some are escaping adverse seasonal conditions; others are on their way to colonize new habitats.

AERIAL EPICS

Many butterflies and moths undertake long journeys to escape the cold weather in winter and to find favorable feeding places in warmer climes. The painted lady butterfly occurs in temperate and tropical regions. Some specimens have been seen over the Atlantic and Indian oceans, more than 500 miles (800 km) from land. During warmer years, they may even cross the Arctic Circle.

Compass bearings Most butterflies are believed to navigate using the Sun. They stay at a constant angle to the Sun, following a curved arc as it moves across the sky.

The major compass cue for migrating moths is the moon. On nights when the moon is not

DRIVER'S SEAT A colony of hundreds of thousands of driver ants moves across the forest floor in search of a more favorable nest site. The eggs, larvae, and queen are carried and fed as they go.

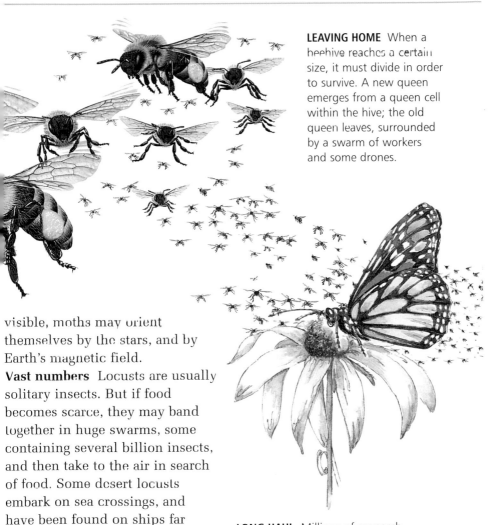

LEAVING HOME When a beehive reaches a certain size, it must divide in order to survive. A new queen emerges from a queen cell within the hive; the old queen leaves, surrounded by a swarm of workers and some drones.

visible, moths may orient themselves by the stars, and by Earth's magnetic field.

Vast numbers Locusts are usually solitary insects. But if food becomes scarce, they may band together in huge swarms, some containing several billion insects, and then take to the air in search of food. Some desert locusts embark on sea crossings, and have been found on ships far from land. Others undertake journeys of 3,000 miles (5,000 km) in five days or less.

LONG HAUL Millions of monarch butterflies travel thousands of miles from North America to Mexico to avoid the freezing winter conditions.

Spiders on the Move

■ Unlike most insects that rely on their wings to carry them to new habitats, spiders and other arachnids use different techniques to help them leave the nest and colonize new lands.

HITCHHIKERS

The spiderlings of many species use threads as sails to launch themselves into the wind from the tops of plants. Others use a technique called ballooning to hitch a ride on the wind. The spiderling stands on tiptoe in an exposed position, such as the end of a branch. It faces the wind and squeezes out a droplet of silk. Pulled by the wind, the droplet expands into threads, and the spiderling floats away. Some spiders travel hundreds of miles in this way, carried by wind currents. Some have been found during aerial surveys at altitudes of up to 3 miles (5 km).

Lucky landings Because of their small size and relative lightness, most spiders are afforded a safe landing after their aerial journey. However, many perish when the breeze drops them in adverse environments, such as the ocean, where they either drown, or become food for fishes.

Easy riders Other arachnids employ different methods to move them from place to place. Pseudoscorpions and mites attach themselves to flying insects or birds, or to the fur of a passing mammal. Wherever the host goes, its cargo travels also.

ON A THREAD The unique "ballooning" technique used by some spiderlings allows them to be carried away on silken threads.

RAGLINE DROP Some spiderlings leave their nest by climbing to a high perch and dropping a dragline. When the dragline breaks, the spider drifts gently to the ground.

INSECTS, SPIDERS, AND US

An investigation of the relationship between people and insects and spiders.

Friend
or Foe?

CROP DESTRUCTION

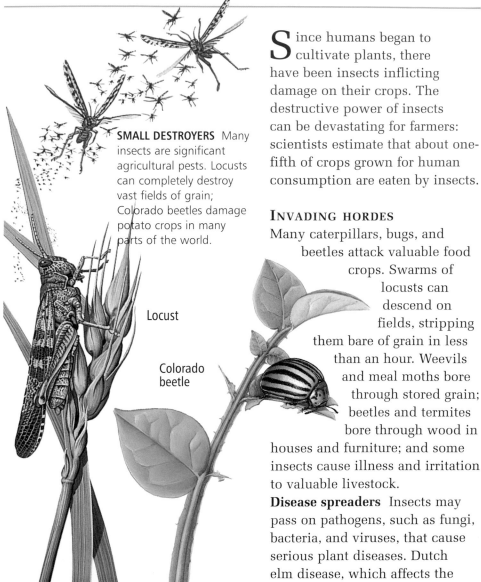

SMALL DESTROYERS Many insects are significant agricultural pests. Locusts can completely destroy vast fields of grain; Colorado beetles damage potato crops in many parts of the world.

Locust

Colorado beetle

Since humans began to cultivate plants, there have been insects inflicting damage on their crops. The destructive power of insects can be devastating for farmers: scientists estimate that about one-fifth of crops grown for human consumption are eaten by insects.

INVADING HORDES

Many caterpillars, bugs, and beetles attack valuable food crops. Swarms of locusts can descend on fields, stripping them bare of grain in less than an hour. Weevils and meal moths bore through stored grain; beetles and termites bore through wood in houses and furniture; and some insects cause illness and irritation to valuable livestock.

Disease spreaders Insects may pass on pathogens, such as fungi, bacteria, and viruses, that cause serious plant diseases. Dutch elm disease, which affects the

American elm tree, is transmitted by the elm bark beetle. This beetle carries on its body the spores of the fungi that cause the disease.
Skin deep The kind of damage inflicted on a plant depends largely on the mouthparts the invading insect possesses. Chewing is the most visible form of destruction, but piercing and sucking of plant fluids probably inflicts the most devastation.

DESERT STORM A swarm of desert locusts may contain more than 40 billion individuals. Usually solitary insects, locusts gather in huge swarms when food is scarce, eating tons of green plant matter.

Many insects damage plants and fruits through egg-laying scars and nest building. Discoloration caused by scale insects can also reduce the commercial value of many fruit and vegetable crops.

DISEASE CARRIERS

I nsects carry many diseases that are harmful to humans and animals. As a result, disease-carrying insects have played an integral role in shaping human history. Until the widespread use of insecticides, and the development of antibiotics and inoculations, twice as many soldiers were struck down by insect-transmitted diseases than were killed during armed conflict.

WORLD SHAPERS

The most serious disease spread by insects is malaria. Female mosquitoes feed on animal blood, and also carry the malaria parasite, called *Plasmodium*, in their salivary glands. Throughout history, malaria has had a major impact on human health. Today, it remains the number one killer of humans throughout the world, and is still responsible for killing between two to four million people every year. Scientists estimate that about half the world's population, mostly in the tropics, either have malaria or are in danger of contracting it. Other

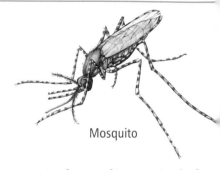

Mosquito

mosquito-borne diseases include yellow fever, dengue fever, and encephalitis. An outbreak of yellow fever in the late 1800s delayed the building of the Panama Canal and killed approximately 18,000 workers.

Lice, mites, and ticks Lice are ectoparasites and most cause irritation and blood loss to their chosen host. Human body lice can also transmit epidemic typhus, especially in times of population stress, and during war and famine.

Dust mites feed on the dead skin and hair cells humans shed

PROBLEM FEEDERS Dust mites (top right) cause allergic reactions, including asthma. Deer ticks (bottom right) carry the bacteria that cause Lyme disease. Symptoms include rashes and fever.

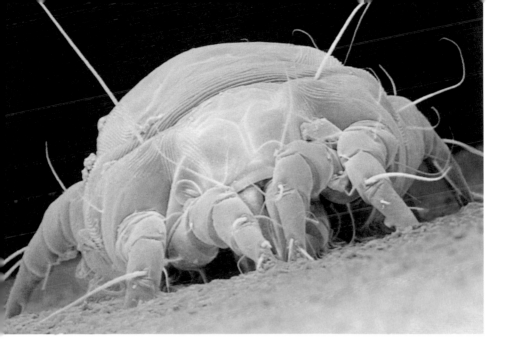

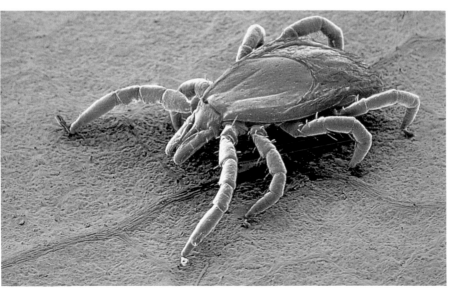

in their thousands every day. Some people are allergic to dust mite droppings, and may suffer from asthma if they inhale them. Some mite species cause severe cases of dermatitis and other allergic reactions.

Many ticks transmit serious diseases to poultry, cattle, sheep, and horses, as well as to domestic pets, such as dogs. They may also carry viruses that cause encephalitis, tick typhus, and Lyme disease in humans.

Black death World epidemics of bubonic plague killed millions of people and, as a consequence, changed the structure of society. The plague, or black death, swept through Europe in the Middle Ages. Between 1346 and 1350, one-third of the population died from this disease, which was spread by fleas living on the black rats of Asia.

Flies on us At present, flies are by far the greatest disease-transmitters of all. House flies passively spread many illnesses, including typhoid, cholera, and gastroenteritis. They walk over feces, rubbish, and other waste products, spreading germs as they go.

The tsetse fly of Africa spreads the trypanosome parasite that causes the debilitating disease known as sleeping sickness. The flies bite infected animals and then pass it on to humans.

FATAL FLEAS Outbreaks of bubonic plague devastated the population of Europe in the 1300s. This 15th century painting from the Toggenberg bible depicts patients suffering from the disease. Fleas were the major vector, feeding on infected rats, and then biting humans.

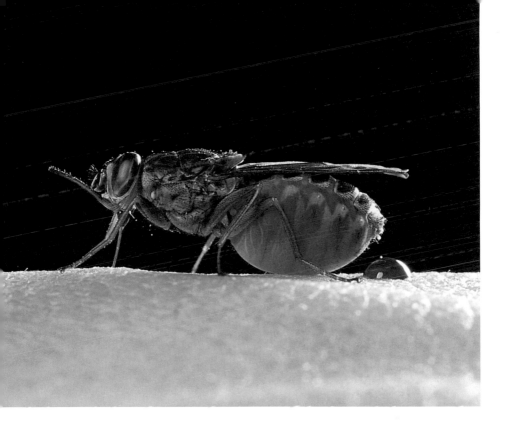

FIRST BLOOD The tsetse fly (above), which feeds on the blood of cattle and humans, can gorge itself until it is hugely swollen. It spreads sleeping sickness disease that affects the nervous system of animals and humans. Ticks (right) often feed in clusters on host animals. They transmit many diseases, including encephalitis and Lyme disease.

ENDANGERED SPECIES

Insects and spiders are vital components of our global ecosystems. In fact, most ecosystems would cease to function without insect and spider species. Earth's biodiversity will be changed forever if humans continue to change and destroy their habitat.

WAR OF THE WORLDS

Chemical insecticides, herbicides, and fertilizers indirectly threaten biodiversity by contaminating air and groundwater. Insecticides kill

COLLECTING JEWELS Many birdwing butterflies are highly prized by collectors. This, coupled with shrinking habitat, has seen the disappearance of many species.

not only the targeted species, but many harmless species as well. Eventually, plants and animals that rely on these insects for pollination, and as a food source, are also adversely affected.

Urban crawl The pressures of rural and urban development have taken their toll. For example, the Texan tooth cave spider is under threat because many of the caves it inhabited have been filled in.

Worth saving Insect and spiders are worth preserving. The best way to protect insect and spider diversity is to preserve habitat. Some countries have also introduced legislation to protect international trade in vulnerable species.

CREEPING THREAT The collection of spiders for pets has endangered some species. The Mexican red-kneed tarantula (left) is now protected by law.

Good Friends

VENOMS AND MEDICINES

Venoms are complex combinations of chemicals that, drop for drop, are among the most toxic substances known. Some insects and many arachnids produce these compounds inside modified salivary glands or vestigial reproductive organs. To help them subdue their prey, and to protect themselves from enemies, they inject their poison using their fangs, stingers, or piercing mouthparts.

DANGEROUS COCKTAIL

Venoms have many effects on the body systems of animals. Some of the most common symptoms are pain, paralysis, interference with blood clotting, and the breakdown of heart and lung tissue.

Male Sydney funnel-web spiders are the only male spiders with venomous bites that are dangerous to humans. Dogs, cats, and other mammals appear to be relatively resistant to their poison. A funnel-web's bite can cause extreme illness, or even death, in a relatively short time. Before an antivenin was developed, many children died from this spider's bite.

The saliva of the Australian paralysis tick contains a toxin that causes progressive paralysis in some humans and a severe allergic reaction in others.

ANT POWER

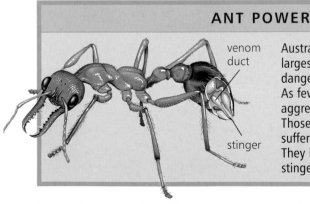

venom duct

stinger

Australia's bulldog ants are the largest, and among the most dangerous ants, in the world. As few as 30 stings from these aggressive ants can kill a human. Those allergic to the venom may suffer life-threatening reactions also. They inject their poison using a stinger on their abdomen.

The North African scorpion is the most deadly of all scorpions. Its venom attacks the nervous system and may cause death within minutes of a sting. **Antidote solution** Venom is collected from spiders, ticks and other poisonous creatures to help develop medicines, or antivenins, to counteract the effects of toxic bites. Antivenins are available for some scorpion, ant, spider, and bee venoms.

GOOD BITE To produce an antivenin, funnel-web spiders are first milked for their venom. The venom is injected into a bite-resistant mammal and the antibodies it produces are purified for use.

Good use Venom research is helping in the development of medicines for illnesses, such as cancer and multiple sclerosis. Honeybee venom may be used to alleviate the symptoms of arthritis and other inflammatory diseases.

USEFUL PRODUCERS

Humans rely on insects to provide them with a wide range of useful products. Insects make honey and wax, oils and silks, natural medicines and dyes. In some countries, insects provide a valuable protein food source for humans. Insects are important in crop production as plant-pollinators. Insects are also useful subjects in scientific research.

SOFT TOUCH Silkworm caterpillars are fed a diet of fresh mulberry leaves. When they pupate, their cocoons are carefully tended by silk farm workers.

SWEET AS HONEY

As well as being Earth's major pollinators, honeybees produce valuable honey and beeswax. In order to produce 1 pound (500 g) of honey, bees may fly more than 5,600 miles (9,000 km). A single hive can produce 110 pounds (50 kg) of honey per year, which means they have traveled more than 615,000 miles (1 million km in total.

Weaving threads Silk is made from the material that silkworm caterpillars use to spin their cocoon. Although commercial silk is produced by a number of species, most comes from the cocoons of the domesticated commercial silkworm moth from Asia. This moth is now used in silk farms all over the world.

When the caterpillars are ready to pupate, they produce saliva that solidifies into thread when it comes into contact with the air. Silkworm caterpillars take approximately three days to spin their cocoons. Once finished, the the cocoons are baked in an oven to kill the insects inside. They are

IN THE BOX Beekeepers place the queen honeybee inside the hive. Honeybee workers seek the queen out, relocating to the same hive to attend to her needs.

SILKEN THREADS Each silk moth cocoon (left) is made from a single silk thread more than 1/2 mile (1 km) long. Silk thread is the strongest natural fiber.

then dropped in boiling water, causing them to unravel into single strands. The single strands are twisted together to make silk thread, and this is then woven into cloth.

Useful variety Several other insects make products that are important to humans. Certain dyes are produced by scale insects—the Asian lac insect, for example, produces substances used in the manufacture of varnishes, such as shellac.

Control agents Predacious insects are now widely used as biological control agents, particularly for insecticide-free crop protection and pest control in domestic gardens. Ladybugs may control aphids that are harmful to many garden plants and vegetable crops. Dung beetles help to decompose the droppings of domestic stock.

Pollination Partnership

■ Insects and flowering plants evolved side by side over millions of years. During this time, some insects became plant-eaters or sap-suckers; others struck valuable partnerships with plants to become their primary pollinators. Many plants are unable to reproduce without the services of their insect partners.

FREQUENT FLIERS
Most flowering plants rely on insects to carry their pollen from one flower to another. Insects, such as honeybees, visit flowers

FLOWER FEAST Beetles carry pollen on their bodies as they move from flower to flower in order to feed. They are attracted to flowers by color and scent.

in search of sugary sweet nectar and pollen. A dusting of pollen grains gets caught on the bee's body as it brushes against the flower's stamens. Some of this pollen rubs off on the stigma of the next flower the bee visits, fertilizing the plant in a process called cross-pollination. Bees rely on the plant's bounty as a food source for the colony; in turn, the plant relies on cross-pollination to bear viable fruit and seeds.

Some plants have evolved flowers that mimic the shape and coloration of a female wasp. When the male attempts to mate with the flower, it receives a dusting of pollen instead.
Bearing fruit One in every three bites we eat is produced thanks to the services of an insect or some other pollinator. Some of the valuable crops that require insect pollination include apples, pears, onions, and potatoes.

SPECIAL DELIVERY
Honeybees deliver pollen to flowers as they collect food for their hive.

Insect and Spider Studies

The best way to understand insects and spiders is to observe them firsthand. Taking the time to study their everyday lives can be a rewarding experience. The most important tools of observation are your eyes and ears. Learn to look and listen closely—the smallest details are often the most fascinating.

UP CLOSE A plastic or glass jar with holes punched in the lid makes a good observation chamber. Provide some moisture using a damp tissue in a dish, and add leaves or twigs. When you have finished, release the insect where you originally found it.

INSECT COLLECTING

Insects and spiders can be observed in their natural habitat, or they can be collected for closer inspection before being returned to their environment. Take a few minutes to listen and look carefully: detecting the presence of cleverly camouflaged animals, such as katydids, may depend almost entirely on aural signs.

Closer look To extend your vision, a hand lens and magnifying glass are valuable pieces of field equipment. A 35 mm single lens reflex camera (SLR) may assist you in recording your observations. A macro lens (50–100 mm) will help ensure well-focussed results. **Identifying insects** Once you have collected interesting specimens, identifying them, especially to order level, can be relatively easy with some practice and an appropriate field guide. **Welcome visitors** One of the best ways to observe insects and spiders is to attract them to the garden. A diverse range of habitats and vegetation will attract a diverse range of insects.

LOOK AND NOTE A magnifying glass can help to zero in on intricate details. Sketching is a satisfying way to record your observations.

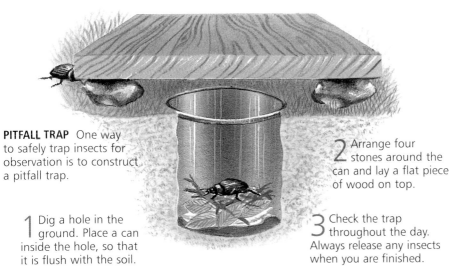

PITFALL TRAP One way to safely trap insects for observation is to construct a pitfall trap.

1 Dig a hole in the ground. Place a can inside the hole, so that it is flush with the soil.

2 Arrange four stones around the can and lay a flat piece of wood on top.

3 Check the trap throughout the day. Always release any insects when you are finished.

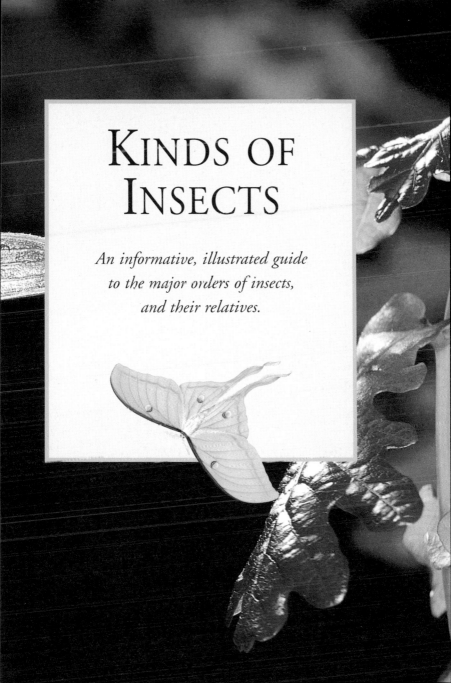

KINDS OF INSECTS

*An informative, illustrated guide
to the major orders of insects,
and their relatives.*

USING THE GUIDE

This guide gives informative and detailed descriptions of the world's major insect and arachnid groups. It is divided into two parts and five main chapters. Each chapter covers an important group of orders, each of which have key characteristics in common. Most entries are arranged by order, although suborders are included, when required, to increase clarity.

The characteristics, life cycle, diet, and habitat for an order or suborder are outlined in each entry. With more than 1,000 families worldwide, each entry includes descriptions of representative or well-known families only.

Illustrations and photographs show the form, coloration, and sometimes behavioral aspects of selected species.

Within the chapters, orders are listed in taxonomic sequence.

The sample page opposite shows the typical layout of an order entry, and is annotated to show the main features.

The order to which the families belong.

The number of families in the order. When a suborder further defines an order, it is listed here.

The common name of each order or suborder.

The approximate number of known species worldwide within the order.

The range of body lengths or wingspans for each order.

Snapshot panels give vital at-a-glance information about each order, including diagnostic features, diet, life cycle, habitat, and distribution.

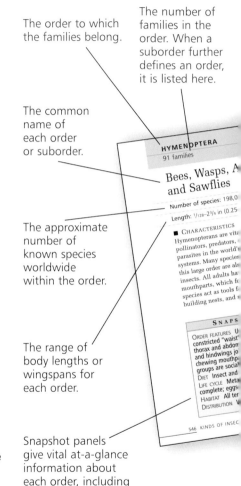

HYMENOPTERA
91 families

Bees, Wasps, A
and Sawflies

Number of species: 198,0
Length: $^1/_{128}$–$2^3/_4$ in (0.25

■ CHARACTERISTICS
Hymenopterans are vita
pollinators, predators,
parasites in the world's
systems. Many species
this large order are als
insects. All adults hav
mouthparts, which fo
species act as tools f
building nests, and

S N A P S

ORDER FEATURES U
constricted "waist"
thorax and abdom
and hindwings jo
chewing mouthpa
groups are socia
DIET Insect and
LIFE CYCLE Meta
complete; eggs
HABITAT All ter
DISTRIBUTION W

546 KINDS OF INSEC

Photographs and illustrations of representative families within the order are a visual aid to the text descriptions.

...IATOR
...ed mining bee is a vital
...many spring flowers. Pollen
... its body hairs as it feeds.

...t have two pairs of
...ous wings that join
...with small hooks during
...d large compound eyes.
...e exception of sawflies,
...ax and abdomen are
...d by a constricted "waist,"
...a pedicel. The ovipositor
...ale bees, ants, and social
...s has evolved into a stinger
...associated poison glands.
...enopterans range in size
...the fairyfly wasp, so small
...uld fly through the eye of a
...dle, to the spider-eating wasp,
...asuring 2¾ inches (70 mm).

LIFE CYCLE AND DIET
...l hymenopterans undergo
...omplete metamorphosis.
...ertilized eggs produce females

NO SWEAT
Also called sweat bees,
members of the family
Halictidae brood their eggs
underground, within cells
that are waterproofed with
a special bee secretion.

LEAF-CUTTERS
Female leaf cutter bees clip
out circular pieces of leaf
with their jaws. These are
taken back to their nests
where they are fashioned
into tube-shaped cells for
the eggs and larvae.

WINGED INSECTS 547

Captions provide extra information on a representative species within an order.

Main text describes the principal characteristics of the order or suborder. Subsequent sub-headings and text describe the characteristics of well-known or representative families.

Primitive Wingless Insects

Proturans

Number of species: 400

Length: $1/64$–$1/16$ in (0.5–2 mm)

Springtails

Number of species: 6,500

Length: $1/32$–$5/16$ in (1–8 mm)

Diplurans

Number of species: 800

Length: $1/4$–$1 1/4$ in (6–30 mm)

■ PROTURANS

Characteristics Proturans are primitive, pale, wingless, and blind. They do not possess antennae. The front pair of legs have a sensory function. The piercing and sucking mouthparts are concealed inside a pouch and are protruded when feeding. **Habitat** Proturans occur worldwide, and are found in moist soil, moss, leaf mold, in decaying wood, and under bark.

■ SPRINGTAILS

Characteristics These pale, wingless insects have elongate or oval bodies. They have a distinctive jumping organ, called a furcula, which helps them "spring" their way out of danger. **Habitat** Springtails live in soil and leaf litter, under bark, and in rotting wood. Some species live on the surface of freshwater ponds or along the seashore.

■ DIPLURANS

Characteristics Diplurans are slender, soft-bodied primitive insects with two abdominal

SNAPSHOT

ORDER FEATURES Pale and wingless; diplurans, proturans, and some springtails lack eyes; elongate body; springtails have furcula
DIET Insect and plant matter
LIFE CYCLE Metamorphosis is incomplete; eggs laid in soil
HABITAT Damp, cool conditions, including soil, leaf litter, moss, in fungi, and around ponds
DISTRIBUTION Worldwide

LINKS IN THE CHAIN
Springtails are among the most abundant of all the insect orders. They are vital components of the food chain.

sensory "tails" or cerci. They have long, segmented antennae and biting mouthparts that are contained within a pouch. Eggs are laid in soil and sometimes females guard their brood.
Habitat They live in soil, under rocks, and in rotting vegetation.

SOIL CREEPER
This dipluran is common in Europe and Asia, and is usually found pushing its way through rotting vegetation and soil.

ARCHAEOGNATHA
2 families

Bristletails

Number of species: 350

Length: Up to 1/2 in (12 mm)

THYSANURA
4 families

Silverfish

Number of species: 370

Length: 1/16–3/4 in (2–20 mm)

SNAPSHOT

ORDER FEATURES Wingless, simple mouthparts, compound eyes

DIET Starchy material, including paper, flour, textiles, and glue

LIFE CYCLE Develop without obvious metamorphosis; continuous lifetime molting

HABITAT Trees, under rocks, in leaf-litter, houses, and nests

DISTRIBUTION Worldwide, mainly in warm areas

■ BRISTLETAILS

Characteristics Bristletails are small, wingless insects, often covered in dark brown or gray scales. In side view, they have a humped-back appearance. They have compound eyes and three ocelli. There are three long tails at the end of the abdomen. Underneath the abdomen are projections called styles, which may help bristletails to move.
Life cycle, diet, and habitat Bristletails molt continuously throughout their lives. There is no change in the insect's shape, and they continue to molt even after they reach sexual maturity. Females lay batches of eggs in small cracks. Bristletails feed on algae, lichen, and other plant material. They live in leaf litter and rotting vegetable matter.

■ SILVERFISH

Characteristics Silverfish are wingless, flat bodied, and sometimes covered in gray or brown scales. They have simple mouthparts and compound eyes, although some species have no

ON THE ROCKS

Bristletails can jump small distances by flicking their abdomen against rocks. Some are common along rocky coasts.

eyes at all. They have three tails projecting from their abdomen.

Life cycle diet, and habitat

Silverfish molt throughout their life, even after they have reached sexual maturity, with no obvious change in shape. Females lay their eggs in crevices. They eat book bindings, flour, and damp cloth. They live in warm areas, under stones, in trees, and in caves. Domestic species are considered pests.

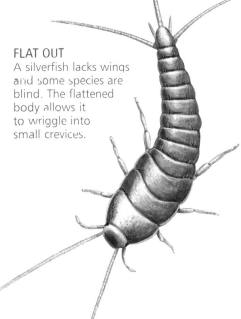

FLAT OUT

A silverfish lacks wings and some species are blind. The flattened body allows it to wriggle into small crevices.

Primitive Winged Insects

Mayflies

Number of species: 2,500

Length: $^5/_{32}$–1$^1/_4$ in (4–34 mm)

■ CHARACTERISTICS

Mayflies are the only insects that molt after they have functional wings. They have soft bodies, long legs, and two pairs of large, triangular wings that cannot be folded back; instead, the wings are held together above the body when the mayfly is at rest. Adults have vestigial mouthparts and therefore do not feed.

SNAPSHOT

ORDER FEATURES **Usually two pairs of triangular wings, long legs, long abdominal tails**
DIET **Adults do not feed; nymphs eat plants and animals**
LIFE CYCLE **Metamorphosis is incomplete; eggs laid in water**
HABITAT **Near streams, rivers, ponds, and lakes; sometimes near brackish water**
DISTRIBUTION **Worldwide**

■ LIFE CYCLE AND DIET

Mayflies mate in huge swarms, usually at dawn or dusk. Females lay their eggs by dipping their abdomen into the water. They lay between 500 and 3,000 eggs. Metamorphosis is incomplete. Nymphs may go through up to 50 molts and live for up to two years in the nymphal stage. They feed on organic material. When fully grown, they rise to the water's surface and molt into a sub-imago—a form that has the appearance of an adult, but with dull-colored wings. Within one hour or several days, the sub-imago molts into a shiny-winged adult. Adults of some species live for one or two days; others have a life span of only a few hours.

■ HABITAT

Mayflies live near streams, rivers, ponds, and lakes. Some species live near brackish water.

MAY OR MAY NOT

Many mayfly species are becoming rare because pollution levels in rivers and streams are affecting mayfly nymphs.

Damselflies and Dragonflies

Number of species: 5,500

Wingspan: $3/4$–$6^3/4$ in (20–170 mm)

■ CHARACTERISTICS
Damselflies and dragonflies are the only surviving representatives of the ancient flying insects. They have large compound eyes, three ocelli, biting mouthparts, and short, bristle-like antennae. The long, cylindrical abdomen has short cerci. They have two pairs of large wings with many veins. The forewings and hindwings are roughly the same size. Damselflies have a broad head with eyes widely spaced; dragonflies have a more rounded head and less space between the eyes. Both beat their forewings and hindwings independently during flight. The hindwings beat at a slightly different speed, increasing flight stability. Dragonflies are strong fliers and active hunters. They hunt by forming a basket with their legs to scoop up prey during flight. Damselflies are weaker fliers; they sit and wait for prey to come within reach.

■ LIFE CYCLE AND DIET
Males transfer sperm from a genital opening on the ninth segment of the abdomen to a storage organ on the third segment. During mating, the male clasps the female behind

---

S N A P S H O T

ORDER FEATURES **Large eyes, two pairs of membranous wings**
DIET **Other insects**
LIFE CYCLE **Metamorphosis is incomplete; eggs laid in water and on aquatic plants**
HABITAT **Near water. Aquatic nymphs have abdominal gills**
DISTRIBUTION **Worldwide**
REMARK **Despite common beliefs, dragonflies do not sting**

WINGS TOGETHER
At rest, damselflies hold their wings together above their body; dragonflies tend to hold their wings outstretched.

the head, while the female bends her abdomen to connect to the genitalia of the male. Sperm is transferred into the female's sperm storage organ. Eggs are deposited inside water plants. Members of this order develop by incomplete metamorphosis. The aquatic nymphs have feathery gills projecting from their abdomen. They feed using modified mouthparts that they shoot forward to grasp prey.

■ HABITAT
Most species are found near fast- and slow-flowing water.

SEEING ALL
The huge compound eyes of dragonflies and damselflies allow them incredible precision when hunting, even at dusk.

BLUE HUE
The exquisite blue color of many dragonflies results from tiny, light-refracting granules on the surface of their body.

SEEING RED
Some male dragonflies develop strong colors as a visual signal to females during breeding.

Winged Insects

Cockroaches

Number of species: 4,000

Length: 5/16–4 in (8–100 mm)

■ CHARACTERISTICS
Cockroaches have a tough, leathery covering and a flattened, oval shape. This shape enables them to scuttle into narrow crevices. They have two pairs of wings; the forewings are toughened and the hindwings are large and membranous. Many species have a shield covering the head, called a pronotum. They are usually brown, red–brown, or dark in color. Most have long, slender antennae. Cockroaches are highly sensitive to vibration. They are fast runners, and some exude or spray toxic chemicals to deter predators. The Madagascan hissing cockroach startles prey by pushing air out of its spiracles to create a hissing sound.

■ LIFE CYCLE AND DIET
Both males and females exude pheromones to signal and attract potential mates. Females lay up

PERFECT SCAVENGERS
Although cockroaches will eat any food scraps, they can survive without food for months.

FEEL THE NOISE
Long antennae and sensitive leg spines can detect minute vibrations.

to 50 eggs at a time. These are often enclosed within a hardened egg case, which protrudes from the female's abdomen until it is dropped when the eggs are ready to hatch.

Cockroaches eat mainly decaying organic matter, as well as bird and mammal droppings. Pest species will eat anything from bread to shoe polish.

■ HABITAT
Nearly all cockroaches live in tropical climates. Some are common household pests.

RAINFOREST ROACH
This large wood cockroach lives in a Costa Rican rainforest.

Mantids

Number of species: 2,000

Length: 3/4–6 in (20–150 mm)

CREEPING THREAT
A mantid's shape
and coloration help
to conceal it from
its victim.

■ CHARACTERISTICS
Mantids derive their common
name, "praying mantis," from the
way they hold their front legs
together, as if they were praying.
All mantids have large wings and
a triangular head equipped with
large forward-facing eyes.
Binocular vision means they can
calculate distances with pinpoint
accuracy, enabling them to seize
prey in a split second with their
strong front legs. Unlike other
insects, mantids can turn their
head to look behind their body.

■ LIFE CYCLE AND DIET
Mantids develop by incomplete
metamorphosis. Females lay their
eggs inside a papery case that
they then attach to twigs. Some
species guard their egg case
from predators. Mantids eat a
wide range of prey, including
lizards and frogs. They lie in wait
for their prey, using camouflage
to conceal themselves.

■ HABITAT
They live mainly in warmer
regions, on foliage and flowers.

BIG BODIES

Most female praying mantises (above) are larger than their male counterparts.

SURPRISE ATTACK

Poised to strike, this orchid mantis blends in with its flowery surroundings.

SNAPSHOT

ORDER FEATURES Triangular, mobile head; large, forward-pointing eyes; front legs modified for catching and subduing prey

DIET Wide range of insects, spiders, even lizards and frogs

LIFE CYCLE Metamorphosis is incomplete; eggs laid in egg case

HABITAT On vegetation

DISTRIBUTION Worldwide, especially in tropical regions

Termites

Number of species: 2,750

Length: $^5/_{32}$–$^5/_8$ in (4–14 mm)

DEMOLITION SQUAD
Termites work in darkness, eating wood from the inside. The damage is often hidden until the wood begins to collapse.

■ CHARACTERISTICS

Termites are social insects. They live in permanent colonies where individuals are differentiated into distinct castes. Typically, they are soft-bodied, pale in color, wingless, with short antennae, chewing mandibles, and reduced eyes. The king and queen have an oval head and two pairs of long wings. Soldier termites are sterile and have larger heads than worker termites.

■ LIFE CYCLE AND DIET

Termites develop through a process of incomplete metamorphosis. They build nests, ranging in size from small structures in trees to extensive underground constructions. A queen termite may produce thousands of eggs each day. Termites are one of the few insects able to digest cellulose.

■ HABITAT

They live in various habitats, including soil, trees, and timber.

S N A P S H O T

ORDER FEATURES **Social insects; pale body, mainly wingless, short antennae; differences between castes**

DIET **Rotting or dead wood, wood fibers, crops**

LIFE CYCLE **Metamorphosis is incomplete; eggs laid by queen**

HABITAT **Tree, mud, and underground nests**

DISTRIBUTION **Mostly tropical**

MUD SPIRES
The structure of a large termite nest allows air circulation that can maintain a virtually constant temperature.

HEAD BANGER
Damp-wood termites bang their heads against the walls of the nest, sending warning vibrations to other members of the colony.

ZORAPTERA

1 family

Zorapterans

Number of species: 29

Length: Less than $3/16$ in (5 mm)

GRYLLOBLATTODEA

1 family

Ice insects

Number of species: 25

Length: $1/2$–$1^1/4$ in (12–30 mm)

SNAPSHOT

ORDER FEATURES Small and wingless; downward-pointing (Zoraptera) or forward-pointing (Grylloblattodea) mouthparts

DIET Plant matter, live prey

LIFE CYCLE Metamorphosis is incomplete

HABITAT Rocks, snow, ice, caves

DISTRIBUTION Worldwide, except Australia (Zoraptera); Northern Hemisphere (Grylloblattodea)

■ ZORAPTERANS

Characteristics Also known as angel insects, the tiny, termite-like adults of this order display two forms. One form is pale, wingless, and has no eyes; the other form is darker in color, has eyes, three ocelli, and two pairs of wings. Both forms have downward-pointing mouthparts, similar in appearance to grasshoppers and crickets.

Life cycle, diet, and habitat Zorapterans undergo incomplete metamorphosis. Eggs are laid in leaf litter or rotting wood. Nymphs differ in appearance, depending on whether they develop into winged or wingless adults. Both adults and nymphs eat small arthropods and fungal threads. They are found in leaf litter, rotting wood, and under tree bark. Zorapterans live worldwide, except Australia.

■ ICE INSECTS

Characteristics These small, wingless, pale brown or gray insects are adapted to alpine conditions. They are also known

as rock crawlers, because they are found under stones and on open ground. Their small head has simple, forward-facing mandibles. The eyes may be quite small or completely absent. Ice insects have slender cerci and thread-like antennae.

Life cycle, diet, and habitat Ice insects undergo incomplete metamorphosis. Eggs are laid in rotten wood, moss, and in soil. It

may take nymphs more than five years to develop to adulthood. Adults eat plant matter and also hunt for insect prey. They live in the cooler mountainous areas of the Northern Hemisphere.

DERMAPTERA
10 families

Earwigs

Number of species: 1,900

Length: $^9/_{32}$–2 in (7–50 mm)

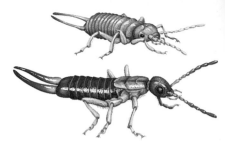

ADULT AND NYMPH
Earwig nymphs molt up to five times before becoming adults. They increase in size, but essentially look like their parents.

■ CHARACTERISTICS
Earwigs are flattened insects with short forewings that cover and protect the larger, fan-shaped hindwings. The abdomen is segmented and mobile. At the end of the abdomen is a pair of pincer-like cerci. The cerci are usually straight in females and curved in males. They have a mainly defensive function, but they can give a relatively painless pinch. Some earwigs are pests of flowers and fruits. Many species produce foul-smelling chemicals to deter predators.

■ LIFE CYCLE AND DIET
Earwigs develop by incomplete metamorphosis. Most females lay eggs in soil or leaf litter; some give birth to live nymphs. Female earwigs protect their eggs and young by licking them clean and guarding them from predators. They may also feed the hatched nymphs by regurgitating a portion of their own meal.

■ HABITAT
They are found in soil and leaf litter, under bark, and in crevices.

S N A P S H O T

ORDER FEATURES **Flat, elongate body; segmented abdomen bearing pincer-like cerci**
DIET **Plant matter and small insects, such as caterpillars**
LIFE CYCLE **Metamorphosis is incomplete; eggs laid in soil**
HABITAT **Leaf litter, sand, debris, riverbanks, crevices**
DISTRIBUTION **Worldwide, in warmer regions**

FEEL THE PINCH
The pincer-like cerci on the abdomen of male earwigs are curved. They are used in prey capture and may also have a defensive function.

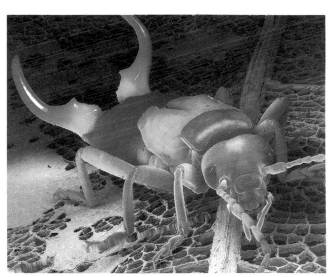

FLOWER POWER
The European earwig is a well-known pest of crops and garden plants, particularly flowers.

Stoneflies

Number of species: 2,000

Length: $3/16$–$2^1/_2$ in (5–65 mm)

■ CHARACTERISTICS
Stoneflies are soft-bodied, slender insects that are usually dull brown to dark brown, although some are pale yellow in color. Most have long cerci on the abdomen and all species have two pairs of similar-size transparent wings. When resting, they fold their wings tightly around their body, giving the rounded appearance of a stone. Most stoneflies have simple mouthparts, although some short-lived, non-feeding adults have none at all.

■ LIFE CYCLE AND DIET
Males court females by vibrating the underside of their abdomen on the ground. Females lay masses of eggs in water, sometimes formed into a sticky ball. Most nymphs live an aquatic existence, feeding on algae and detritus. They have two, long filaments on their abdomen. Nymphs may molt 30 times and take up to 5 years to become adults. Adults usually emerge from the water in midwinter or early spring. Many adults are short-lived and do not feed.

■ HABITAT
Most prefer cool climates, and are always found near water.

S N A P S H O T

ORDER FEATURES Flat, slender bodies, long cerci; dull coloration; transparent wings
DIET Plant matter, small insects, such as caterpillars
LIFE CYCLE Metamorphosis is incomplete; eggs laid in water
HABITAT Near lakes, springs, on vegetation near running water
DISTRIBUTION Worldwide, but mostly Northern Hemisphere

STONE'S THROW
At rest, and usually close to a stream, adult stoneflies roll their transparent wings tightly around their body.

Grasshoppers and Crickets

Number of species: 20,000

Length: 3/16–3 1/4 in (5–85 mm)

■ CHARACTERISTICS

These large and easily recognizable insects include grasshoppers, crickets, mole-crickets, cave crickets, and katydids. They all have chewing mouthparts and highly modified hindlegs for jumping. Most have small, tough forewings covering the larger, membranous hind-wings. Many species "sing" by rubbing pegs on the hindlegs against hard ridges along the wings. These mating songs are used to attract females.

■ LIFE CYCLE AND DIET

All species undergo incomplete metamorphosis. Most lay eggs on the ground, in soil, on bark, or on vegetation. They eat plant and animal matter.

■ HABITAT

Orthopterans are found in a wide range of terrestrial habitats, including deserts, grasslands, forests, caves, and underground.

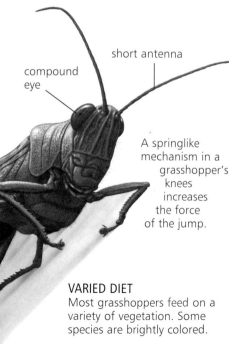

short antenna

compound eye

A springlike mechanism in a grasshopper's knees increases the force of the jump.

muscular hindleg

VARIED DIET
Most grasshoppers feed on a variety of vegetation. Some species are brightly colored.

Snapshot

ORDER FEATURES **Chewing mouthparts; strong hindlegs adapted for jumping**

DIET **Plant and animal matter**

LIFE CYCLE **Metamorphosis is incomplete; eggs laid in soil, under bark, or in detritus**

HABITAT **Grasslands, woodlands, underground, on vegetation**

DISTRIBUTION **Worldwide, in subtropical and temperate areas**

■ GRASSHOPPERS

Characteristics Grasshoppers have relatively short antennae. Females are usually larger than males and they do not have a conspicuous ovipositor. Males sing during the daytime to attract females, who pick up the calls with "ears" (tympanal organs) on their abdomen. Many grasshopper species have camouflage coloration; others produce poisonous chemicals for defensive purposes. Pest species, called locusts, swarm in vast numbers—sometimes comprising several billion individuals— to devastate food crops.

Life cycle Females lay egg masses in the ground, often surrounded by a foamy, protective secretion.

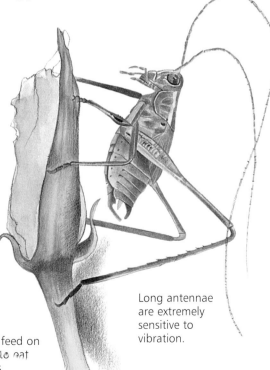

DINING OUT
American tree crickets feed on caterpillars that come to eat evening primrose buds.

Long antennae are extremely sensitive to vibration.

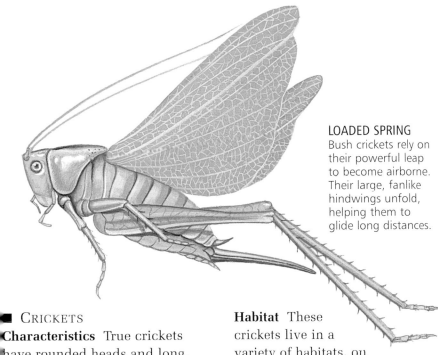

LOADED SPRING
Bush crickets rely on
their powerful leap
to become airborne.
Their large, fanlike
hindwings unfold,
helping them to
glide long distances.

■ CRICKETS
Characteristics True crickets
have rounded heads and long,
spindle-like antennae. Most
species are black or brown. The
female's ovipositor is usually
round and shaped like a needle.

Leaf-rolling crickets roll leaves
to make a nest, which becomes a
hiding place during the day.

Mole-crickets are burrowers,
and have front legs adapted
for digging. They have short,
toughened forewings. The males
produce a song that is amplified
by their special Y-shaped burrow.
Some cricket species are pests on
cereal crops.

Habitat These
crickets live in a
variety of habitats, on
vegetation and under the ground.

■ CAVE AND KING CRICKETS
Characteristics Cave crickets
are wingless and have very long
antennae. Some have soft bodies
and reduced eyes. They lay their
eggs in sand on the cave floor.

King crickets (also known as
Jerusalem crickets or wetas) are
large, wingless insects with short
antennae. Adults venture out of
their burrows after nightfall.
Habitat They live in caves, in
rotten wood, and underground.

■ KATYDIDS

Characteristics Katydids (also called bush crickets or long-horned grasshoppers) communicate using sharp clicks and buzzes; only both sexes of the "true" katydids of North America sing "*katy*-DID." Males produce their song by scraping their wings across their hindlegs. Females of some species have a large, sickle-shaped ovipositor. Most katydids are green or brown in color. Their veined, leaf-like front wings, which cover most of their body,

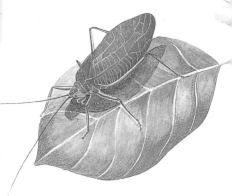

TRUE KATYDID
Male katydids sing the characteristic "katy-did" call often heard on warm summer evenings. Most females are mute, but some respond with a chirp.

provide excellent camouflage. Many species mimic the shape and color of bark and leaves. Some startle enemies by flashing colored hindwings. **Life cycle, diet, and habitat** After mating, katydids lay their eggs in soil or inside plants. Nymphs may go through up to six nymphal stages before adulthood. Katydids are mainly found in dense foliage.

KATYDID CONFUSION
Katydids (left) transform themselves by flicking open their colorful, patterned wings to startle predators. Some species, such as this mountain katydid (right), also take on a defensive posture.

Stick Insects and Leaf Insects

Number of species: 2,500

Length: 1–11½ in (25–290 mm)

S N A P S H O T

ORDER FEATURES Stick-like or leaf-like body; mostly nocturnal and slow-moving
DIET Plant matter
LIFE CYCLE Metamorphosis is incomplete; eggs scattered or laid in soil or glued to plants
HABITAT Among the foliage of trees and shrubs
DISTRIBUTION Mainly tropical regions or warm, temperate areas

■ CHARACTERISTICS

Stick insects and leaf insects are mostly nocturnal. They protect themselves from daytime predators by hiding among foliage. Most remain motionless when they are disturbed, holding their legs alongside their body. Others produce smells, noises, or regurgitate food to repel predators. Males are usually smaller than females.

■ LIFE CYCLE AND DIET

Females usually scatter their eggs from the abdomen. Development is via incomplete metamorphosis. Most species eat plant matter.

■ HABITAT

Members of this order are usually found among thick vegetation.

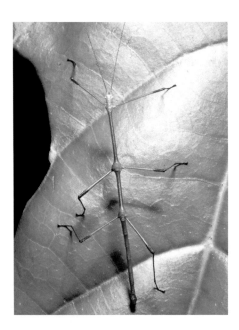

RED-KNEED WALKING STICK
This colorful stick insect lives in the dense foliage of Mount Kinabalu, Borneo. Most stick insects feed on plants at nighttime.

ORANGE FLASH
This orange walking stick displays a flash of its fan-shaped wings. Only the males possess wings.

LOOSE LEGS
Some stick insects shed a leg when seized by a predator. The lost limb usually grows back again.

Webspinners

Number of species: 300

Length: 1/8–3/4 in (3–20 mm)

■ CHARACTERISTICS
Webspinners are small, soft-bodied, gregarious insects that are not often observed. Their common name reflects the females' ability to make large, protective, silk tunnels in soil, under bark, and in leaf litter.

Webspinners have short legs. They have a swollen segment on their front legs that contains silk glands. The silk is extruded through structures on the underside of the body. The webspinner moves its front feet through the silk and a sheet gradually forms.

Males usually have two pairs of narrow, same-size wings; females are wingless. They have chewing mouthparts and round compound eyes. Females have smaller eyes than males.

Webspinners are nocturnal, living inside their tunnels during the day and coming out at night to feed. Males enter the tunnels only to mate with the females.

■ LIFE CYCLE AND DIET
Webspinners undergo incomplete metamorphosis. Females show a degree of maternal care. They lay small clusters of eggs along the sides of the tunnel, and then cover them with silk and detritus. The female may guard her eggs, licking and moving them. Once hatched, she may feed the nymphs pre-chewed food.

Some individuals congregate in one area, each within their silk

---

S N A P S H O T

ORDER FEATURES **Small, elongate body; swollen segment on front legs containing silk glands.**

DIET **Rotting or dead wood, wood fibers, crops**

LIFE CYCLE **Metamorphosis is incomplete; females show degree of parental care**

HABITAT **Wide variety, including in bark, tree holes, under stones**

DISTRIBUTION **Worldwide**

tunnel. Females and nymphs
remain with this "colony;" adult
males fly off to other colonies to
mate with females.

Females and nymphs feed on
a variety of vegetation, including
bark, leaf litter, moss, and
lichens. Males are probably
non-feeding and are short-lived.

SILKEN HOME
Webspinners have swollen areas on their
front legs that contain silk glands. This
silk is made into a protective tunnel.

■ HABITAT
Webspinners are found in a
wide variety of habitats, from
deserts to rainforests.

Booklice and Barklice

Number of species: 3,000

Length: $1/64$–$1/4$ in (0.5–6 mm)

Parasitic Lice

Number of species: 6,000

Length: $1/32$–$1/4$ in (1–6 mm)

■ BOOKLICE AND BARKLICE

Characteristics These small, soft-bodied insects have two pairs of membranous wings (if present), a large, bulging forehead, and long, slender antennae. When folded, the wings are held up over the body like a roof.

Life cycle, diet, and habitat Most species lay eggs, although some give birth to live young. Some lay batches of eggs on dead leaves and then cover them with silken threads; others lay their eggs in leaf litter, tree bark, or birds' nests. They develop through incomplete metamorphosis. Nymphs are usually similar to adults. Adults and nymphs feed on lichen, fungi, molds, and pollen. Some are considered pests, particularly those that feed on books. These insects live in dry leaf litter, under bark or stones, in debris, and inside buildings and food stores.

LARGE GATHERING
Barklice are small and usually incon-spicuous, but enormous populations can be found on some trees.

Parasitic lice

Characteristics Parasitic lice have flattened, wingless bodies. They use their specialized mouthparts for biting skin, fur, or feathers.

Life cycle, diet, and habitat These lice develop through incomplete metamorphosis and are exclusively blood feeders. They live permanently on the exterior of mammals (including humans) and birds. The human body louse lives in clothing and then latches onto the host's body; head lice spend their entire lives in human hair.

HAIR CEMENT

This head louse, magnified 100 times, lays its eggs (nits) singly and then cements each one to the base of a hair.

SNAPSHOT

ORDER FEATURES **Wings held rooflike above body (Psocoptera); flattened, wingless (Phthiraptera)**

DIET **Pollen, paper (Psocoptera); blood, skin (Phthiraptera)**

LIFE CYCLE **Metamorphosis is incomplete**

HABITAT **Leaf litter, food stores (Psocoptera); skin, feathers, and fur (Phthiraptera)**

DISTRIBUTION **Worldwide**

Bugs

Number of species: 82,000

Length: 1/32–4 in (1–100 mm)

■ CHARACTERISTICS
Members of this order range in size from minute, wingless aphids to giant, frog-catching water bugs. All possess specialized sucking and piercing mouthparts, consisting of a central tube

(rostrum) and four, sharp-tipped stylets. To feed, a bug pierces the food source with its stylets and then pushes its rostrum into the wound. It pumps in saliva, which partly digests the food, and then sucks up the liquid. A bug's front wings are often leathery at the

WELL SHIELDED
This hawthorn shield bug feeds on ripe hawthorn berries. Some female shield bugs guard their eggs until they hatch.

base and clear at the tips. Its transparent hindwings are shorter than its front wings.

This guide covers three of the four suborders of the Hemiptera, representing some of the best-known families in the order.

■ LIFE CYCLE AND DIET

Most bugs develop by incomplete metamorphosis. Females lay their eggs in soil, under bark, and on vegetation. Some produce live young; others reproduce asexually. Most are plant-eaters; some feed on blood and animal fluids.

■ HABITAT

Bugs live in all terrestrial and aquatic habitats, including the surface of some oceans.

OFF THE SCENT
Stink bugs produce defensive odors from special glands on the thorax. Their bright colors warn predators to stay away.

True Bugs

Number of species: 36,000

Length: 1/32–4 in (1–100 mm)

■ CHARACTERISTICS
True bugs vary widely in shape, size, color, habitat, and diet. All have specialized piercing and sucking mouthparts. They also have long antennae with five or fewer segments.

■ LIFE CYCLE AND DIET
All true bugs undergo incomplete metamorphosis. They usually lay their eggs on or in plants, in soil, on bark, or in cracks or crevices. Only true bugs have species that are blood-feeders and insect predators. Most species

UNDERCOVER BUGS
As their name and appearance imply, bark bugs live on or under bark. They feed on fungus growing on the bark.

suck sap and other plant fluids from vegetation. Many are significant crop pests.

■ HABITAT

The majority of true bugs live on vegetation and many spend winter hibernating in leaf litter or clumps of grass. Some true bugs are exclusively aquatic, while others live in close association with birds and mammals, including humans.

SNAPSHOT

ORDER FEATURES **Piercing and sucking mouthparts (rostrum); tips of forewings transparent**

DIET **Sap, other plant fluids, blood, animal body fluids**

LIFE CYCLE **Metamorphosis is incomplete; eggs laid in soil, on vegetation, under bark**

HABITAT **All terrestrial habitats, freshwater and ocean surface**

DISTRIBUTION **Worldwide**

MOVING INCUBATOR

A female giant water bug glues her eggs onto the back of a male. While carrying the eggs, he is unable to use his wings.

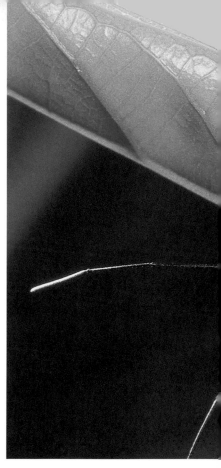

HEMIPTERA
Heteroptera

■ SHIELD BUGS

Characteristics Shield bugs (or acanthosomatids) have a distinctive, triangular shield on their thorax, tipped with a pale, Y-shaped mark. Most are green, gray, or brown in color.

Life cycle, diet, and habitat One of the best-known species is the parent bug. Female parent bugs guard their eggs and nymphs under their body. Most shield bugs suck sap from foliage. They live in warm areas, often in woodland and scrubland.

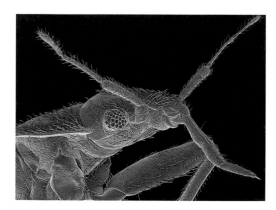

MIDNIGHT SNACK
Bed bugs are nighttime feeders. They pierce their host with their needlelike rostrum and feed on blood.

■ BED BUGS

Characteristics These wingless insects are oval and flattened. They feed by sucking blood from humans, other mammals, and from birds. They can be serious pests, but because of improved hygiene and modern pesticides they are now less common.

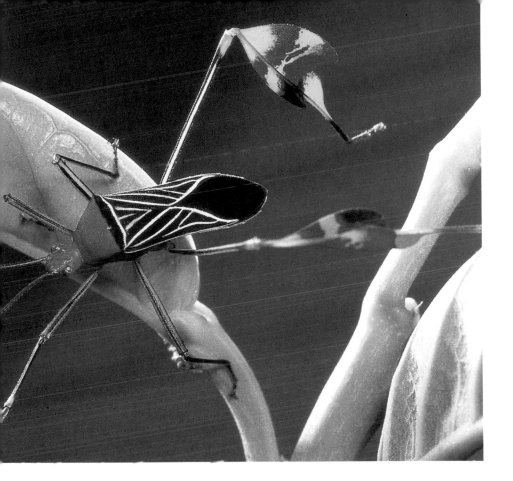

Life cycle, diet, and habitat

Bedbugs lay their eggs close to a host. They have five nymphal stages; each stage relies on a large blood meal for its survival. These nighttime feeders sense their host by body heat. Although there are only 90 species, bedbugs are widely distributed.

FLAG FLYING
The colorful expansions on the hindlegs of this flag-footed bug may be used to distract predators.

■ SQUASH BUGS

Characteristics Some species display bright colors and flag-like expansions on their hindlegs.

Life cycle, diet, and habitat
Some species of squash bug use squash plants as hosts for their nymphs. They are found in warmer regions, and live on a wide variety of plants. Some species are crop pests.

GLIDING STROKE
Water boatmen use their fringed hindlegs as oars to push them through the water.

■ AQUATIC BUGS
Characteristics Aquatic bugs, such as water boatmen, use their hindlegs like oars to move them across the water. Their forelegs are used for catching prey, while their middle legs are used to grip plants. The long, thin, hair-fringed legs of water striders and ripple bugs enable them to spread their weight evenly on the water without falling through the surface of a pond.

Life cycle, diet, and habitat Most species lay eggs in or on aquatic plants. They live in streams, ponds, marshes, and swamps.

WATER SKATING
The water strider uses surface tension to skate on the water's surface. Hairs on its feet help to repel water, thus keeping it afloat.

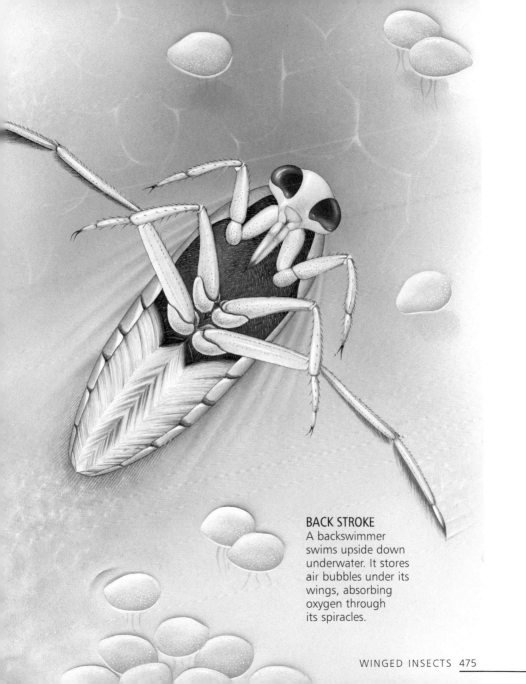

BACK STROKE
A backswimmer
swims upside down
underwater. It stores
air bubbles under its
wings, absorbing
oxygen through
its spiracles.

■ STINK BUGS AND ALLIES
Characteristics Stink bugs are a large and well-known group. Many species are very common and abundant. Most can produce strong odors as a defensive measure. Shield-backed bugs are mostly colorful, and often resemble beetles. The middle section of the thorax (scutellum) is large and almost covers the body. Assassin bugs have long, thin hindlegs and strong, short forelegs for grasping prey.

Life cycle, diet, and habitat The majority glue their eggs onto plants. Stink bugs and shield-backed bugs are sap-suckers. Assassin bugs are predators of other insects, stabbing them with their sharp rostrum. All are found on a wide variety of vegetation.

NO JOKE
Jester bugs use their piercing mouthparts to suck nectar. Their mouthparts are tucked away in a groove on the underside of the body when they are not feeding.

QUICK CHANGE
Australian harlequin bugs are bright orange as adults, but may be orange and steely blue as nymphs.

TOUCHÉ!
An assassin bug uses its sharp beak to stab its victim. It then sucks out the insect's body fluids.

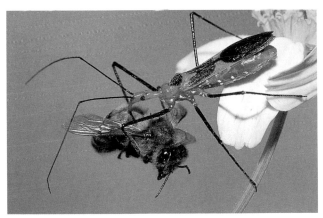

Cicadas and Allies

Number of species: 35,000

Length: 1/8–4 in (3–100 mm)

■ CHARACTERISTICS
Members of families in this
suborder include the froghoppers,
leafhoppers, treehoppers, and the
cicadas. Most species have stout
bodies, broad and blunt heads,
and large, wide eyes. Many
display camouflage or warning
coloration. Some produce mating
calls in special abdominal organs.

■ LIFE CYCLE AND DIET
All cicadas and hoppers develop
by incomplete metamorphosis.
Eggs are laid inside plants or
in soil. Most feed on sap from
plant stems and roots.

■ HABITAT
These bugs are found on a wide
variety of vegetation, including
trees, shrubs, and flowers.

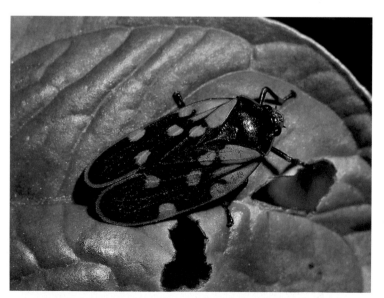

BRIGHT BUGS
Froghoppers (left)
often display
bright warning
colors. They live on
a variety of trees
and shrubs,
particularly in
warm climates.

MATING CALLS
Male cicadas
(right) produce
their loud
mating songs in
abdominal organs.
Males can produce
a number of
different songs.

CUNNING DISGUISE
The peanut bug's shape and dull coloration help to conceal it from hungry birds.

■ FROGHOPPERS
Characteristics Froghoppers are excellent jumpers. They have squat bodies and large, round eyes. Some species are drab brown in color; others display bright red-and-black, or yellow-and-black patterns.
Life cycle, diet, and habitat Froghoppers lay their eggs in soil. The nymphs live under the ground, covered by a frothy, spittle-like mass of bubbles. They live on a wide variety of plants and shrubs, feeding on plant sap.

■ CICADAS
Characteristics Cicadas are more often heard than seen. Only the males produce a song in special organs on their abdomen. Usually green or dark brown in color, they have a wide head and prominent eyes.
Life cycle, diet, and habitat Females lay eggs inside slits that they cut in trees and shrubs. The hatchlings drop onto the ground and burrow into the soil. The nymphs then emerge, crawling up trees before their final molt

into adulthood. Some species have a life cycle of 13 to 17 years.

■ FULGORIDS

Characteristics Many fulgorids, including the bizarre peanut bug, have strangely shaped heads. They remain camouflaged in their surroundings until disturbed, suddenly flashing the eyespots or bright colors on their wings.
Life cycle, diet, and habitat Fulgorids surround their eggs with a protective secretion. They live in tropical and subtropical regions and feed on plant sap.

LIVING THORNS
Treehoppers, or thorn bugs, feed in clusters, sucking up plant sap. Their spiny shape deters birds from eating them, but also provides them with an extremely effective disguise.

■ LEAF- AND TREEHOPPERS

Characteristics Leafhoppers have triangular heads and slim bodies. Treehoppers can be distinguished from leafhoppers by their dome- or thorn-shaped pronotum.
Life cycle, diet, and habitat These bugs lay their eggs inside plant tissue. They live on foliage and feed on plant fluids.

Aphids and Allies

Number of species: 11,000

Length: $^1/_{32}$–$1^1/_2$ in (1–30 mm)

■ CHARACTERISTICS

Aphids, scale insects, and whiteflies belong to different families within the suborder Sternorrhyncha. Aphids are tiny, soft-bodied bugs, with short tubes on their abdomen, called cornicles, capable of making substances to deter predators. Scale insects are usually flat, wingless females that form a protective, scalelike covering over their bodies. Whiteflies look similar to small, white moths and have a powdery substance coating their wings.

■ LIFE CYCLE AND DIET

Aphids reproduce both sexually and asexually. Winged females fly to host plants and then reproduce by a process—parthenogenesis—whereby eggs develop without fertilization, with females giving birth to live nymphs. Like aphids, scale insects have sexual and asexual reproduction, and are able to build up enormous colonies in a very short time. Adult whiteflies lay their eggs on the undersides of leaves. Aphids, scale insects, and whiteflies are significant plant pests.

■ HABITAT

These bugs are found on a wide variety of plants. Scale insects and whiteflies live in warm areas; aphids tolerate cooler climates.

LIVE BIRTH
Female aphids produce billions of offspring without mating. Here, wingless adult females are giving birth to nymphs.

Thrips

Number of species: 5,000

Length: $^{1}/_{32}$–$^{1}/_{2}$ in (0.7–12 mm)

FAMILY GROUPS
Adult and nymph tube-tailed thrips feed alongside each other. Some species eat fungi, while others feed on plants or rotting wood.

■ CHARACTERISTICS
Thrips are slender, black or pale-yellow insects with short antennae and large compound eyes. They have two pairs of narrow wings, fringed with long hairs. They are weak fliers. Their distinctive sucking mouthparts are asymmetrical; one mandible is small and the other is slender and needle-shaped.

■ LIFE CYCLE AND DIET
Thrips undergo a similar reproductive pattern to the Hymenoptera (bees, wasps, and ants), whereby unfertilized eggs produce males and fertilized eggs produce females. Females lay their eggs inside plant tissue. Most thrips feed on plant sap. Banded thrips, however, feed on small insects or pollen grains

■ HABITAT
Thrips are commonly found on a variety of vegetation. Many species are major crop pests.

SNAPSHOT

ORDER FEATURES **Slender bodies; two pairs of fringed wings; asymmetrical mouthparts**
DIET **Sap, pollen, other insects**
LIFE CYCLE **Neither incomplete nor complete metamorphosis; fertilized eggs produce females, unfertilized eggs produce males**
HABITAT **On foliage and flowers; some live in soil**
DISTRIBUTION **Worldwide**

Alderflies and Dobsonflies

Number of species: 300

Length: 3/8–3 in (10–75 mm)

■ CHARACTERISTICS

Members of this order have soft bodies, two pairs of similar-size wings, and are weak fliers. At rest, they hold their folded wings in a "roof" over the body.

■ LIFE CYCLE AND DIET

Alderflies and dobsonflies are considered the most primitive insects to develop by complete metamorphosis. Larvae pupate

inside a chamber made from moss, sand, or soil. Although adults have large mandibles, they do not feed. The aquatic larvae have gills on their abdomen, and feed on small, water-dwelling insects.

■ DOBSONFLIES

Characteristics Dobsonflies' wings are either clear, or gray or brown in areas. Males have very large mandibles.

Life cycle, diet, and habitat Dobsonflies lay their eggs near water. The aquatic larvae eat small aquatic animals and may take years to develop to adulthood. They occur in temperate regions, and are most often found near running water.

■ ALDERFLIES

Characteristics Smaller than dobsonflies, alderflies have dark-veined wings and no ocelli.

FIGHTING CHANCE

Male dobsonflies have huge mandibles, which are thought to be used in combat with other males, or to hold the female.

LONG DROP
Female alderflies lay their large masses of eggs near water. As they hatch, the larvae drop into the water below.

Life cycle, diet, and habitat
Females lay their egg masses near water. The hatched larvae take up to one year to mature, and feed on small pond life. Adults are often found resting on plants near slow-moving water.

Snakeflies

Number of species: 150

Length: 1/4–1 1/4 in (6–30 mm)

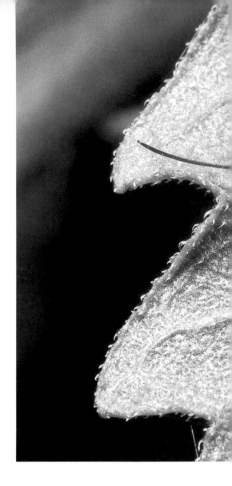

■ CHARACTERISTICS

Snakeflies are dark in color, with two pairs of similar-size wings and a distinctive "neck," consisting of a long pronotum and a shiny, flat head. The head can be raised and lowered on the pronotum. Snakeflies get their name from the snakelike way in which they hold their prey. They move their head up and forward to strike at their victim. They have forward-pointing, chewing mouthparts. Female snakeflies are larger than males.

■ LIFE CYCLE AND DIET

These insects develop by complete metamorphosis. Females lay several hundred eggs through a slender ovipositor, usually under bark or in rotting wood. The strong-limbed larvae forage for food under loose tree bark, in rotten trees, and in leaf

TO THE POINT
Female snakeflies are usually larger than males. They have a long, slender ovipositor to lay eggs in tree bark.

litter. Unlike the larvae of the closely related alderflies (Order Megaloptera), snakefly larvae are land-dwellers and do not possess

gills. Adults and larvae are predators, both feeding on other soft-bodied insects and larvae, but they may also scavenge for food.

■ HABITAT
Most snakefly species live in the Northern Hemisphere, in wooded areas among lush vegetation.

SNAPSHOT

ORDER FEATURES Snakelike head and neck; two pairs of clear, similar-size wings

DIET Other soft-bodied insects and insect larvae

LIFE CYCLE Metamorphosis is complete; eggs laid under bark; larvae are terrestrial

HABITAT On vegetation, in bark

DISTRIBUTION Mostly Northern Hemisphere

NEUROPTERA

17 families

Net-veined Insects

Number of species: 4,000

Wingspan: 1/4–43/4 in (6–120 mm)

■ CHARACTERISTICS
Most members of this order have large compound eyes and long antennae. The two pairs of wings are of similar size and are held over the body like a roof when the insect is at rest. The major wing veins are "netted" or forked.

SNAPSHOT

ORDER FEATURES Long antennae, large compound eyes, wings held rooflike over body at rest
DIET Flying insects; aphids, mites, and thrips
LIFE CYCLE Metamorphosis is complete; eggs are laid on vegetation, in soil; some species parasitize other insects
HABITAT On vegetation
DISTRIBUTION Worldwide

■ LIFE CYCLE AND DIET
All species develop by complete metamorphosis. Most are active hunters of flying insects. Some eat aphids, mites, and thrips; others eat nectar or pollen.

■ HABITAT
Most live on vegetation— usually near water—in tropical, temperate, or semi-arid regions.

■ LACEWINGS AND OWLFLIES
Characteristics Lacewings are usually green in color, with large

WISE OWLS
Owlflies can be identified by their long antennae with clubbed ends. They are skilled nocturnal predators, deftly seizing insect prey on the wing.

LION HEART
Antlions resemble damselflies, but can be distinguished by their conspicuous, knobbed antennae.

gold or red eyes. Adults are attracted toward lights shining from houses. Owlflies have distinctive, clubbed antennae and patterned wings. Adults seize prey in the air.
Life cycle, diet, and habitat Both insects lay eggs on vegetation; lacewing eggs are laid on stalks and owlflies lay eggs in spirals. Both eat insects and live on vegetation in dry habitats.

■ ANTLIONS
Characteristics Antlions have clubbed antennae and large eyes.
Life cycle, diet, and habitat Their eggs are laid in soil. The larvae construct pits to trap insect prey. Most live in warm, dry areas.

Beetles

Number of species: 370,000

Length: $1/32$–$7 1/2$ in (1–190 mm)

BREAK OUT
Weevils have sharp, chewing mouthparts. Most feed by boring into grain.

■ CHARACTERISTICS

The Order Coleoptera is the largest in the animal kingdom. In fact, almost one in every four animals on Earth is a beetle. Arguably the most successful insects, beetles have colonized every terrestrial and aquatic habitat. They vary enormously in size, ranging from the minute feather-winged beetle, only just visible to the naked eye, to the male hercules beetle from Central America, which can be more than $7 1/2$ inches (19 cm) long.

HEAD-TAPPER
The deathwatch beetle's head-tapping mating signals were often heard in quiet rooms during a funeral wake.

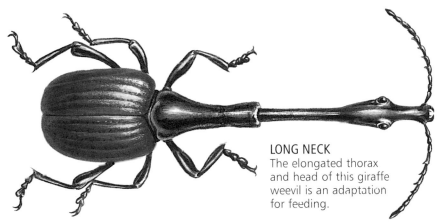

Despite this amazing variation in color and shape, beetles have one important feature in common—all have hardened forewings, called elytra, that protect the delicate, membranous hindwings folded underneath. In all species, the elytra meet down the middle of the body. A beetle's elytra protect its spiracles and fragile hindwings from being damaged as it clambers around in search of food. Aquatic insects use the space under their elytra to store air for breathing. Most beetles have large compound eyes and antennae composed of ten or more segments.

This guide covers a selection of representative families within this huge order, from wood-borers to flesh-eaters.

HIDDEN JEWELS
Many weevils have bright patterns and colors, produced by light reflecting off microscopic hairs, and by the structure of their body case.

■ LIFE CYCLE AND DIET
Beetles undergo complete metamorphosis. The male usually clings to the female's back during mating. She then lays eggs on or inside suitable vegetation, on soil or bark, inside wood or dung, in leaf litter or fungi, or near a host insect. Some beetle species have

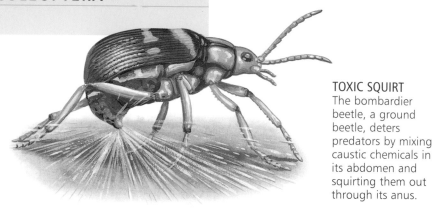

TOXIC SQUIRT
The bombardier beetle, a ground beetle, deters predators by mixing caustic chemicals in its abdomen and squirting them out through its anus.

lengthy larval stages. Most beetle species are plant-eaters, and will consume anything from hardwood to nectar. Carpet beetles feed not only on rugs but also on stored grain, upholstery, fur, and stuffed toys. Some, such as tiger beetles, are predators of other insects; specialized parasitic species are also known. Many beetles are significant crop and timber pests.

■ HABITAT

Beetles are found in all habitats, from rainforests and streams to deserts and caves. Some rove beetles live only in the fur of beavers; others live on birds or in the nests of bees. Some clerid beetles live in termite nests, or on carrion. Many beetles make their home in damp leaf litter.

■ WOOD-BORING BEETLES

Characteristics These small beetles are elongate to oval. The best-known species are the furniture beetle and the common wood-borer. They can fit their short legs into special grooves on the underside of the body.

Life cycle, diet, and habitat
The eggs are laid on a food source, usually dry wood. The larvae bore circular tunnels as they eat through the wood. They are able to digest the fibers with the assistance of yeasts found within their gut. Wood-borers live in wooded areas, warehouses, and inside buildings.

DAPPER UNIFORMS
Soldier beetles get their common name from their yellow-and-black coloring, similar to military uniforms.

LONG HORNS
This longhorn beetle has extremely long antennae, typical of family members.

VIOLIN BEETLE
With its flattened elytra and semi-transparent "wings," this ground beetle squeezes between bracket fungi.

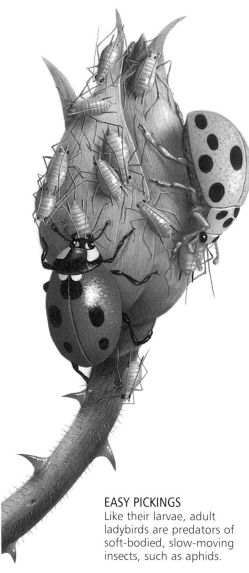

EASY PICKINGS
Like their larvae, adult ladybirds are predators of soft-bodied, slow-moving insects, such as aphids.

■ JEWEL, SOLDIER, AND GROUND BEETLES

Characteristics Most jewel beetles are metallic green, red, or blue, with large eyes and short antennae. Soldier beetles have distinctive, curved jaws, long, thin antennae, and are usually red and black, or yellow and black. Ground beetles are long and flattened, sometimes with a metallic sheen. A few produce caustic substances, which they blast out from the end of their abdomen, to deter predators.

Life cycle, diet, and habitat Some jewel beetles have heat-detecting organs at the base of their legs, used to seek out their preferred egg-laying sites in burned forests. They lay their eggs in wood. When the larvae hatch, they chew tunnels through dead trees. Adults eat flowers, nectar, and pollen. Soldier beetles scatter their eggs on the ground. Both the adults and larvae are predators. Ground beetles lay their eggs on soil or vegetation. The larvae and adults are primarily predacious.

POLLEN FEAST
Some checkered beetles (above) are pollen-feeders. They are found mainly in tropical areas.

GRUB UP
The grub of the seven-spot ladybird (below) needs strong legs to climb after the aphids that it feeds on.

EGG CLUSTERS
Female ladybirds (left) lay egg clusters on foliage. After about one week, the first larvae begin to emerge from the eggs.

CLICK BEETLE
A click beetle escapes danger by lying on its back and keeping still. It suddenly snaps upward, hurling itself out of harm's way.

■ LADYBIRDS AND CHECKERED BEETLES

Characteristics Ladybirds are mostly brightly colored, often with black spots or stripes. They are round-bodied and have short legs. Checkered beetles have a flat, elongate shape. They are often covered with long hairs and some have clubbed antennae.

Life cycle, diet, and habitat Ladybirds glue single eggs or egg clusters to plants. Both adults and larvae eat soft-bodied insects. They are sometimes used as biological controls on insect pests. Checkered beetles lay their eggs in rotting wood. Larvae feed on the larvae of other insects.

■ CLICK BEETLES

Characteristics These elongate beetles are mostly dull in color. Some have distinctive markings on the thorax. Click beetles can propel themselves into the air, producing a loud, clicking sound that deters predators.

Life cycle, diet, and habitat Click beetles lay eggs in soil, with their larvae taking a year to develop. The larvae of some species are called wireworms, and may cause damage to potato crops.

■ DIVING BEETLES

Characteristics Diving beetles have many adaptations for aquatic life, including a smooth

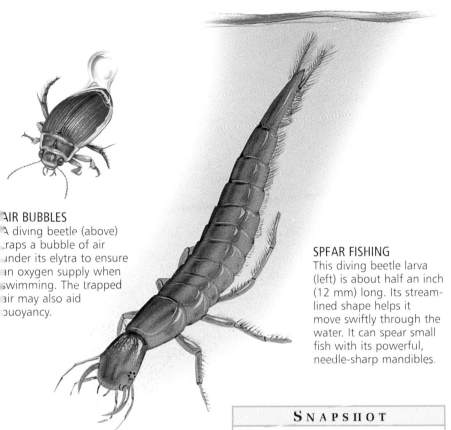

AIR BUBBLES
A diving beetle (above) traps a bubble of air under its elytra to ensure an oxygen supply when swimming. The trapped air may also aid buoyancy.

SPEAR FISHING
This diving beetle larva (left) is about half an inch (12 mm) long. Its stream-lined shape helps it move swiftly through the water. It can spear small fish with its powerful, needle-sharp mandibles.

body and fringed hindlegs to help propel them through the water.

Life cycle, diet, and habitat

Female diving beetles lay eggs inside aquatic plants. The larvae pupate in wet soil. Adults and larvae are fierce predators, eating insects, frogs, and small fish.

SNAPSHOT

ORDER FEATURES **Hardened forewings (elytra) that meet down the middle of the body**
DIET **Most eat plant matter; some are predators and scavengers; a few are parasitic**
LIFE CYCLE **Metamorphosis is complete; eggs laid in terrestrial and aquatic habitats**
HABITAT **All habitats**
DISTRIBUTION **Worldwide**

■ FIREFLIES

Characteristics These small, flat beetles are also called lightning bugs. The adults of many species communicate using flashes of green light produced in luminous organs on the abdomen. Males have fully developed wings; some females are wingless.

Life cycle, diet, and habitat Fireflies lay their eggs on vegetation. The larvae are known as glow-worms. They feed on invertebrates and live on plants.

AERIAL ILLUMINATION
Male fireflies flash coded signals to the wingless females on the ground. Females sometimes signal closely related species, luring them and then attacking and eating them.

SEEING THE LIGHT
Fireflies recognize their own species,
usually by signaling at specific times
of day. Some always signal at dusk
for about half an hour; others signal
after sunset for several hours.

CARDINAL FLIGHT
As this cardinal beetle takes to the air, it displays the functional use of its elytra as stabilizers during flight.

■ STAG AND FIRE-COLORED BEETLES

Characteristics Stag beetles have large, shiny bodies. Males are always larger than females and have huge mandibles equipped with prominent "teeth." These mandibles are used in courtship combat for mating rights. They are designed to clip over a rival beetle and assist in flipping it over during conflict. The best-known fire-colored beetles are the cardinals. They have black, red, or yellow coloring, flat bodies, and serrations on their antennae.

Life cycle, diet, and habitat Female stag beetles lay eggs in rotting tree stumps. Larvae pupate inside cells composed of chewed wood fibers. Adults are sometimes non-feeding or they feed on plant juices. Fire-colored beetles lay eggs under bark. They feed on other insects.

■ BLISTER BEETLES

Characteristics These beetles produce an oily fluid that may cause human skin to blister. They secrete the fluid from their

LONG DEVELOPMENT

Stag beetle larvae take several years to reach adulthood (below). Eggs are laid on rotting wood and the nymphs pupate inside a cell made from wood fibers.

JOUSTING JAWS

The ferocious-looking jaws of male stag beetles (above) are used for grappling with other males for mating rights.

Egg   Larva   Nymph   Adult

leg joints as a deterrent to predators. Many species are soft and leathery; most have red or yellow markings.

Life cycle, diet, and habitat Females lay their eggs in soil. The larvae of some species hide among flowers and grab on to visiting bees. The bees then carry them back to their nest, where they eat the bee's eggs. Adults feed on plant matter. They live mainly on flowers and foliage.

■ SCARAB BEETLES
Characteristics This large family contains more than 16,000 species, and displays a wide variety of shapes, colors, and sizes. All species have distinctive antennae that end in a club shape, and consist of several movable parts. The males of many species have horns, which they use in courtship battles over females. Scarab beetles were important religious symbols in

ON A ROLL
A male and female dung beetle fashion animal droppings into a ball, before the female lays one or more eggs inside it.

Ancient Egypt. Many of the
brightly colored species are
under threat from over-collection,
especially in Central America.

Life cycle, diet, and habitat
Females lay eggs in soil, decaying
wood or animal remains, and
in the dung of plant-eating
mammals. Some roll dung into
balls before burying it and laying
eggs inside. Some species stay in
a nest with the dung balls until
the young emerge. Both adults

and larvae eat the moist fungi and
yeast in dung. They are usually
found on decaying matter, on
dung, under bark, or in ant nests.

◼ Weevils

Characteristics Weevils form
the largest family in the animal
kingdom. These beetles have a
long rostrum, equipped with
sharp mouthparts at its tip. Most
have camouflage coloring, but
some are brightly patterned.

SWEET FOOD
Rose cockchafers, also known as
May beetles, are frequent visitors
to gardens across southern Europe.
They feed on nectar and pollen.

Life cycle, diet, and habitat
Weevils drill a hole in a plant
using their rostrum and then lay
their eggs inside. The larvae are
grub-like. Many adults and larvae
are pests of cereal crops, cotton,
and timber.

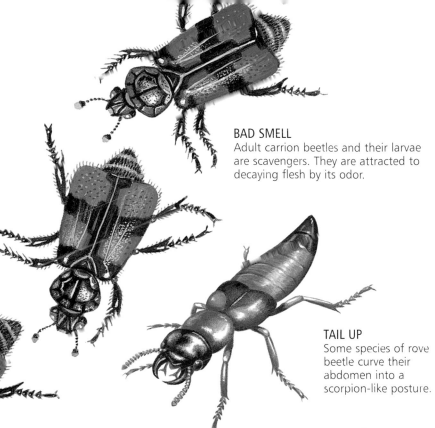

BAD SMELL
Adult carrion beetles and their larvae are scavengers. They are attracted to decaying flesh by its odor.

TAIL UP
Some species of rove beetle curve their abdomen into a scorpion-like posture.

■ CARRION BEETLES
AND ROVE BEETLES

Characteristics Carrion beetles are usually flat and soft-bodied, with yellow, orange, or red markings. They have short elytra, exposing some of their segmented abdomen. All rove beetles have short elytra and an exposed, mobile abdomen. Many species have a covering of black and yellow hairs.

Life cycle, diet, and habitat
Carrion beetles lay eggs in the corpses of small mammals that they first bury. They eat rotting plant and animal material. Rove beetles lay their eggs in leaf litter, soil, or fungi. Larvae and adults usually live in the same area. Both eat insects or invertebrates. Some species live in decaying plants, in ant colonies, or on the fur of some mammals.

Twisted-winged Parasites

Number of species: 560

Length: 1/64–5/32 in (0.5–4 mm)

Scorpionflies and Allies

Number of species: 550

Length: 1/16–1 1/2 in (2–40 mm)

■ TWISTED-WINGED PARASITES

Characteristics As the common name suggests, the hindwings of these males have a twisted appearance. Females are wingless and legless, and usually live inside the bodies of other insects as a parasite. They mostly favor bees, wasps, and bugs as hosts.

Life cycle, diet, and habitat Males and females communicate using pheromones. The male mates with the female while she is inside the host's body. The eggs hatch inside the female and the legged larvae emerge and move on to new hosts.

■ SCORPIONFLIES

Characteristics These insects have long and slender bodies, with two pairs of narrow wings. In some species, the males have an upturned abdomen with enlarged genitalia, resembling

WEB RAIDER
Some scorpionfly males appropriate insects captured in spiders' webs, and then present them as a gift to a potential mate.

a scorpion's tail. The head is lengthened downward to form a beak-like rostrum.

Life cycle, diet, and habitat

Males sometimes present females with a gift of food before mating. Females may refuse males that offer small or inferior gifts. Scorpionflies undergo complete metamorphosis. They lay their eggs in soil and the larvae usually pupate under the ground. Most scorpionflies eat insects, fruit, nectar, and mosses. Some species, called hangingflies, dangle from vegetation, catching passing insects with their hindlegs.

HANGING AROUND
These scorpionflies, called hangingflies, mate at night. Males often present courtship gifts of food to females.

SNAPSHOT

ORDER FEATURES **Females are endoparasites (Strepsiptera); upturned abdomen (Mecoptera)**

DIET **Females eat host's body fluids (Strepsiptera); insects and nectar (Mecoptera)**

LIFE CYCLE **Metamorphosis is complete**

HABITAT **Endoparasitic females (Strepsiptera); among vegetation (Mecoptera)**

SIPHONAPTERA
18 families

Fleas

Number of species: 2,000

Length: $^{1}/_{32}$–$^{5}/_{16}$ in (1–8 mm)

S NAPSHOT

ORDER FEATURES Small, wingless, laterally flattened; sucking mouthparts; specialized jumping mechanism
DIET Adults suck blood; larvae eat dried blood and detritus
LIFE CYCLE Metamorphosis is complete; eggs laid near host
HABITAT Ectoparasites on mammal and bird hosts
DISTRIBUTION Worldwide

■ CHARACTERISTICS
Fleas are wingless, laterally flattened insects, with tough, shiny bodies covered in bristles. Their mouthparts are modified for sucking blood. Adult fleas are sensitive to heat. They use their small antennae to sense the body heat of a passing mammal or the presence of a mammal's exhaled carbon dioxide. Fleas have a unique mechanism for moving from host to host. Before a jump, muscles squeeze protein pads in the thorax. When the pads are released, they spring back into shape and catapult the flea into the air. Many species are disease spreaders; rodent fleas carried the bacterium that caused bubonic plague in Europe in the 1300s.

■ LIFE CYCLE AND DIET
Fleas undergo complete metamorphosis. Females leave

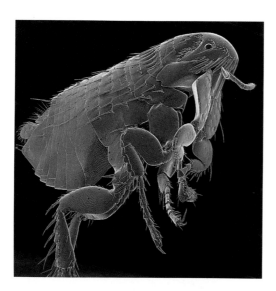

HAIR-RAISING
A flea's body is flattened laterally, making for easier movement between the hairs or feathers of its host.

their host to lay sticky eggs in a host's nest or burrow. Pupation takes place inside a cocoon, which is sometimes composed of silk. The pupae remain in their cocoon until a potential host is nearby. Adult fleas suck blood from their hosts, although they can survive long periods without a meal. The larvae are scavengers, feeding on the host's dried blood, the excrement of the adult fleas, and other detritus.

UNWANTED GUEST
Heavy infestations of fleas may cause the serious illness of a host, in this case a small bird called a house martin.

■ HABITAT
Fleas are ectoparasites. They live on the outside of hosts—usually mammals, but sometimes birds—and feed on them without causing death. Some species feed on a large number of host species (up to 30 in some cases).

Flies

Number of species: 122,000

Length: $^1/_{32}$–$2^3/_4$ in (1–70 mm)

■ CHARACTERISTICS

Flies belong to the fourth-largest order of insects. They are characterized by having only one pair of wings. The hindwings are reduced to small, knob-shaped organs called halteres. The halteres vibrate at high speed during flight to keep the fly's body balanced and level. All flies are similar in basic shape. They

WELCOME BREATH
Some non-biting midges have hemoglobin in their blood, which may assist them to carry the oxygen required to survive in stagnant water.

range in size from tiny midges to the Trinidad horse fly, which is the size of a walnut. Most flies have a large head, large compound eyes, and excellent vision. All eat liquid food. They have mouthparts that act like straws or sponges to suck or mop up food. Each foot has hairy pads that secrete oily fluids, enabling flies to stick to glass and ceilings. Because of their dietary habits, many species transmit a variety of bacteria and parasites.

■ LIFE CYCLE AND DIET

Most members of this order undergo complete metamorphosis, transforming

SNAPSHOT

ORDER FEATURES **Two pairs of wings, hindwings modified into halteres; sucking mouthparts**
DIET **Adults take fluids; larvae take fruit, flesh, dung, vegetation**
LIFE CYCLE **Metamorphosis is complete; eggs laid in soil, plants, water, carrion, dung**
HABITAT **A wide range of terrestrial and aquatic habitats**
DISTRIBUTION **Worldwide**

from blind, legless maggots to winged adults. Females lay eggs in soil, under bark, in rotting fruit, inside a host insect, or in flesh or dung. Larvae eat a wide variety of food.

■ HABITAT

Flies are found in virtually all habitats, from aquatic to alpine,

MIDGE ON THE MOVE
Biting midges suck fluids from larger insects or vertebrates. Adults never stray far from their preferred marshy areas.

and from cave to desert. Some species are parasitic; others play an important role in the detritus cycle. Many pest species are found near raw or cooked food.

■ MIDGES

Characteristics Biting midges may be slender or rounded, with a rounded head and feathery antennae. Their bites can cause severe irritation to the skin of humans and other mammals. Non-biting midges can be delicate or stocky. They look very similar to mosquitoes, but do not possess functional mouthparts.

Life cycle, diet, and habitat Male and female biting midges mate in large swarms. Their eggs are laid in damp soil, water, and rotting organic matter. Non-biting midges lay their eggs in a sticky jelly, and deposit them onto aquatic vegetation. Some remain in the larval stage for up to three years, adults live for only a few weeks. Midges are common by ponds, bogs, and near the seashore.

■ MOSQUITOES

Characteristics Some tropical mosquitoes are brightly colored; most are gray, white, and brown. They have long, narrow wings and long, slender, piercing mouthparts. Females are carriers of organisms that cause serious diseases, such as malaria, dengue fever, and encephalitis.

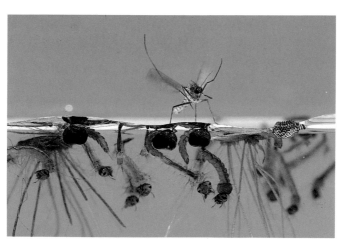

ON THE SURFACE
Mosquitoes lay their eggs on the surface of puddles or stagnant ponds. The writhing larvae breathe from a siphon on their abdomen. Tiny brushes on their head sweep food particles into the mouth.

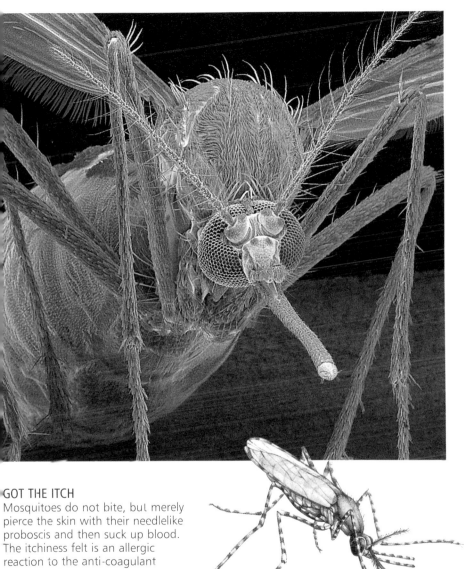

GOT THE ITCH
Mosquitoes do not bite, but merely pierce the skin with their needlelike proboscis and then suck up blood. The itchiness felt is an allergic reaction to the anti-coagulant chemicals the mosquito injects to make the blood flow more freely.

FRAGILE FLIERS
Craneflies are often mistaken for mosquitoes, but they do not bite or suck blood. Instead, these fragile, short-lived flies feed on nectar.

Life cycle, diet, and habitat The life cycle of a mosquito lasts less than three weeks. Females lay eggs on the water's surface, in groups of up to 300 or singly. The larvae eat other mosquito larvae. Adult females feed on the blood of vertebrates; males drink nectar and plant fluids. They live in mainly warm areas, and are found near fresh water, from roadside puddles to mountain lakes.

■ CRANEFLIES
Characteristics Most are gray, black, or brown, with very long legs that they shed if captured.
Life cycle, diet, and habitat Eggs are usually laid in soil. The larvae eat fungi, mosses, and decaying vegetable matter. Many adults feed on nectar. They typically fly at twilight and are short-lived. They are most often found near water or among damp vegetation.

■ BLOWFLIES
Characteristics Blowflies are stout-bodied and bright metallic green or blue. Males and females can be different colors. This group includes the well-known bluebottle and greenbottle flies.

Life cycle, diet, and habitat

Female blowflies lay their eggs—hundreds in a lifetime—in carrion, flesh, and dung. Some species lay larvae instead of eggs. They are found around carcasses, on vegetation, and are also attracted to raw and cooked meat. Some carry diseases, and may lay their eggs on livestock and humans. Because they burrow into flesh, blowfly maggots have been used to remove necrotic tissue after surgery.

LONG SHOT
Bee flies resemble bumblebees, with their fuzzy, broad body and nectar-feeding habits. Their proboscis may be three times longer than the head.

■ BEE FLIES

Characteristics Some bee fly species are small, but most have broad and furry bodies. They have brown, yellow, or red coloration, and some have bright markings.

Life cycle, diet, and habitat Bee flies are often seen at rest, wings outstretched, on flowers. Some species are important pollinators. The larvae of most species parasitize the larvae of other insects, particularly bees, grasshoppers, and beetles. Females lay their eggs close to the hosts' nests. Adults eat nectar. They are found around flowers or resting on the ground.

■ ROBBER FLIES

Characteristics Robber flies are the most active predators in this order. They are large and beelike, with bulging eyes that give the top of their head a concave appearance. Most species have long facial and body hair, a thick, stout proboscis, and well-developed, spiny bristles on their legs. These bristles assist in the capture of prey. When hunting, robber flies can quickly accelerate from 0 to 25 miles per hour (40 km/h) to snatch a bee or other flying insect in midair. They do not chase prey, but intercept it by darting out from a perch—usually a leaf or a twig.

Life cycle, diet, and habitat Eggs are laid inside plants or in soil. Looking like minute, flattened worms, the larvae eat the eggs and larvae of other insects as they move through soil and leaf litter. Adult robber flies use their sharp proboscis to stab insect prey, usually in the neck. They inject the prey with paralyzing saliva,

MIDAIR ATTACK
A robber fly can suck its victim completely dry within a matter of seconds. Its legs are covered with bristles, some of which are used to hold on to captured prey.

and then suck up the victim's body fluids. Robber flies are found in a variety of habitats, mostly in dry areas.

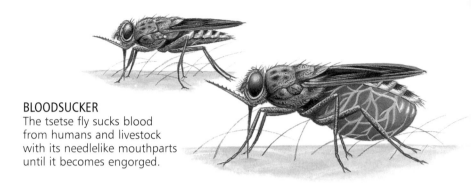

BLOODSUCKER
The tsetse fly sucks blood from humans and livestock with its needlelike mouthparts until it becomes engorged.

■ TSETSE FLIES

Characteristics Tsetse flies are gray or brown in color, with needlelike mouthparts used for sucking up animal and human blood. Some species transmit the trypanosome parasite that causes sleeping sickness, a disease that makes humans so exhausted they can barely move. The parasite does not affect wild animals, but can be debilitating to livestock.

Life cycle, diet, and habitat
Females lay single eggs, and the larvae hatch inside the mother's body, feeding on her secretions. When a larva emerges from the female's body, it immediately pupates. These flies live in open forests and savanna in Africa.

■ STALK-EYED FLIES

Characteristics These unusual flies have eyes and tiny antennae on the tips of long stalks extending from their head. Females of some species sometimes lack eye stalks.

Life cycle, diet, and habitat
When males meet, they compare eyes; the male with the longest stalks wins the right to mate with the female. Stalk-eyed flies stick their eggs on foliage or on rotting plant matter. The larvae are tapered at both ends of the body and often bore into the stems of grasses. These flies are found near vegetation or close to running water in tropical regions of Africa and Southeast Asia.

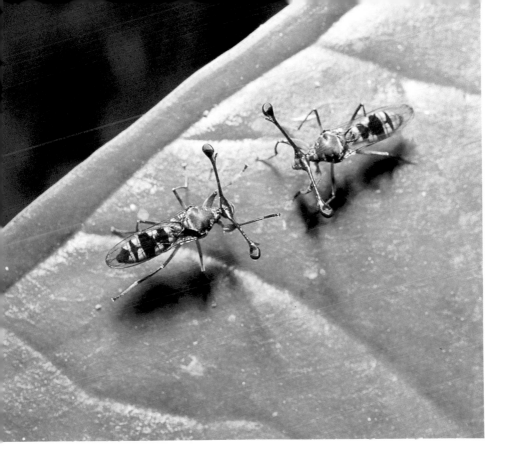

EYES WIDE OPEN

Male stalk-eyed flies from Southeast Asia use their strange eye stalks to threaten rivals and measure their size. The largest male gets to mate.

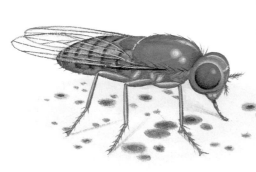

FRUIT FEEDER

Vinegar flies—both maggots and adults— favor rotting fruit. They sponge up the liquid with their proboscis.

■ HOUSE FLIES

Characteristics Most house flies are dull in color, with dark bristles and long legs.

Life cycle, diet, and habitat Females lay masses of eggs in feces, decomposing matter, on plants, or in birds' nests. The larvae are fast growing and can pupate in a week. Adults lap up anything organic, including dung, with their sponge-like mouth parts. They are found on excre-ment and decaying matter. House flies spread diseases, including cholera, typhoid, and dysentery.

■ VINEGAR FLIES

Characteristics These flies are also known as pomace flies. They are black, yellow, or brown flies with bright red eyes. Their body may also bear stripes or spots. The best-known species, *Drosophila melanogaster,* is used in genetic studies because of its fast breeding rate and large chromosomes.

Life cycle, diet, and habitat They lay their eggs on or near their food source, including rotting vegetation and fermenting fruit.

■ MYDAS FLIES

Characteristics Mydas flies have smooth bodies and are black in color. Their orange antennae may end in a club shape.

Life cycle, diet, and habitat Little is known of their life cycle, except that females lay their eggs in soil. The larvae eat beetle larvae. They are found in warm, sandy regions.

LIQUID SPONGER
House flies vomit saliva over their food to dissolve it, sopping up the mush with their sponge-like mouthparts.

MYDAS MIMICS
Some mydas flies mimic hoverflies or
spider-hunting wasps. After mating,
the female lays her eggs in soil.

IN THE FLESH
The streamlined shape of these blowfly
maggots allows them to burrow quickly
into decaying flesh.

■ HOVER FLIES

Characteristics So called because they can hover and dart among flowers, hover flies sport yellow stripes, spots, or bands. They are wasplike in shape, with large eyes and short antennae.

Life cycle, diet, and habitat Females lay eggs where their larvae will feed, in a variety of habitats, including boggy pools and heathland. Some larvae eat aphids or scale insects; others feed on plants and fungi. Adults eat nectar. Many species are important plant pollinators.

■ SOLDIER AND HORSE FLIES

Characteristics Soldier flies are slightly flattened, with metallic markings. Males have large eyes. Some species are aquatic. Horse flies are hairless, with patterned, sometimes iridescent eyes. The female's mouthparts can cut skin.

Life cycle, diet, and habitat Soldier flies lay their eggs on the surface of water or in dung, leaf litter, or soil. Adults live in a variety of habitats. Horse flies lay eggs in soil and rotten wood.

DARTING FLIGHT
Hover flies (right) are often seen darting and hovering over flowers. Their colors mimic those of wasps, giving them protection from predators.

SOLDIERING ON
Some aquatic soldier fly larvae can survive in salty water or in hot springs.

DARK HORSE
Certain horse fly species transmit damaging viruses to cattle and other livestock.

Caddis Flies

Number of species: 8,000

Length: $1/16$–$1\,1/2$ in (2–40 mm)

■ CHARACTERISTICS
Caddis flies are closely related to moths and butterflies (Order Lepidoptera), but are distinguished by having short hairs on their wings instead of scales. They hold their wings over their body like a roof when at rest. During flight, the hindwings and forewings are connected by curved hairs.

Most caddis flies are drably colored; some have black, gray, or white speckles. They have an elongate body with triangular wings, and a small head with large, compound eyes. The long, slender antennae consist of many segments. Adults have chewing mouthparts, but they are reduced, and used only for drinking water and nectar.

■ LIFE CYCLE AND DIET
Caddis flies undergo complete metamorphosis. Eggs are deposited in water, sometimes in gelatinous masses, and attached to water plants. The larvae are active, sometimes sucking the juices of water plants, or eating debris, algae, and small organisms. The aquatic larvae pupate inside a case—often characteristic of the species—constructed from wood, leaves, sand, or stone. The particles are melded together with silk from the salivary glands. Net-spinning caddis fly larvae spin a cup-shaped net between stones to ensnare algae and small

---

S N A P S H O T

ORDER FEATURES **Mothlike appearance; hairs on wings**
DIET **Larvae eat insect and plant matter; adults may take liquids; some are non-feeding**
LIFE CYCLE **Metamorphosis is complete; eggs laid in water**
HABITAT **Adults found near ponds, streams, marshes, and bogs; larvae are aquatic**
DISTRIBUTION **Worldwide**

AQUATIC COCOONS
Caddis fly larvae pupate underwater, inside their case, finally emerging and undertaking a final molt to adulthood.

organisms. The larval cases of northern caddis flies look like small log cabins. Adults are nocturnal and short-lived.

■ HABITAT
Caddis flies are found near sunny ponds and streams, and in temporary pools and bogs.

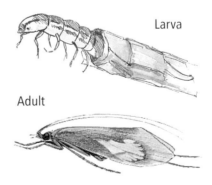

Larva

Adult

IN THE TUBE
Caddis fly larvae encase themselves in tubes made of sand, sticks, or leaves for protection. Adults are nocturnal and only live long enough to breed and lay eggs.

Moths and Butterflies

Number of species: 180,000

Wingspan: $^1/_{16}$–12$^1/_2$ in (2–320 mm)

■ CHARACTERISTICS

The name Lepidoptera, which means "scaly wing," refers to the millions of tiny, overlapping, colored scales covering the wings and body of all moths and butterflies. The scales are actually flat, hollow hairs. Many are filled with pigment absorbed from the insect's food; others reflect light to produce a metallic sheen. For all their variety in color and pattern, the Lepidoptera are remarkably uniform in their morphology. Of the 180,000 species in this order, moths outnumber butterflies ten to one. Both moths and butterflies have two pairs of wings that beat in unison. When flying, the forewings and hindwings link together with tiny hooks. At rest, butterflies hold their wings folded up over their backs; moths rest

SNAPSHOT

ORDER FEATURES Wings covered in overlapping scales; most with long proboscis for nectar-feeding

DIET Most adults feed on nectar; larvae eat plant matter

LIFE CYCLE Metamorphosis is complete; eggs glued to plants; caterpillars pupate within cocoon

HABITAT Among foliage in a wide variety of habitats

DISTRIBUTION Worldwide

MOTH OR BUTTERFLY?

Moths and butterflies (below) can be distinguished from each other by looking at antennae: Butterflies have threadlike antennae, ending in a club, whereas most moths have feathery antennae.

88 butterfly

Ornate tiger moth

TIGER MOTH

Some tiger moths (right) can detect bat sonar with special sense organs, and fly off to avoid capture.

with their wings spread flat. Moths mostly fly at night and have elaborately plumed or feathery antennae. Butterflies are daytime fliers and their slender, threadlike antennae are clubbed at the tips. Most butterflies have mouthparts that form a long tube, or proboscis, which can uncurl to feed on nectar and coil away again when not in use. Some moths have short, stabbing mouthparts; in some short-lived species they may be absent.

Lepidopterans have compound eyes that are sensitive to color patterns and to movement of flowers; they are also sensitive to other moths and butterflies.

■ LIFE CYCLE AND DIET
Moths and butterflies undergo complete metamorphosis. Courtship may involve flying displays and pheromones. The scent signals are detected by the mate's antennae. After mating, the eggs are scattered on the ground or laid on plants. The larvae, called caterpillars, are mainly plant-eaters, with strong, chewing mouthparts, three pairs of legs on the thorax, and a number of abdominal prolegs; the prolegs have minute hooks to help to grip onto plants. Adults drink nectar, fruit juice, and tree sap. Caterpillars pupate in an underground, silk-lined chamber, encased in a silk cocoon, inside a seed or plant stem, or in a bare case called a chrysalis.

WITCHETTY GRUBS
The larvae of carpenter moths are called witchetty grubs. They live in the roots of certain trees and are eaten by Australian Aboriginals as a sought-after delicacy.

WELL SPOTTED

Hidden by the forewings when the owl moth is at rest, its eyespots are revealed when danger threatens (above).

CHEMICAL DEFENSE

Caterpillars (below) defend themselves from predators with toxins, "horns" that release a foul smell, or stinging, hairlike spines, like those of this silk moth larva.

LEPIDOPTERA

■ HABITAT
Moths and butterflies are found on all continents, except Antarctica. In alpine areas, where temperatures are too cold for night-flying, moths have adapted to fly and feed during the day. They live in well-vegetated areas or wherever host plants grow.

HANGING AROUND
The bagworm caterpillar incorporates twigs and other debris into its cocoon design. It can then pupate unnoticed among the tree branches.

■ TIGER MOTHS
Characteristics These moths have thick, hairy bodies and bright red, yellow, orange, and black coloration.
Life cycle, diet, and habitat Females lay their eggs around the host plants. Many of the caterpillars are hairy and poisonous. They mainly feed at night on a wide variety of plants and live among foliage.

■ SILK MOTHS AND CLOTHES MOTHS
Characteristics Silk moths are pale cream or brown, with a profusion of hairs. They do not have functional mouthparts. Clothes moths are tiny, dull-brown scavengers that feed on a wide range of organic material, such as fabric, wool textiles, and skins. They are significant pests.

CRAWLING PROCESSION
Processionary moth caterpillars are the larvae of noctuid moths. They follow each other in single file.

COOL CAT
The vaporer moth caterpillar (a noctuid) is armed with a battery of hairs that can irritate skin.

Life cycle, diet, and habitat
Silk moths lay their eggs on food plants suitable for their larvae. The caterpillars pupate within a silk cocoon, and these are used in commercial silk production. They live in well-vegetated areas. Clothes moths live among cloth.

■ CARPENTER MOTHS
Characteristics These moths are cream or brown, with a large body and speckled or spotted wings.
Life cycle, diet, and habitat
The eggs are laid on bark. The caterpillars tunnel into wood and eat the fibers. They pupate inside cocoons made of silk and chewed wood fibers. They are found in wooded areas.

■ NOCTUID MOTHS
Characteristics The largest family in the order, these nocturnal moths have quite narrow forewings and broader hindwings. Noctuids usually have dull forewings and often more brightly colored hindwings.
Life cycle, diet, and habitat Eggs are laid singly or in numbers in the soil or on host plants. The caterpillars attack plants, chewing their way inside. Many are serious pests of crops, such as maize, cotton, and rice. Adults of some species have unusual food preferences; the vampire moth pierces the skin of mammals and feeds on their blood. Noctuids live in a variety of habitats.

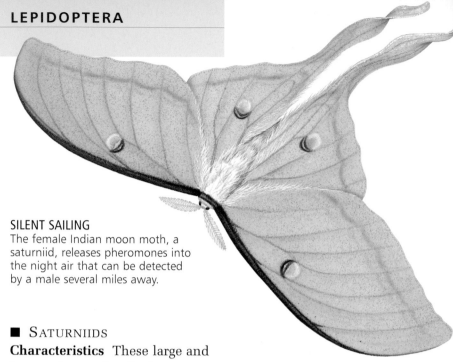

SILENT SAILING
The female Indian moon moth, a
saturniid, releases pheromones into
the night air that can be detected
by a male several miles away.

■ SATURNIIDS

Characteristics These large and
impressive moths display a
variety of colors and patterns,
including prominent eyespots
and wing patches. Pale green
saturniids with long tails and
eyespots are known as moon or
luna moths. Other well-known
species include the royal and
emperor moths. The world's
largest moth, *Attacus atlas*, is a
saturniid. Many species in the
genus *Attacus* are protected in
some countries. Males have
expansive, feathery antennae to
help them detect the scent signals
of the females; the females'
antennae are threadlike. All
these moths are night-fliers.
Life cycle, diet, and habitat
Females lay their eggs on foliage.
The larvae feed on a wide variety
of trees and shrubs. Cocoons may
be attached to twigs or left among
leaves on the ground. Adult
saturniids are non-feeding and
they do not possess working
mouthparts. They live in wooded
areas and are often seen fluttering
around street lights.

POWERFUL JAWS
The hickory horned devil is the caterpillar of the regal moth, a saturniid. The powerful muscles of its large mandibles can chew through the leaves of hickory and walnut trees.

BAD TASTE
The red spots on this five-spotted burnet moth advertise that it has an unpleasant taste, and predators tend to avoid it.

■ HAWK MOTHS

Characteristics Hawk moths are renowned for their powerful and speedy flight. They can hover at flowers to suck nectar with their long proboscis. The proboscis is curled up under the body when they are not feeding. They have a thick, rounded body that tapers to a point.

Life cycle, diet, and habitat The eggs are laid singly on plants. The caterpillars eat the foliage of host plants. Most larvae have a soft spine at the end of the body, resulting in the common name of hornworms. Some are pests of tomatoes and other crops. They usually pupate in the ground. Adults are nectar-feeders; the death's head hawk moth eats honey from hives. Most adults feed at dusk or at night; some feed during the day. They inhabit subtropical and tropical environments, wherever their host plants are found.

■ BURNET MOTHS

Characteristics Also known as foresters, these dark-bodied moths often have bright or metallic blue, green or red

HAWK MOTHS
During the time from hatching to pupation, this sphinx moth caterpillar (left), like other caterpillars, increases its size about 30,000 times. Hawk moths (right) are often so heavy that they cannot land on flowers. Instead, they hover like bumblebees to collect nectar.

coloration. They have thick antennae and small, hairy bumps above the eyes. Many species display warning coloration to signal that they contain poisons and that they are harmful to eat.

Life cycle, diet, and habitat
Females lay their eggs on suitable food plants for their hatched larvae. The larvae pupate inside an elongate cocoon. These moths feed and fly during the day.

■ SKIPPERS

Characteristics Skippers are daytime feeders and fliers. They are considered to be butterflies and take their common name from their distinctive, strong and darting flight. They have a thick body and a long or curved club

IN THE WOODS
The golden-banded skipper prefers moist, wooded areas near wetlands.

on the tip of their antennae. The forewings are triangular; a few species have long tails on their hindwings, similar to those of luna moths.

Life cycle, diet, and habitat

Skippers lay single eggs on host plants. The larvae feed at night on leaves, herbs, and grasses, and usually live in a shelter made from rolled-up leaves. Adults feed on nectar. Because they feed

ON THE WING
At rest, many skippers, such as this least skipper, hold their forewings and hindwings at slightly different angles.

at flowers, they cross-pollinate many plants. Some species fly great distances. Skippers live in a variety of habitats, usually near grassland and farmland. They are found worldwide, except in New Zealand.

■ HAIRSTREAKS, BLUES AND COPPERS

Characteristics These butterflies have a small, slender body and show a wide variety of wing colors and patterns. The upper side of the wings may be brown or orange, or iridescent blue, copper, or purple; the undersides are dull. Males and females are often differently colored. Some blues and coppers have white, hairlike scales on the body and fringing on their wings.

Hairstreaks usually have streamers on their hindwings that may be long and trailing, or short and dark-edged. Many hairstreak species are commonly seen perched on plants, rubbing their hindwings back and forth.

Life cycle, diet, and habitat Females lay their eggs on host plants. The caterpillars may feed on plants or on small insects, such as aphids. The caterpillars of many species have "honey glands" on their abdomen. These glands secrete a sweet liquid (honeydew) that attracts ants. A beneficial relationship results for both insects: The caterpillar gains protection from parasitic wasp attack and the ant derives a regular source of nutrition. Larvae pupate on plants or underground. They live around host plants or in ants' nests, in warmer regions. Some species of coppers are found in vacant lots, landfill, fields, and gardens.

NECTAR FEAST
The roemer acacia, found in North America's southwest, provides nectar for butterflies, such as the marine blue.

LUSTROUS COPPER
This lustrous copper (above) shows the hairlike fringing of the wings displayed by a number of species.

BUCKWHEAT MEAL
Bramble green hair-streak caterpillars (left) feed on the leaves of wild buckwheat. They are found on the west coast of North America.

LEPIDOPTERA

■ BRUSH-FOOTS

Characteristics These butterflies, also known as nymphalids, vary greatly in color and size. The front legs are markedly reduced,

WIDE-RANGERS
Fritillaries (Nymphalidae) inhabit a wide range of habitats, including alpine meadows, roadsides, and marshy areas.

hence their common name. The upper side of the wings is brightly colored and patterned; the underside has camouflage coloration. Members of this family include the following well-known species: red admiral, viceroy, monarch, painted lady, mourning cloak (Camberwell beauty), blue morpho, and

fritillaries. Some fritillaries are sluggish fliers; others have strong flying abilities, and sometimes travel long distances. Monarchs and painted ladies are famous for their migratory habits. The monarch migrates thousands of miles, from Canada to Mexico.

Life cycle, diet, and habitat

Females lay their ribbed eggs on trees, shrubs, and herbaceous plants. In temperate regions,

BLUE BEAUTY

The iridescent colors on the wings of the exquisite blue morpho are produced not by pigmentation, but by bending light.

some adult species hibernate during the harsh winter months. Brush-foots live in a variety of habitats—usually forests or meadows with abundant foliage—from the arctic tundra to tropical rainforests.

■ SWALLOWTAILS

Characteristics Swallowtails include the largest and most strikingly colored butterflies. They typically have dark wings, with spots and patches of green, blue, yellow, or orange. Many species have tails on their hindwings. Most swallowtails are fast and powerful fliers. The larvae have a forked scent organ, called an osmeterium, on their head, which secretes a foul-smelling substance. The caterpillars of some species, such as the giant swallowtail *Papilio cresphontes,* eat citrus leaves, and their osmeterium exudes an orange scent. The most spectacular members of this family (Papilionidae) are the birdwing butterflies from the tropical regions of Southeast Asia. Some are so large (wingspans of 8 inches [20 cm]) that early butterfly collectors would shoot them with fine shot. Birdwings are now protected by law.

Life-cycle, diet, and habitat The round eggs are laid on a variety of host plants. Caterpillars pupate on host plants. Most swallowtails live in tropical regions, in open or shaded flower-filled areas.

MIMICRY
The black swallowtail (left) mimics the color and flight patterns of the pipe vine swallowtail, a butterfly that predators avoid.

TRUE BEAUTY
At nearly 6 inches (15 cm) wide, the giant swallowtail (right) is one of the largest butterflies in North America.

■ SULFURS AND WHITES
Characteristics These common butterflies have representatives in most parts of the world. They usually have white, yellow, or orange wings. The wing scales are filled with pigments that are a by-product of the caterpillar's food. The caterpillars are usually hairless and green, with a yellow line down each side. Some adults migrate in large numbers.

ORANGE AND WHITE
Orange sulfurs (above) can often be seen drinking from puddles. The cabbage white butterfly (below) is unpopular with gardeners and farmers; its larvae can strip cabbage plants bare.

Life cycle, diet, and habitat

Many species engage in spiral flights that may be associated with mating. Females usually lay elongate eggs on host plants. One of the most common species in this family (Pieridae) is the cabbage white. Cabbage white caterpillars feed on cabbage leaves and are serious agricultural pests. Whites and sulfurs are very

common and are often found sipping fluids from around puddles and bird droppings. The caterpillars feed mostly on legumes and clovers. They are found in a wide range of habitats.

Bees, Wasps, Ants, and Sawflies

Number of species: 198,000

Length: $1/128$–$2^3/4$ in (0.25–70 mm)

SPRING POLLINATOR
The hairy-legged mining bee is a vital pollinator of many spring flowers. Pollen is trapped on its body hairs as it feeds.

■ CHARACTERISTICS
Hymenopterans are vital plant pollinators, predators, and parasites in the world's eco-systems. Many species in this large order are also social insects. All adults have chewing mouthparts, which for some species act as tools for digging, building nests, and slicing up food. Most have two pairs of membranous wings that join together with small hooks during flight, and large compound eyes. With the exception of sawflies, the thorax and abdomen are divided by a constricted "waist," called a pedicel. The ovipositor of female bees, ants, and social wasps has evolved into a stinger with associated poison glands. Hymenopterans range in size from the fairyfly wasp, so small it could fly through the eye of a needle, to the spider-eating wasp, measuring $2^3/4$ inches (70 mm).

■ LIFE CYCLE AND DIET
All hymenopterans undergo complete metamorphosis. Fertilized eggs produce females

---

SNAPSHOT

ORDER FEATURES **Usually constricted "waist" between thorax and abdomen, forewings and hindwings joined by hooks; chewing mouthparts; many groups are social**
DIET **Insect and plant matter**
LIFE CYCLE **Metamorphosis is complete; eggs laid in nests**
HABITAT **All terrestrial habitats**
DISTRIBUTION **Worldwide**

NO SWEAT
Also called sweat bees, members of the family Halictidae brood their eggs underground, within cells that are waterproofed with a special bee secretion.

LEAF-CUTTERS
Female leaf-cutter bees clip out circular pieces of leaf with their jaws. These are taken back to their nests where they are fashioned into tube-shaped cells for the eggs and larvae.

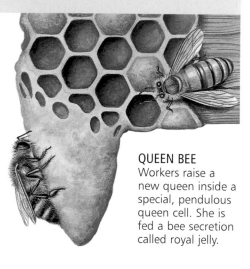

QUEEN BEE
Workers raise a new queen inside a special, pendulous queen cell. She is fed a bee secretion called royal jelly.

and unfertilized eggs result in males. Adults are usually fruit- or nectar-eaters; larvae eat insect or plant matter.

■ HABITAT
Hymenopterans live on all continents except Antarctica. Many groups are adapted to arid and semi-arid regions.

■ HONEYBEES AND ALLIES
Characteristics Honeybees and bumblebees are the best-known species in this family (Apidae). Most females have a pollen-storing basket on the outside of

each hindleg called a corbiculum. Many species have black and yellow banding, or a metallic blue or green sheen. Honeybees are highly social and live in colonies of up to 60,000 individuals. In contrast, bumblebees form small colonies, usually on or under the ground. A typical honeybee hive includes the egg-laying queen, workers (sterile females), who tend the young and the queen, find food, and look after the hive, and drones (males).

Life cycle, diet, and habitat
Honeybees have special glands on the underside of their bodies that ooze a waxy substance. They scrape this off and use it to make honeycomb—double-sided wax combs divided into hexagonal cells. These cells are used to brood the bee larvae and store honey and pollen. A queen can lay over 1,000 eggs a day,

POLLEN BASKETS
Worker honeybees collect pollen in basket-like notches on their back legs. Pollen is taken back to the hive and stored for periods when food is scarce.

every day of her life. She lays two kinds of egg: fertilized eggs develop into workers or queens, and unfertilized eggs become drones. Eggs hatch in approximately three days and the larvae are fed by workers for six days before being capped inside cells for a pupation lasting twelve to fourteen days. Future queens are fed an enriched diet consisting mainly of royal jelly, a creamy substance formed by special glands in the heads of the young worker bees. When the hive has reached its size limits, a young queen flies off to found a new colony, followed by a swarm of as many as 70,000 workers.

Unlike wasps, honeybees and their allies are strictly vegetarian, feeding only on nectar and pollen. Workers use a special dance to communicate the direction, distance, and abundance of a food supply.

Honeybees and their allies are found worldwide, except in sub-Saharan Africa. They live and feed in flower-rich habitats.

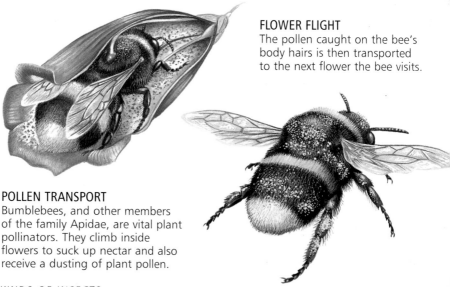

FLOWER FLIGHT
The pollen caught on the bee's body hairs is then transported to the next flower the bee visits.

POLLEN TRANSPORT
Bumblebees, and other members of the family Apidae, are vital plant pollinators. They climb inside flowers to suck up nectar and also receive a dusting of plant pollen.

■ MINING BEES

Characteristics Most members of this family are solitary. Many species have a hairy thorax and abdomen, and are red-brown or dark brown to black in color.

Life cycle, diet, and habitat Females make cells in soil burrows, each supplied with pollen and honey, into which they lay their eggs. They live worldwide, except Australia.

OVERFED
Parasitic bees, such as cuckoo bees, lay eggs in the larval cells of other bees. The cuckoo bee's larvae eat the host's larvae, as well as their stored food supply.

■ CUCKOO AND DIGGER BEES

Characteristics Most cuckoo bees are solitary and wasplike in appearance, with black and yellow coloration. The solitary digger bees are round and hairy.

Life cycle, diet, and habitat
Cuckoo bees parasitize the larvae of soil-nesting bees. Digger bees build nests in the ground, providing their larval cells with honey and pollen. Both these bees are found near flowers.

■ HALICTID BEES
Characteristics Also called sweat bees, most species are dark brown or black, but some species have metallic green or blue coloration. Usually solitary, some show a degree of societal structure.
Life cycle, diet, and habitat
Females lay their eggs in underground tunnels or in rotten wood. The larvae that mature are all females and they make tunnels as offshoots of their mother's

VELVET ANT
The females of this wasp family (Mutillidae) are wingless, covered in velvety hairs, and ant-like in appearance.

JEWEL THIEF
This brilliantly colored jewel wasp is also called a cuckoo wasp. Its larvae steal the food provided for the host's larvae.

tunnel, raising a brood without mating. These larvae develop into males, and then mate with a brood laid by the original female. Halictid bees are found worldwide in flower-rich habitats.

■ VELVET ANTS
Characteristics These "ants" are actually wasps that take their common name from the appearance of the female, who is covered with soft, velvety hairs and is wingless. Males have fully developed wings.
Life cycle, diet, and habitat
Velvet ants parasitize the nests of other wasps and bees. A female seeks out the nest of a suitable host, bites open a larval cell, lays her own egg inside, and reseals it.

■ JEWEL WASPS
Characteristics These wasps are bright metallic green, red, or blue in color. Their body surface is

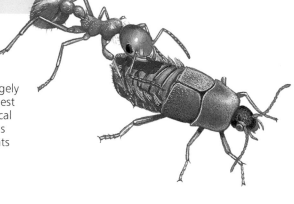

INSECT ILLUSIONS
Ant colonies are controlled largely by chemical signals. This ant-nest beetle (right) secretes a chemical to fool ants into accepting it as a colony member, and then eats their eggs and larvae.

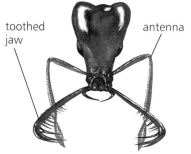

toothed jaw   antenna

HEAD AND TAIL
The trap-jaw ants, a tropical genus, have large and menacing jaws, and they also are capable of inflicting a painful sting.

hard and dimpled, which protects them from wasp and bee stings. They are also called ruby wasps, because of their coloration, or cuckoo wasps, because they steal the food that the host species has provided for its larvae.

Life cycle, diet, and habitat
Jewel wasps parasitize solitary bee or wasp larvae. The females lay an egg in the host's nest, and the larva eats the host's larvae and food provisions.

■ ANTS
Characteristics Ants are members of a highly social family of insects (Formicidae). Some ant colonies contain only a few hundred individuals; others, such as driver ants, have colonies consisting of more than 20 million insects. Most species are brown, red-brown, or black in color, although there are yellow and green species. The second abdominal segment is constricted to form the characteristic "waist,"

HEADSTRONG BULLDOG
The mandibles of the bulldog ant are large and heavily toothed. After ambushing its katydid prey, the ant may sting its victim with the poisonous stinger on its abdomen.

or pedicel possessed by most members of this order. The pedicel has a spiny process or a small, scale-like bump. Ants have large heads and large eyes, and generally three ocelli. The antennae have 11 or 12 segments, and may be long in some species. Most have chewing mouthparts.

Like social bees, ants have very sophisticated sensory systems. Pheromones are used to recognize individual colony members and the queen is able to control the reproductive status of her workers using these pheromone signals.

Members of individual castes have different physical attributes: The queen is large with a rounded abdomen; reproductive males and females have wings at certain stages of their lives; workers are small and compact; and soldiers often have large heads or enlarged mandibles.

Ants protect themselves from attack by stinging and biting, or by spraying formic acid from a gland at the rear of their abdomen. When the nest is attacked, workers carry the larvae to safety deeper underground.

Life cycle, diet, and habitat Each year a new colony is founded by a winged female and male. When conditions are optimal, these flying ants swarm out of the nest in search of new homes. The male dies soon after mating, but the female lives for many years. She never leaves the nest, and continues to produce huge numbers of eggs. Most of the queen's eggs hatch as sterile female worker ants. These workers collect food, look after the nest, raise the young, and tend the queen.

Most ants build permanent nests, and spend their lives in the same area. Nests are usually

BIG-HEADED ANTS
Ant societies are divided into castes, each with a defined purpose within the colony. Winged males fertilize the queen's eggs, workers tend the young, and soldiers protect the nest from harm.

Queen

Worker

Male

This worker ant lives in the darkness of the nest. It has small compound eyes, containing only a few hundred eyelets, and relies on other sensory signals, including pheromones, to communicate with fellow workers.

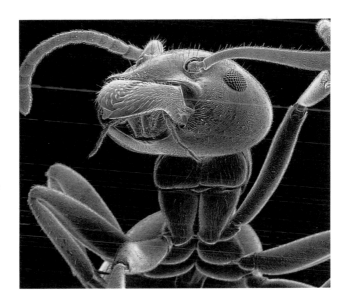

constructed from soil, leaves, or wood. Army ants and driver ants, however, form marauding hordes, sweeping across the ground, killing and eating any other insects in their path.

Not all ants are carnivores. Adult bulldog ants also eat tree sap and honeydew, and leaf-cutter ants grow fungus gardens (see page 98). Honey ants feed nectar to specialized workers; the workers store the nectar in their balloon-like abdomens.

Ants play an important role in ecosystems. Some species help to break down plant material and refine soil; others spread seed or help to decompose carrion. In contrast, some species—fire ants and leaf-cutter ants, for example—are serious crop pests.

Ants live in all habitats, including desert and alpine areas.

Soldier

■ SOCIAL WASPS

Characteristics Probably the best-known members of this large family (Vespidae) are the hornets, yellow jackets, and paper wasps. They can be recognized by the way they hold their wings when at rest—they are rolled along the length of the wing and held out slightly to each side of the body. (Other wasps hold their wings flat over their back.) Many species are social, making a papery nest for their colony from chewed up

DIRTY WORK
Mud daubers are solitary wasps. They construct small nests using pellets of mud, molded into place by the wasp's mandibles.

wood fibers (see page 67). Mason wasps make underground, mud-lined nests.

Life cycle, diet, and habitat Adult wasps feed on nectar and rotting fruit; the larvae, called grubs, eat spiders and insects. Yellow jacket and paper wasp colonies have queens to lay eggs and workers to rear young, as well as overlapping generations.

■ DIGGER WASPS

Characteristics Also known as mud daubers and sand wasps, these solitary wasps nest in plants, soil, or rotting wood; some nest inside the burrows of insects. Most have yellow markings or a metallic blue-green sheen.

A HORNET'S NEST
Hornets nest inside hollow trees, with only a few hundred individuals in the colony. True to the adage, they get aggressive if their nest is threatened.

FRUIT DRINK
Worker social wasps hunt for insects to feed their colony's larvae, but they will also take fruit juice for themselves.

PARALYZING POWER
A spider-hunting wasp avoids a tarantula's fangs by stabbing it with a long stinger that administers a paralyzing poison.

Life cycle, diet, and habitat
Females capture an insect or spider, paralyze it with a sting, and take it to a nest. The prey is buried, along with a single egg. The emerging wasp larva feeds on the stored prey. Adult digger wasps eat a variety of insect prey, including butterflies. They are found in a range of habitats.

■ SPIDER-HUNTING WASPS
Characteristics Some members of this family (Pompilidae) are very large. Many are dark blue or black in color, with wing patterns ranging from white patches to a purplish sheen. They have a slender body and long legs.

HEARING MOVEMENT
A torymid wasp uses its antennae to feel the vibrations of insect larvae as they move within their nesting chamber. The wasp uses its long ovipositor to reach inside, laying an egg on the host larvae.

Life cycle, diet, and habitat The females of some species search for spider prey on the wing. They use their strong poison to subdue the spider, and then place it inside a mud nest. They lay a single egg, usually on the spider's abdomen, and the larvae hatch and eat their host. These wasps live in tropical areas, in habitats where spiders are found.

■ ICHNEUMON WASPS
Characteristics The distinctive feature of most of these slender wasps is the long, thin ovipositor used for drilling into tree trunks or tree galls. Most have long, slender antennae. They are brown to black in color, with either brown and black or yellow and black patterns.
Life cycle, diet, and habitat Using their ovipositor, ichneumon wasps lay their eggs in or on the larvae of other insects, usually beetles, moths, and sawflies. They live in the world's warmer regions, in a wide range of habitats wherever their hosts occur.

■ TORYMID WASPS

Characteristics Many torymid wasps have shiny, metallic green or blue coloration, and a long, slender ovipositor.

Life cycle, diet, and habitat The ovipositor is used to parasitize gall-forming flies and wasps. Plant-eating species lay their eggs

FINE DRILLING
An ichneumon wasp's ovipositor is as fine as a human hair. It is, however, strong enough to drill through wood.

in the seeds of certain trees, where their larvae develop. They are found in a variety of habitats, wherever hosts can be found.

■ SAWFLIES

Characteristics Sawflies are considered the most primitive member of this order. They do not have the marked narrowing and fusing of abdominal segments displayed in other families of hymenopterans. The ovipositor of female sawflies is, as their common name suggests, saw-like.

SPOTTED SURPRISE
Figwort sawflies resemble spotted caterpillars. This warning coloration gives them some protection from predators.

Life cycle, diet, and habitat

Females cut slits in the leaves and shoots of plants and lay their eggs inside. The larvae feed on the outside of the plant, and pupate inside a silk cocoon. Horntails use their ovipositor to drill into trees, laying eggs and, at the same time, infecting the tree with a fungus. The larvae eat both the wood and fungus before pupating inside a cocoon composed of silk and chewed wood fibers. Some larvae produce substances to repel predators.

OVER-EATING
Adult pergid sawflies lay their eggs on Australian eucalypt trees. The larvae are voracious eaters, and can cause the total defoliation of a forest.

ON GUARD
These pergid sawfly larvae cock up their tails in a defensive posture, and regurgitate their stomach contents to deter predators.

KINDS OF ARACHNIDS

*An informative, illustrated guide
to the major orders of spiders,
scorpions, mites, and their allies.*

Spiders

ARANEAE

101 families

Spiders

Number of species: 40,000

Length: $1/32$–$3^1/2$ in (1–90 mm)

HIDING PLACE
This long-jawed orb weaver lies along grass stems, head pointing downward, to hide from predators.

SNAPSHOT

ORDER FEATURES **Relatively short pedipalps; first pair of legs similar in size to others; non-segmented abdomen; silk organs**
DIET **Mostly insects; occasionally small vertebrates**
LIFE CYCLE **Round eggs laid in silk cocoon; some carry young**
HABITAT **All habitats (except marine), including houses**
DISTRIBUTION **Worldwide**

■ CHARACTERISTICS

Like insects, spiders are one of the most abundant groups in the animal kingdom. They are characterized by their general body shape and by their ability to spin silk into webs and other structures. They range in size from money spiders no bigger than a pinprick, to tarantulas nearly twice the size of a human hand. All spiders have hinged, hollow fangs at the end of their jaws, called chelicerae, through which they can inject poison into prey. Fangs not only bite, but they also hold and crush prey. The cephalothorax and abdomen are joined together by a stalk, called the pedicel. Spiders have a variable number of eyes (six to

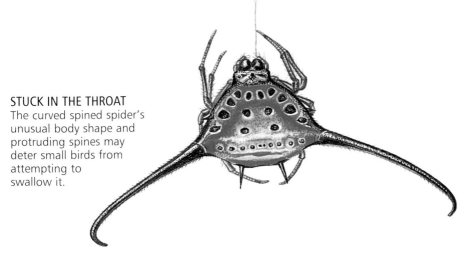

STUCK IN THE THROAT
The curved spined spider's unusual body shape and protruding spines may deter small birds from attempting to swallow it.

eight) on the cephalothorax. A spider's pedipalps are important sensory organs; in males, they also transfer sperm to females. Each of the eight walking legs is made up of seven segments.

Spiders have an unsegmented abdomen, which carries the silk-spinning organs called spinnerets. Spiders build an enormous variety of webs in which they catch flying insect prey. Webs vary from tripwires and untidy cobwebs to intricate orbs. A high percentage of spiders do not weave webs, but instead rely on stealth and speed to hunt their prey. Some chase down their preferred prey; others use a "sit-and-wait" strategy, pouncing when prey is in range.

■ LIFE CYCLE AND DIET
Some spiders have elaborate courtship behaviors (see page 58). Most spiders lay their eggs in a silk sac (up to 1,000 eggs in some tarantula species). Many carry these sacs with them until the eggs hatch; others camouflage them with debris and keep them in the web or buried in leaf litter. The hatched young are called spiderlings. They do not undergo metamorphosis, but molt at periods during their lifetime to increase in size and to reach sexual maturity. Many leave the silk egg sacs via silken threads that float them to the ground.

Most spiders eat small insect prey; larger species tackle fish, frogs, birds, and small mammals.

Spiders cannot chew, but instead inject digestive enzymes and paralyzing poison into their prey, dissolving their body tissues and sucking up the resultant liquid. Prey items that are not eaten immediately may be wrapped in a silk shroud and stored for later consumption.

BODY SPOTS

This male eresid spider has a distinctive, orange abdomen with black spots. They are found in Africa, Europe, and Asia.

■ HABITAT

Spiders live on all continents except Antarctica, in forests, grasslands, deserts, cliffs, caves, fresh water, and in houses. Most are nocturnal, although some are active during the day. They live among moss and low vegetation, such as grasses and flowers, in bushes, and in the lower foliage of trees. Many web-builders make silk-lined burrows to rest in during the day; nocturnal hunters shelter under stones or debris.

The water spider actively hunts for insects and then brings them back into its silk-shrouded bubble to be eaten.

■ ORB-WEB SPIDERS AND FUNNEL WEAVERS

Characteristics Orb-web spiders have a large abdomen that is often distinctively patterned or strangely shaped. They have eight eyes. Females are often larger than males. They make a web with a central hub, criss-crossed with radiating lines and spirals. Funnel weavers have long legs and many hairs on their bodies. Their cephalothorax bears eight eyes. They construct a funnel-shaped shelter on the edge of a flat web.

Life cycle, diet, and habitat
Orb-web spiders have complex courtships. They attach their silk egg sacs to bark, inside the web, or conceal them in leaf litter. Funnel weavers keep their egg sac in the web. The newly hatched young may be fed regurgitated food. Both spiders live in forests, grasslands, and gardens.

■ WATER SPIDER
Characteristics This spider—the only species in its family—lives mostly underwater. Its third and fourth pairs of legs have specialized tufts of long hairs that help it trap air. The water spider makes a domed diving bell out of silk and fills it with bubbles of air from the surface. It stays within the dome during the day, leaving only to find food at night.

Life cycle, diet, and habitat Eggs are laid and then wrapped in silk and placed in the top of the bell. Water spiders capture small fish and tadpoles and eat them inside the bell. This spider lives in still or slow-flowing water, in parts of Asia and in Europe.

LETHAL WEAPON
One of the most aggressive and toxic spiders in the world, the Brazilian wandering spider's venom is extremely dangerous to humans.

ERESID SPIDERS

Characteristics These round, hairy spiders have a squarish cephalothorax with eight eyes. The males of some species are brightly colored. Some species build webs in the ground, attached to funnel-shaped webs on the surface.

Life cycle, diet, and habitat Females carry their egg sacs on their body or keep them inside their burrow. Eresids live among shrubs and on the ground in parts of Asia, Europe, and Africa.

HUNTSMAN SPIDERS

Characteristics Most species have mottled coloration. They have long legs relative to their body, which are covered in stout spines. They have eight eyes.

Life cycle, diet, and habitat These spiders have complex courtship rituals. The females hide egg sacs under bark or stones until the eggs hatch. They hunt at night, hiding under bark, stones, and vegetation during the day. They live mainly in warmer regions in various habitats.

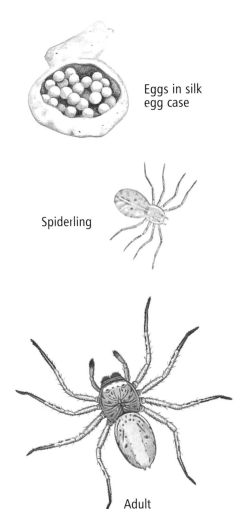

Eggs in silk egg case

Spiderling

Adult

WATCHFUL MOTHER
Female huntsman spiders guard their egg sacs until the young are ready to hatch, months after laying them. She then opens the sac to release her spiderlings.

■ WANDERING SPIDERS

Characteristics Very similar in appearance to wolf spiders, these spiders are usually gray or brown, with a distinctive groove running lengthways on the cephalothorax. The toxin of some species is dangerous to humans.

Life cycle, diet, and habitat
Eggs are laid inside a silk case, carried under the female's body. Wandering spiders are active nocturnal hunters. They search for their prey on the ground and are usually found on low-growing shrubs, or on the ground.

■ WOLF SPIDERS

Characteristics These pale gray to dark brown spiders may have bands, or black spots, and thick, stout legs. They have eight eyes: four large and four small.

Life cycle, diet, and habitat
Wolf spiders may have complex courtship behavior, involving leg-lifting and other visual signals. Females of most species carry their egg sacs with them. When the eggs hatch, the mother carries the spiderlings on her body for a time, sometimes brushing them from her eyes so that she can see. These active hunters have excellent eyesight, searching for prey at night among leaf litter.

■ NURSERY-WEB SPIDERS

Characteristics Similar in some features to wolf spiders, nursery-web spiders are large and long-legged, with eight eyes. They

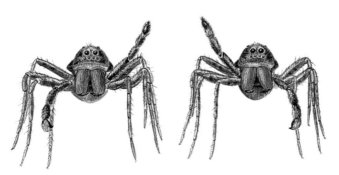

LEGS IN THE AIR
Male wolf spiders perform a courtship dance to impress a potential mate. If the dance is carried out satisfactorily, the female allows the male's advance.

vary in color from gray to dark brown, with brown or white legs covered with black hairs. The abdomen and cephalothorax have stripes running down each side. **Life cycle, diet, and habitat** A female carries her silken egg sac in her chelicerae. Just before the eggs hatch, she spins a silk "tent" web to enclose the emerging spiderlings. She will guard them for a time, even chasing away small predators if they threaten. Adults run across the ground to catch prey. They live in a variety of habitats, on the ground and at the water's edge. Some species are semi-aquatic, catching tadpoles, small fish, and insects at the surface.

■ JUMPING SPIDERS
Characteristics Jumping spiders are relatively small and mostly drably colored. Some have a

pattern of dark and light banding on their legs. They have eight eyes, four of which form a row on the cephalothorax. The two middle eyes are much larger than the rest. Their common name comes from their habit of jumping at prey. With their good vision, these daytime hunters stalk their prey at close range and then pounce on them.

Life cycle, diet, and habitat Most lay their eggs under stones and bark, and in vegetation, encased in a silk cell. Mothers guard the eggs until they hatch. They live in many habitats, including sunny spots on walls or on the ground.

SPLENDID VISION
Jumping spiders have relatively good vision. They can detect prey up to 8 inches (20 cm) away.

ONE GIANT LEAP
A jumping spider can leap four times the length of its own body. It often secures itself with a silk safety line.

■ CRAB SPIDERS
Characteristics These spiders get their common name from their crab-like appearance and the sideways movements of some species. Many have a broad abdomen. The first two pairs of legs, used to catch and grasp prey, are larger and armed with more spines than the other two pairs. Many crab spiders are colorful, often matching the pink, white, or yellow flowers that they hunt on. One common species spends its time among yellow or white flowers, and can alternate its color from one to the other so that it blends in with its surroundings.

Life cycle, diet, and habitat Crab spiders attach their egg sacs to plants and then guard them until they hatch. They feed on insects, especially those that visit flowers. Crab spiders are found mainly in gardens and meadows, around flowers, but also on vegetation.

SAFETY NET

A female nursery-web spider carries her egg sac until her young are ready to hatch. She then spins a nursery area out of silk to enclose and protect her spiderlings.

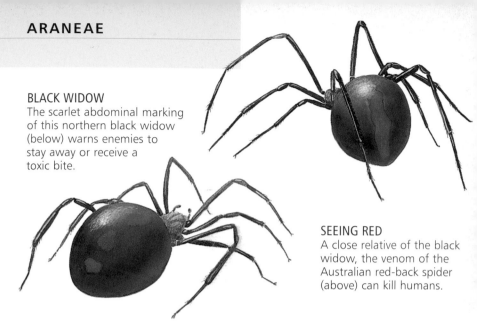

BLACK WIDOW
The scarlet abdominal marking of this northern black widow (below) warns enemies to stay away or receive a toxic bite.

SEEING RED
A close relative of the black widow, the venom of the Australian red-back spider (above) can kill humans.

■ COMB-FOOTED SPIDERS
Characteristics This family (Theridiidae) includes the infamous American black widow and the Australian red-back. They have a globular abdomen and are brown or black in color. Most are nocturnal hunters, moving along the ground in search of suitable prey. They build webs in vegetation, in cracks and crevices, and under buildings.
Life cycle, diet, and habitat After mating, females may eat the male, earning the black widow her name. They attach their egg sacs, containing up to 250 eggs, to their webs. These spiders are found among vegetation, under stones and leaf litter, and in and around buildings.

■ TARANTULAS
Characteristics Members of this family (Theraphosidae) are large, hairy, nocturnal hunters, with pink, brown, white, red, or black markings. They have relatively poor vision, provided by a group

GRAB AND STAB
Camouflaged crab spiders lurk among flowers with their front legs wide open. They strike when prey comes into range.

of eight small eyes on the front of the cephalothorax. Some species, such as the Mexican red-legged tarantula, are ground-dwellers that actively hunt prey, usually after dusk. Using their large, downward-stabbing fangs, they

OPEN WIDE
Trapdoor spiders live in silk-lined burrows, with a silk door. They pounce on prey and eat it inside the burrow.

crush their victims and then suck up their body fluids. Tree-living species hunt among the foliage of forest trees. A tarantula's body hairs have microscopic barbed spines that make skin itch and burn. When threatened, it scrapes hairs off its abdomen and showers them on its enemy.

Life cycle, diet, and habitat
Females lay up to 1,000 eggs in a burrow. Most tarantulas hunt

on the ground, capturing arthropods, small frogs, and mice; tree-dwelling species eat insects and small reptiles. Tarantulas live in a variety of habitats, including deserts and forests.

OLD AGE
Most spiders have a life span of only 2 or 3 years, but some tropical tarantulas live to 17 years or more.

■ FUNNEL-WEB AND
   TRAPDOOR SPIDERS

Characteristics These usually dark brown spiders have six or eight eyes, and long spinnerets. They have large fangs and highly toxic venom, that may be fatal if antivenin is not administered quickly. Their silk-lined burrows incorporate a series of silken trip wires at the front, alerting them to nearby prey. Trapdoor spiders wait in their tunnels, just beneath their circular trapdoor made from silk and soil, ready to pounce on passing prey.

Life cycle, diet, and habitat Females lay disk-shaped eggs with a tough casing. They keep the eggs in their burrows until they hatch. They live in various habitats, in Asia, Australia, Africa, and North America.

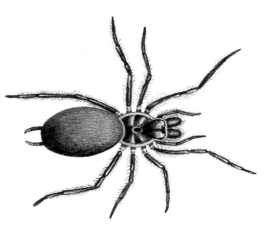

DANGEROUS MALE
The male Sydney funnel-web spider has extremely toxic venom. Its bite is far more deadly than that of the female.

Scorpions, Mites and Allies

Scorpions

Number of species: 1,400

Length: $^5/_{16}$–$8^1/_4$ in (80–210 mm)

■ CHARACTERISTICS

Scorpions are the most ancient group of arachnid. Like spiders, scorpions have eight walking legs attached to their cephalothorax. They differ from spiders in having an abdomen divided into 12 segments. The last five segments of the abdomen make up the distinctive, mobile "tail" or telson. The telson bears a stinger and poison gland, which is used to paralyze prey, and in defense. The sting of some species is lethal to humans. The modified pedipalps, resembling large, lobster-like pincers, are used to seize and subdue prey. Scorpions have 12 eyes; the main pair is situated on top of the head and a

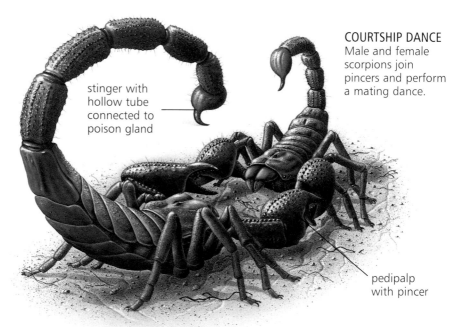

stinger with hollow tube connected to poison gland

COURTSHIP DANCE
Male and female scorpions join pincers and perform a mating dance.

pedipalp with pincer

BACK HOME
Scorpion eggs hatch inside their mother's body and then emerge as live young. They then climb onto her back.

variable number around the sides. Despite this number, scorpions have poor vision; some species are blind. Instead, scorpions use sensory leg hairs, and a pair of sense organs, called pectines, on the tip of their abdomen, to detect vibrations caused by prey.

SNAPSHOT

ORDER FEATURES **Flattened body; large pedipalps with pincers; segmented abdomen, elongated into a tail tipped with a stinger**
DIET **Insects and other arthropods**
LIFE CYCLE **Eggs hatch inside female's body; nymphs emerge from genital pore**
HABITAT **Under rocks, logs, bark**
DISTRIBUTION **Worldwide**

SCORPIONES

■ LIFE CYCLE AND DIET
Scorpions have complex mating
rituals. A male's pectines sense
the pheromone trail left by a
female. They interlock pincers
to perform a circling dance,
during which the male produces
a spermatophore. He then
maneuvers the female over it so

that she can pick up the packet
with her genital pore. The eggs
develop and then hatch inside the
female's body. The young are
born live and climb onto their
mother's back. Most species are
carried until their first molt about
two weeks later; some scorpions
take several years to mature.

Scorpions emerge from their
daytime retreats at dusk to hunt
for insects, spiders, and small
vertebrates. They usually crush
their victim using their pedipalps;
with larger prey they also use
their sting. Scorpions cannot
ingest solid food. They pour
dissolving digestive juices onto
the prey's tissues and then suck
up the liquid.

IMPERIAL SCORPION
Because daytime temperatures in deserts
are so extreme, scorpions venture out to
hunt only in the cool of the evening.

■ HABITAT
Scorpions live in dark crevices
under bark, stones, or leaf litter,
in mainly warm, dry, or humid
areas. Some are cave-dwellers.

Pseudoscorpions

Number of species: 3,300

Length: $^1/_{32}$–$^1/_2$ in (1–12 mm)

■ CHARACTERISTICS

These small arachnids, also called false scorpions, are similar in shape to scorpions (Scorpiones), but lack their abdominal tail and stinger. Most species have poison glands in their pincer-like pedipalps. The pedipalps are used to capture prey and in defense. They vary in color from brown and black, to dark green. Pseudoscorpions have up to four eyes, although in some species eyesight is poor or non-existent. They produce nests of silk in burrows for protection when hibernating or molting.

■ LIFE CYCLE AND DIET

Mating and courtship can be complex, sometimes involving a male and female gripping each other by the pedipalps in a courtship dance. Males deposit a spermatophore that is picked up by the female's genital pore. Eggs are laid into a silk sac that is carried under the female's body. In some species, the hatched young cling to their mother's sides; in others, larvae leave the sac and move into soil, bark, or leaf litter.

■ HABITAT

Most species live in warm, humid conditions among leaf litter, bark, and debris. Some live in caves, in birds' nests, the burrows of small mammals, and inside buildings; others live in coastal habitats, in rock crevices, and under stones.

SNAPSHOT

ORDER FEATURES **Flat body; pedipalps with pincer-like claws; oval abdomen with 12 segments**

DIET **Insects, small arthropods**

LIFE CYCLE **Eggs laid in silk sac, carried under female's body**

HABITAT **Among leaf litter, under stones, in caves, birds' nests, and greenhouses**

DISTRIBUTION **Worldwide, except in extreme north, in warm regions**

RIDING HIGH
This rainforest pseudoscorpion is hitching a ride on a harlequin beetle's antenna.

LOADED PINCERS
Most pseudoscorpion species are equipped with venom glands in their pincers.

Harvestmen

Number of species: 5,000

Length: 1/16–6 in (2–150 mm)

■ CHARACTERISTICS
Members of this order lack a "waist" between the abdomen and cephalothorax. The pedipalps have six segments and the pincer-like chelicerae have three. The paired eyes are often elevated on small protuberances. Most are dull colored, although some tropical species display bright colors, even changing to blend with their surroundings. Harvestmen have glands in the

REAP THE HARVEST
Most harvestmen are nocturnal hunters. Members of the family Leiobunidae (below) descend from trees to hunt for insects and arthropods on the ground.

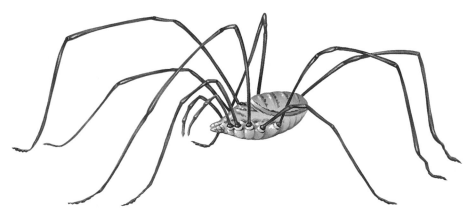

cephalothorax that produce toxic secretions that are smeared on attackers as a deterrent.

■ LIFE CYCLE AND DIET
Unlike other arachnids, male harvestmen have a penis for transferring sperm to the female. Some females have an ovipositor and lay their eggs into crevices in the soil or under bark. In some species, the eggs are laid in damp areas. In one species, the female encloses herself and her young within a mud wall.

SPINY LEGS
This harvestman, a native of Venezuelan cloud forest, has long, sharp spines on its large hindlegs.

■ HABITAT
Harvestmen live among moist debris, under stones and leaf litter, and in caves, usually in grassland and forests. They are found worldwide, mainly in temperate and tropical regions, with the largest number of species concentrated in South America and Southeast Asia.

Mites and Ticks

Number of species: 30,000

Length: $1/128–1\,1/4$ in (0.2–30 mm)

■ CHARACTERISTICS

This huge and diverse order (known collectively as acarians) has members with varied habits. Most acarians are rounded, with no distinct body division. Their short abdomen is non-segmented and the chelicerae are adapted for piercing and sucking. Adults and nymphs have four pairs of walking legs, although larvae have only three pairs.

■ LIFE CYCLE AND DIET

In some families, males transfer sperm with their chelicerae. Acarians lay their eggs wherever they are feeding: either on plant material, on food products, in beehives, in nests and burrows, or in mattresses, to name a few. Adults eat a variety of foods, including plant fluids, blood, skin, and stored food products.

■ HABITAT

Acarians live in a wide range of terrestrial and aquatic habitats, including marine environments.

VELVET UNDERGROUND
Velvet mites emerge from the soil at certain times of the year to mate and lay eggs, often after a rain shower.

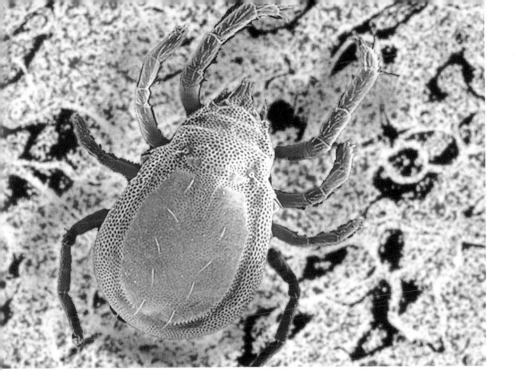

■ Mites

Characteristics There are probably more mite species on Earth than any other arthropod group. Most species are microscopic. Many are translucent, with long abdominal hairs; others are red, orange, green, yellow, or brown, with hairy or spider-like bodies. There is little or no distinction between body parts. They have needle-like chelicerae for sucking blood and plant fluids from host plants or animals.

BIZARRE LIVING
Mites are found in the most unlikely habitats: Some live inside the ears of seals, or inside the lungs of monkeys; others live on the jaws of ants.

Life cycle, diet, and habitat
In some families, males transfer sperm using their chelicerae. Eggs are laid wherever the mites feed. Most have three nymphal stages. Mites are found in almost every terrestrial and aquatic habitat; many are animal parasites.

■ TICKS

Characteristics Ticks are generally larger than mites, especially after a blood meal. Like mites, they have an unsegmented body. Most have three pairs of legs as larvae and four pairs as nymphs and adults. Ticks take in liquid food using their piercing

TICK TOXIN
This microscopic view of a tick shows its piercing mouthparts. Tick saliva contains a toxin that can paralyze some animals.

SHEEP TICK
Hard ticks are serious pests of domestic animals and humans. These sheep ticks attach themselves to a host as it brushes through grass and other vegetation.

and sucking mouthparts. They anchor themselves to a host with a small hook.

Life cycle, diet, and habitat Eggs are laid in the nests and burrows of the hosts, or in vegetation. Most are blood feeders; many species carry diseases.

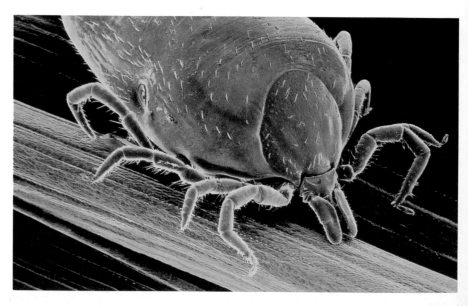

UROPYGI

2 families

Whipscorpions

Number of species: 99

Length: 3/8–3 in (10–75 mm)

AMBLYPYGI

3 families

Tailless Whipscorpions

Number of species: 130

Length: 3/16–2 1/2 in (5–60 mm)

■ WHIPSCORPIONS

Characteristics Also known as vinegaroons, because of their ability to spray acetic acid from abdominal glands, whipscorpions have a flattened abdomen with 12 segments and a long cephalothorax. The abdomen ends in a whiplike tail. The large and powerful pedipalps, armed with spines, are used to catch and crush prey, and to dig tunnels. Three of the four pairs of legs are used for walking; the first pair have a sensory function.

Life cycle, diet, and habitat A courtship dance precedes mating, where the male places his spermatophore inside the female. The hatched young are carried on her back. They eat insects and other arthropods. They are found in India, Malaysia, and in parts of North and South America, usually in soil, leaf litter, rotting wood, and in caves.

DANCE PARTNERS
Like their relatives the scorpions, male and female whipscorpions lock pincers and perform a courtship dance.

ORDER FEATURES **Squat body, large pedipalps with spines, long front legs (Amblypygi); powerful pedipalps, abdomen with whiplike tail (Uropygi)**
DIET **Insects and other arthropods**
LIFE CYCLE **Hatched young carried on female's back**
HABITAT **Leaf litter, under bark**
DISTRIBUTION **Tropical areas**

■ TAILLESS WHIPSCORPIONS

Characteristics Also known as whip-spiders, these squat-bodied arachnids have a broad cephalo-thorax and a flattened abdomen. They have large, sharply spined pedipalps that fold toward the mouth to hold prey. The long first pair of legs are sensory organs.

Life cycle, diet, and habitat Females pick up the spermato-phore deposited by the male. The young develop in a brood sac. They prefer moist areas in leaf litter, caves, and under bark, and are found in tropical areas.

SAFE AND SOUND
This female tailless whipscorpion, from a Peruvian rainforest, carries the young on her back to protect them from predators.

ACID SQUIRT
Whipscorpions do not sting, but instead spray out acetic acid from special glands on their abdomen.

Windscorpions

Number of species: 1,000

Length: $5/32$–$2^3/4$ in (4–72 mm)

■ CHARACTERISTICS

Also called sun spiders, these arachnids have a slightly rounded head with huge, forward-facing chelicerae used to kill and slice up prey. Their leg-like pedipalps are without claws, but instead have tiny suction pads that assist in grasping prey. Windscorpions have a segmented, mobile abdomen, small paired eyes, and many sensory body hairs. Most are nocturnal, although some are active during the day.

■ LIFE CYCLE AND DIET

In some families, mating includes males carrying the females. Males place a spermatophore into the female's genital pore. Eggs are laid in burrows in the ground, sometimes in several batches. Most species eat insects and other arthropods, including termites.

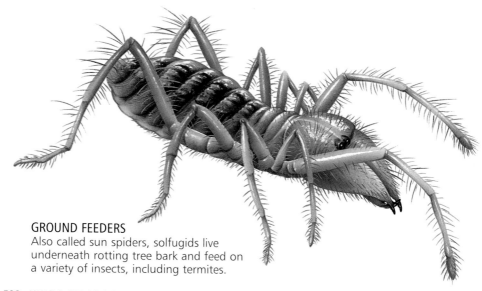

GROUND FEEDERS
Also called sun spiders, solfugids live underneath rotting tree bark and feed on a variety of insects, including termites.

SLICING FANGS
Unlike spiders, solfugids have only one pair of eyes. The sharp, forward-pointing chelicerae are used to macerate prey.

■ HABITAT
Windscorpions live under rocks, on soil, and in leaf litter. They are found mainly in dry areas, including deserts, savanna, and mountainous areas of Central, South, and North America.

SNAPSHOT

ORDER FEATURES **Forward-facing chelicerae; leg-like pedipalps**

DIET **Small insects, mainly termites, and small arthropods**

LIFE CYCLE **Eggs laid in burrow, in several batches**

HABITAT **Nocturnal; inside termite colonies; in soil during day**

DISTRIBUTION **In deserts and mountainous areas of Central, South, and North America**

INDEX

Page numbers in *italics* indicate illustrations and photos.

W

Z

Picture Credits

K. Atkinson, Auscape (V. Steger/P. Arnold, E & P Bauer, D. Bringard/Bios, B.S.I.P, J. Cancalosi, D. Clyne, J. P. Ferrero, P. Geotgheluck, G. Harold, C. A. Henley, H. Van Ingen, L. E. Lauber/OSF, J. McDonald, M. Macconacchie, C. Milkins/OSF, S. Miller, R. Morrison, R. Williams, F. Polking, A. & J. Six, S. Wilby & C. Ciantar); APL (Bruce Coleman, J. Burton, J. Cancalosi, G. Dore, F. Labhardt, Dr. F. Sauer, A. Stillwell, K. Taylor, M. P. L. Fogden, P. Zabransky); Australian Museum (C. Bento); Corbis; Corel; Frank Lane Picture Agency (G. E. Hyde, D. Jones, W. Rohdich, M. Rose, Silvestris, L. West, A. Wharton); Hemera Studio; NHM Picture Library; Oxford Scientific Films (N. Bromhall, M. Fogden, S. Kuribayashi, London Scientific Films, S. Morris, P. de Oliveira, J. H. Robinson); PhotoDisc; photolibrary.com (W. Ervin/SPL, A. Evrard, S. Holt, K. H. Kjeldsen/SPL, Nurdsany & Perennou/SPL, D. Scharf/SPL, A. Syred/SPL); Planet Earth Pictures (B. Kenney, K. Lucas, D.P. Maitland); PhotoDisc; Photo Essentials; Premaphotos Wildlife (R. Brown, K. Preston-Mafham, J. Preston-Mafham, R. Preston-Mafham); Ronald A. Nussbaum, Science Gallery (O.S.F./Auscape); Stock Photos; and Tom Stack & Associates (D. M. Dennis).

Illustration Credits

Susanna Addario, Alistair Barnard, Anne Bowman, Martin Camm, Sandra Doyle/Wildlife Art, Simone End, Christer Eriksson, Alan Ewart, Giuliano Fornari, John Francis/Bernard Thornton Artists UK, Jon Gittoes, Ray Grinaway, Tim Hayward/Bernard Thornton Artists UK, Robert Hynes, Ian Jackson/Wildlife Art, David Kirshner, Frank Knight, Angela Lober, John Mac/FOLIO, Rob Mancini, Iain McKellar, James McKinnon, Colin Newman/Bernard Thornton Artists UK, Nicola Oram, Tony Pyrzakowski, Luis Rey/Wildlife Art Agency, John Richards, Edwina Riddell, Steve Roberts/Wildlife Art, Trevor Ruth, Claudia Saraceni, Peter Schouten, Chris Shields/Wildlife Art, Kevin Stead, Thomas Trojer and Genevieve Wallace.